Job Loss, Identity, and Mental Health

Job Loss, Identity, and Mental Health

DAWN R. NORRIS

RUTGERS UNIVERSITY PRESS

NEW BRUNSWICK, NEW JERSEY, AND LONDON

LIBRARY OF CONGRESS CATALOGING-IN-PUBLICATION DATA

Names: Norris, Dawn R., author.
Title: Job loss, identity, and mental health / Dawn R. Norris.
Description: New Brunswick, New Jersey : Rutgers University Press, [2016] |
    Includes bibliographical references and index.
Identifiers: LCCN 2015035674 | ISBN 9780813573809 (hardcover : alk. paper) |
    ISBN 9780813573816 (e-book (epub)) | ISBN 9780813573823 (e-book (web pdf))
Subjects: LCSH: Unemployment—Social aspects—United States. |
    Unemployment—United States—Psychological aspects. | Unemployed—Mental
    health—United States. | Job stress—United States. | Identity (Psychology)
Classification: LCC HD5708.2.U6 N67 2016 | DDC 305.9/06940973—dc23
LC record available at http://lccn.loc.gov/2015035674

A British Cataloging-in-Publication record for this book is available from the British
Library.

Portions of some of the quotations in this book, as well as table A.1, were previously
published in "'Maybe If I Was 25, But I'm 40': Age Identities, Work-Related
Problems, and Distress Management," *Sociological Spectrum:
Mid-South Sociological Association* 35 (5) (2015): 399–418. DOI:
10.1080/02732173.2015.1064796.

Visit our website: http://rutgerspress.rutgers.edu

Manufactured in the United States of America

This book is dedicated to the kind people
who shared their stories with me.
Thank you.

CONTENTS

Acknowledgments   ix

1   Introduction   1

2   Why Identity?   13

3   "That's Not the Way We Do It at Gentay":
Feedback Mismatches   25

4   "I Wasn't the Same Person": Time Mismatches   46

5   "Me Caveman . . . I Club Deer": Status Mismatches   62

6   "On the Mommy Track": Shifting   78

7   "It Was Like I Was Still Working": Sustaining   99

8   "Like You're Dead and Nobody Told You":
Identity Void   120

9   Conclusion   142

Appendix A: Methodology   155
Appendix B: Additional Considerations   161
Notes   171
References   173
Index   183

ACKNOWLEDGMENTS

It took five years from the start of this project to developing the full manuscript of this book, and there are many people who helped me make it happen. Melissa Milkie, Annette Lareau, Bill Falk, Jeff Lucas, and Jinhee Kim provided helpful feedback and assisted me in producing rigorous, yet accessible, work. My colleagues at University of Wisconsin–La Crosse encouraged me along the way with good spirit and humor as I worked to balance writing with a 4/4 teaching load.

A number of people read and commented on various drafts of this book. First and foremost, Jon Wallace at Princeton University served as a phenomenal developmental editor. For two years, he helped me think about my audience, find my voice, organize my material, and craft a book proposal before I even began to approach publishers. I also owe a debt of gratitude to Peter Mickulas, acquisitions editor at Rutgers University Press. His enthusiasm in our first discussion about this book encouraged me to bring it to fruition; his feedback on the written material helped ensure clarity and focus and built my confidence in what can be a daunting process. I also greatly appreciate the constructive feedback given by Linda Francis and Tim Strangleman.

Students in some of my undergraduate courses at Saint Mary's College of Maryland and at University of Wisconsin–La Crosse (UWL) also provided feedback on the research and some of the book chapters. It was their initial excitement about the participant quotes that helped me realize that undergraduates would really enjoy this material in book form. Additionally, Samantha Gregory at UWL gave several chapters a thorough review and provided insightful commentary from the undergraduate perspective. I would also like to thank Robyn Gurria and Jack Flinchum at UWL for their assistance in finalizing the references section.

I am truly grateful for the trust placed in me by the many people who candidly told me their stories about being out of work. At times, their stories moved me to tears. At other times, we shared the simple joys of a cup of coffee and laughter. I think of all of them fondly and with appreciation.

Most importantly, without my husband, Eric, I could not have completed this book. Eric, you have supported me in my hopes and dreams as if they were your own. I love you with all my heart.

Job Loss, Identity, and Mental Health

1

Introduction

This book looks at the social problem of job loss from an unusual perspective: identity. Most books on job loss focus on the very real material hardship that occurs during unemployment, trends and policy recommendations, or the overall experience of being unemployed. Written from an identity perspective, *Job Loss, Identity, and Mental Health* offers insights into how unemployment, identity, and emotional pain are interrelated, sometimes in ways we would not expect.

Our jobs are often a big part of our identities. Consequently, losing our jobs can threaten our identities, and these threats can harm our mental health. When you are fired or laid off, you may feel confused, hurt, and powerless, and may lose a sense of who you are. Many of the people who told me their stories, such as Lorna and Charlie, described those kinds of experiences:

> I kinda lost my whole music identity. . . . So that kinda hurts. It hurts. . . . Now it's all gone.
>
> —Lorna, former supervisor in the broadcasting industry,
> unemployed for six months

> I think for men especially, you are pretty much your job. If you have a reasonably good job, to dissociate that from who you are I think can make you feel weak and impotent and just at sea in terms of your identity.
>
> —Charlie, former director of training at a nonprofit organization,
> unemployed for three months

This book explores specific identity threats that can occur after losing a job, the strategies we may use to cope with these threats, and the factors that may ease or restrict the use of these coping strategies. However, this sociological examination of these seemingly individual experiences also takes into account the social and historical framework in which people's experiences occur.

Like every social problem, job loss and unemployment are situated in specific historical contexts. This book focuses on the time period just after the Great Recession, which occurred between December 2007 and June 2009. During the Great Recession, an economic crisis second in severity only to the Great Depression, the unemployment rate reached markedly high levels (Grusky, Western, and Wimer 2011a), and remained high in its aftermath. Between February 2009 and August 2010, the lowest unemployment rate was 8 percent, and the rate peaked at 10 percent in October 2009 (U.S. Department of Labor 2015a).

People had a hard time recovering from the Great Recession, partially because periods of unemployment lasted longer than they had in previous recessions. There has been a sharp increase in the percentage of unemployed people who remain out of work "long term," or for twenty-seven or more weeks. In 1990, only about 10 percent of all unemployed people were without work long term. By 2004, this increased to 23.6 percent. But by September 2011, it had skyrocketed to 45.1 percent of all unemployed people, or more than 6.2 million people in the United States (U.S. Department of Labor 2014a). People simply could not find jobs. Even more than three years later, by January 2015, a full 31.5 percent of all unemployed people still qualified as being unemployed long term (ibid. 2015b).

The official unemployment rate underestimates the full extent of unemployment because it does not count "discouraged workers"—people who want to work and are available for work, but have stopped looking because they do not believe any jobs are available (U.S. Department of Labor 2015b). Discouraged workers totaled in excess of 1.3 million in December 2010, and alternated between more than 800,000 to more than one million between January 2011 and May 2013 (ibid. 2015c). As of January 2015, there were still 682,000 discouraged workers (ibid. 2015b).

Even when people found new jobs after the Great Recession, they often became underemployed, meaning they only worked part-time hours when they would have preferred full-time employment. Underemployment increased sharply starting around mid-2006 (U.S. Department of Labor 2008). By November 2009 there were 8.9 million underemployed people in the United States (Sum and Kahtiwada 2010), and as of January 2015, this count remained high at 6.8 million (U.S. Department of Labor 2015b). Underemployment hints at the "jobless recoveries" that have been typical of the new millennium (Kalleberg 2008). As with discouraged workers, underemployment also makes the official unemployment rate appear lower than it actually is.

Economic deregulation was at the root of the larger transformation of the economy (prior to the Great Recession) and began to gain traction by the 1980s.

But deregulation specifically of the housing and mortgage industries was especially relevant to the Great Recession because it tied these industries tightly to the greater economy. This meant any failure in these sectors could (and did) lead to a more widespread economic collapse (Krugman 2012). Regulations for banks that had been in place since the 1930s began to be removed by the 1980s (55). For example, the Glass-Steagall Act that had limited banks' risks by ensuring the separation between regular, everyday personal banking and riskier investment banking was weakened in the 1980s and 1990s by several acts (for example, the Garn-St. Germain Act) (59–62). This move toward deregulation culminated in the Gramm-Leach-Bliley Act of 1999, which generally repealed Glass-Steagall (85). This meant that everyday people's loans (including mortgages) could now be subject to more risk than they had been in the past.

The Great Recession happened (seemingly) very suddenly (Grusky et al. 2011a) at a time when many people thought prosperity from the booming housing market had no foreseeable end. But this interconnectedness between the housing industry and the rest of the economy was what actually led to the economic collapse (Fligstein and Goldstein 2011, 23). Many banks were highly leveraged, meaning they borrowed a lot of money that they then invested in areas (such as housing and mortgages) they believed would bring in substantial profits. Because of deregulation, lenders could even buy and sell this kind of debt to other companies (Krugman 2012, 54–55).

Many individuals were also borrowing against the value of their homes (taking out home equity loans) because they thought their homes could only increase in value and the loans would thus be easy to pay off (Krugman 2012). When the housing bubble finally burst, this high level of borrowing by many banks and individuals froze. Both lending and borrowing came to a halt as everyone tried desperately to save money or pay off debt. Spending overall also came to a stop, leaving the economy in a downward spiral as banks, insurance companies, and investment companies began to fail and many employers laid people off (126).

Many employees who worked in what had been a thriving sector of the economy—banks and mortgage companies—suddenly and unceremoniously found themselves without jobs, and the wealth that people had built up as the housing market boomed suddenly was gone when housing prices tumbled. Housing values, which had doubled between the late 1990s and 2005, fell to half their value between 2006 and 2009 (Grusky et al. 2011a). This left many people owing banks money from loans they took out against their home equity (the portion of their houses that they owned outright) during the same time they found themselves without work. Some even lost their homes. Additionally, even many of those people who did not take out home equity loans found themselves with underwater mortgages—that is, owing the bank more on the home than the home was actually worth—because they had bought their home and taken out the loan during a time when the home had been worth more money. By the end of 2009, 16.4 percent of all mortgages were underwater (Grusky et al. 2011a, 13). Because the bulk of most people's wealth is in their homes, households lost one-quarter of their wealth between 2007 and 2009 (Iceland 2013, 121).

The Great Recession left people in bad economic shape and was much more severe and much longer lasting than previous recessions (Grusky et al. 2011a, 22, 63). Whereas the average duration of unemployment in previous recessions was about nine weeks, that average had increased to twenty-one weeks (or about five months) by June 2010 (when the recession was technically over!) (68). This duration, while tragic, was what allowed me to study transitions in identity and mental health over a longer time period than has been done in most past unemployment research.

By 2009, the number of jobs lost was the highest since World War II, and there were almost seven job seekers for every open position (Grusky et al. 2011a, 64, 78). The economy after the Great Recession was slower to recover than those that followed previous recessions (Grusky et al. 2011a, 3–4; Krugman 2012, 13). Median household income (in 2011 constant dollars) declined between 2007 and 2011 (DeNavas-Walt, Proctor, and Smith 2012). Home foreclosures reached record highs in 2007 (U.S. Department of Labor 2014b, 12), and between 2007 and 2010 people getting close to retirement lost about one-third of what they had in their retirement accounts (Wolff, Owens, and Burak 2011, 128–129).

Although the Great Recession seemingly initiated these high unemployment and underemployment rates, the problem runs deeper than that. Broader structural factors play an important role, and the mainstream view has been that these are unlikely to change much anytime soon. For example, as early as the 1970s (but intensifying during the new millennium), technology made it possible to outsource jobs to other countries (Sullivan 2004), leading to layoffs in the United States. Companies have also been increasing the number of part-time and/or temporary workers instead of hiring permanent workers (Kalleberg 2000). Although at the time of this writing, some jobs have returned to the United States because of increasing costs in China (Fishman 2012), most available U.S. jobs are at one of two ends of the skill/pay spectrum—either they require highly specialized education or they are low-paid service jobs (Kalleberg 2009; Sorenson 2000). This leaves much of the "middle-section" workforce—including skilled manual laborers and mid-level managers—unemployed. In essence, even though the recession is over, the structural forces that created unemployment and underemployment, as well as the problems caused by them, remain in place.

Beyond the large-scale statistics, unemployment and underemployment influence individual lives. The national news often highlights stories of the "disgruntled worker" returning to the workplace with a firearm, or reports suicides that occur after someone has lost his or her job. But losing a job also affects people in a variety of ways that may be "under the radar" of the national news. When people lose jobs or are underemployed, their mental health suffers. (See, for example, Dooley 2003; Kalleberg 2009; Newman 1999 [1988].) Unemployment is connected to depression, anxiety, and anger. It negatively affects the emotional well-being of both blue-collar and white-collar workers, and historically it has been especially harmful to men's mental health (Creed and Moore 2006; Thoits 1986). Similarly, underemployment has been linked to low self-esteem, depression, alcohol abuse, and anger.

The causes of these declines in mental health are multifaceted. Although economic deprivation is certainly stressful and relevant to mental health problems, it is worth asking what other factors trigger the depression, anxiety, and anger that are so common after losing a job.

Job Loss, Identity, and Mental Health uses sociological concepts to examine what losing a job means for people's identities, how unemployment produces distress by threatening identity, how people may (or may not) use identity itself to cope with this distress, and how social institutions and social status may ease or hinder the use of identity-based coping strategies.

Detailed documentation exists on unemployment trends prior to, during, and after the Great Recession. Researchers who study these aspects of unemployment typically use quantifiable data from national surveys to demonstrate the extent of economic damage to individuals, communities, and the nation, and to suggest policy solutions at the societal level. For example, *The Great Recession* (Grusky et al. 2011b) illustrates the widespread decimation of retirement funds, wealth, and home values wrought by that economic crisis, as well as the accompanying delay of life transitions such as marriage and childbearing. Nobel Prize–winning economist Paul Krugman (2012) furthers this idea in his book *End This Depression Now!* by proposing policy solutions to these problems. Most notably, he suggests increasing federal spending to create jobs, tightening regulations on the banking industry, and boosting government's role in granting mortgage assistance to individuals and families.

Other books focus on the psychological experience of unemployment. Some notable examples are Tom Clark and Anthony Heath's (2014) *Hard Times: The Divisive Toll of the Economic Slump* and Clare Bambra's (2011) *Work, Worklessness, and the Political Economy of Health*. As with books whose main focus is economic damage, most books in the psychological vein are chiefly concerned with identifying widespread patterns and identifying policy solutions; they rarely use narratives or give explicit attention to the role of identity in unemployment.

These books that outline large-scale trends and policy solutions provide important insights into the ways that social structure may affect entire communities or nations, as well as individuals. *Job Loss, Identity, and Mental Health* builds on this base by using in-depth interviews and observations that offer insight into the individual's experience of losing a job—what it means for daily life, how they feel about it, and the process they go through as they try to deal with job loss and their new identities as unemployed people.

There are several foundational works that use qualitative methods similar to mine and have helped structure my thinking about the experience of unemployment. For example, in Katherine Newman's (1999 [1988]) *Falling from Grace*, she primarily describes middle-class people who lost their jobs and became downwardly mobile, giving in-depth detail on how this affects distress and relationships with friends and family. Similarly, Dale Maharidge's (2013) *Someplace Like America* and Tracy E. K'Meyer and Joy L. Hart's (2009) *I Saw It Coming* illustrate what it is like when working-class people lose their jobs. Maharidge weaves a discussion of the macro-level causes of job loss (for example, NAFTA) with critically important individual experiences related to the loss of money, such as what it is like to wait in a food bank line or face homelessness. K'Meyer and Hart describe the emotional, cognitive, and material experiences of former factory workers. In the tradition of these authors, I use in-person interviews and observations to focus more narrowly on the experience of identity as it relates to distress and coping after experiencing job loss.

An identity-based approach to the relationship between losing a job and mental health promises to be fruitful (Ezzy 1993; Feldman 1996; Kalleberg 2009). A few theoretical models hint at the connections between identity and losing a job. For example, Marie Jahoda's (1981, 1982) "functional model" proposes that work provides us with an identity, which promotes well-being. Similarly, Peter Warr's (1987) "vitamin model" states that work provides us with a valued social position and clearly defined roles, both of which are important to mental health. These models support taking an identity-based approach to job loss, but posit that work itself or work conditions are objectively "good" or "bad," thus suggesting that the same conditions produce the same outcomes for everyone. My book expands on their models by doing as Douglas Ezzy (1993) suggests: taking a symbolic interactionist approach that emphasizes the meaning of losing a job, and systematically exploring the subjective aspect of work (identity) and how it relates to distress. As Ezzy (1993) also suggests, I go beyond determining cause and effect and instead delve deeply into the process through which other factors (for example, age and gender) may produce mental health differences after job loss.

For people who identify strongly with their jobs, unemployment and underemployment can have a strong psychological impact (Probst 2000), partially because work stressors do the most harm when they "threaten salient aspects of the self" (Warr 2005, 560). As for theoretical approaches, some authors promote using a role-based (Feldman 1996) or identity-based (Ezzy 1993) standpoint, or using stress theory to understand job loss (Feldman 1996). For the most part, calls for this type of work have gone largely unheeded. (See Ezzy's 2001 book, *Narrating Unemployment*, for a notable exception.) My book takes these approaches to exploring the connections between unemployment, identity, and distress.

Empirical research also suggests that job-related problems can challenge identity (Tausig 1999, 259) and that this harms mental health. Specifically, when people's various identities are "mismatched" in some way, this can be detrimental. For example, unemployed people are more likely than employed people to claim there is a difference between who they would like to be and who they currently are (Sheeran and Abraham 1994; Sheeran and McCarthy 1990). These kinds of mismatches increase depression (Sheeran and McCarthy 1992). Underemployed people show a similar pattern. For example, recent college graduates who were working in a job that did not require a college degree—a potential challenge to "educational identity"—were more bored, lonely, and angry, and were less satisfied with life, than those who were not underemployed (Feldman and Turnley 1995).

Several books have documented unemployment from the perspective of unemployed people themselves, and have spoken to the idea of the importance of identity in this process. Thomas J. Cottle (2001) hints at threats to identity in his book *Hardest Times: The Trauma of Long-Term Unemployment*. Using data from unemployed people's narratives, a portion of Cottle's book illustrates how job loss threatens the masculine identity, which results in distress. I extend this idea by overtly examining the meaning of manhood (and womanhood) as they relate to employment, and I expand on this to include other aspects of identity that may be threatened by losing a job. Further, in *Job Loss, Identity, and Mental Health*, I incorporate sociological theory to guide my analysis, and address how identity may be used to cope with distress.

Ofer Sharone's (2013a) work, *Flawed System/Flawed Self: Job Searching and Unemployment Experiences*, also provides strong justification for an identity-based approach. Sharone compares the job search strategies of unemployed American and Israeli former white-collar workers. He finds that the typical American strategy is to present oneself on resumés as a good personal match ("the job is who I am"), whereas the Israeli strategy is to emphasize skills and send out as many resumés as possible. In essence, he establishes that for Americans, jobs have meaning for identity, and when they do not find work, they chalk up their failure to a "flawed self." My book extends Sharone's ideas about the connections between self and emotion by examining other types of unemployment experiences that can harm identity, and by looking at the specific link between distress and the meaning people give to identity and their jobs. My book also examines how job seeking may intensify or become more restricted as people try to cope with identity threats.

I also work with Sharone's themes of how social structure links to people's subjective experiences. Although Sharone centers his analysis on national structures that organize the job seeking process, my focus tends more toward mid-level institutions such as workplaces, family, and job seekers' networking groups, as well as how these may either help or get in the way of repairing identities damaged by job loss.

Notably, Sharone (as well as Carrie M. Lane [2011] in her book *A Company of One*) touches on the importance of job seekers' groups for helping American job seekers sustain a sense of work-related identity. *Job Loss, Identity, and Mental Health* adds to this analysis by addressing the circumstances under which job seekers' groups do or do not help sustain a work-related identity. Identity consistency over time was important to many of the job seekers with whom I spoke. Lane's book also hints at the importance of this by documenting unemployed professionals' individualistic tendencies to self-describe and behave like "entrepreneurs," which may have helped them maintain professional work-related identities. I build on Lane's work by systematically exploring why consistency over time is important for identity, and I connect this to stress process and identity theories.

Given that structural changes, time, and historical context are important to how people think about and experience unemployment (Walkerdine 2006), it is fruitful to compare and contrast today's unemployment with the waves of factory layoffs that occurred in the 1970s and 1980s. The era in which those layoffs occurred shaped unemployed people's experiences through the cultural expectations of that generation's workers and the positions available to them after losing a job. Specifically, factory employees at that time had earned middle-class wages even without a high school diploma if they were willing to work hard (Dudley 1997 [1994]; Milkman 1997), but once those jobs were gone the bulk of positions remaining for people with little formal education consisted of low-paying, unskilled work (Milkman 1997). They could no longer count on a social contract that promised good pay for hard work (Dudley 1997 [1994]; Milkman 1997; Walley 2013).

Is there a parallel between the experiences of the working-class factory employees forty years ago and what has happened to middle-class people after the Great Recession? Has the social contract that virtually guaranteed employment if you had a college degree (Dudley 1997 [1994], 181) been breached? If so, how do middle-class people cope with this breach? I argue (and explore more thoroughly in the final chapter) that, like the working-class people who grew up believing that hard work would always ensure that they had a job, these middle-class people of a later generation grew up thinking that a college degree was a promise of employment. And, like the working-class members of the generation before them, that assumption no longer matches society's reality.

I also argue that in order to cope with this broken promise, today's unemployed middle-class people use individualistic strategies—specifically, two strategies I call shifting and sustaining—to try to cope with the threats that job loss poses to their identities. However, when examined more closely, elements of social structure (in particular, social status and social institutions) influence whether shifting and sustaining can help resolve these identity threats and improve people's mental health.

I use interviews and observations from twenty-five unemployed people who were once in middle-class professions to tell the story of how job loss, identity, and mental health are related. I explore three challenges to identity that may occur during the job loss process and the distress that each produces. I revisit these same people three to six months later to show how they may actively use identity in particular ways (that is, engage in "identity work") to cope with and repair the initial identity damage and alleviate their distress. I also explore the mental health consequences that may occur when they are unable to do so.

I show how identity work is a coping strategy that is not equally available to everyone; it depends on one's resources. I focus on structural resources, such as social status (for example, gender or age) and involvement in and access to social institutions other than the workplace (for example, family or sports teams). Certain social statuses, and/or greater access to social institutions, provide a better chance to successfully use identity work, and therefore a better chance to reduce distress. For those who lack these valuable resources, efforts to cope with job loss through identity work usually do not succeed, and mental health may decline.

Overall, this book is a qualitative exploration of the social psychological experience of unemployment and how individual subjective thoughts and feelings connect to the larger social structure. The book illustrates the utility of incorporating identity into models of distress and coping, and shows how structural factors expand or constrain options for identity work, which can play an important part in overall levels of mental health.

In this study, I aimed to answer three questions:

1. How does identity relate to distress and coping after losing a job, and what role do statuses (such as gender and age) play in this process?
2. How do structural factors (such as involvement in job seekers' networking groups or family) expand or constrain the ways we can cope with identity threats?
3. How does time relate to identity, distress, and coping after losing a job?

Between July 2010 and August 2011, in the aftermath of the Great Recession, I conducted a total of forty-eight face-to-face in-depth interviews with twenty-five participants. I conducted these interviews at two points in time (median time = three months between interviews) with unemployed or underemployed (working less skilled jobs, fewer hours, or for lower pay than their past jobs) former white-collar employees. I limited my study to middle-class, white-collar professionals. In other words, their last job must have primarily involved non-manual "knowledge work" that typically requires a college degree (whether or not the participant had one).

I supplemented these interviews with eight formal observations conducted at job seekers' networking groups and at an unemployment office. I also spent time observing less formally in places that participants asked me to be with them (and sometimes their families): church, their homes, restaurants, former workplaces, and organizations where they currently volunteered.

Because I was interested in a very specific type of person, my sample was purposive. I intentionally recruited people who had lost their jobs and whose work had been and/or was currently relevant to their identities. I recruited participants at two separate job seekers' networking groups and a local unemployment office, as well as through personal contacts, snowball sampling (study participants referring others who might wish to participate), and referrals from personnel recruiters, or "headhunters."

My screening procedures also worked toward obtaining the purposive sample necessary for my work. I limited participation to people who had been regularly employed (for example, not a temporary worker) for at least thirty-five hours per week in their previous job. This was done to ensure that participants had ample opportunity for their jobs to become a strong part of their identities.

I also required participants to be age thirty or older because older people are more likely than younger people to have identities that are strongly invested in work (Fraccaroli et al. 1994; McFadyen 1995). I screened participants to ensure that they were not considering retirement prior to my first interview with them. People who are ready to call themselves retired could easily avoid the stigma associated with unemployment (McFadyen 1995); this could mean that their jobs are less relevant to their identities because they may be preparing to "become someone new."

Because people who have been unemployed for more than six months are likely to have high distress levels simply because of the amount of time they have been without work (Sheeran and McCarthy 1990), I limited participation to people who had lost their jobs within the past six months prior to my first interview with them. This helped ensure that any distress I found was not simply due to being without work for very long periods of time.

To ensure that work had been or was currently important to participants' identities, I asked potential participants to use a 1–10 scale to rate how strongly they identified with their former jobs: (1) when they were still employed; and (2) at the present time (at the time they gave their ratings). Only people who gave a 5 or higher on at least one of these dimensions (indicating at least moderate identity involvement) qualified to be interviewed.

Sixteen study participants were white and nine were African American; fifteen were women and ten were men. All lived in or near a major mid-Atlantic city, were between the ages of thirty and sixty-three (median = 52), and had at least some college education. All but three had at least a bachelor's degree and, reflecting the relative wealth of the geographical region, more than half of participants had annual pre-tax household incomes that exceeded $100,000 (within the past year from the date of my first interview with them). Most participants were in the middle or later stages of their careers. Participants' family situations varied. Some were single, whereas others were married, separated, or divorced. Most of them had children and were the primary breadwinners for their families. All participants lost their jobs involuntarily: some had been laid off; some were fired for cause; and some were forced by managers to resign. Additional detail about my sample is contained in appendix A.

I made audio recordings of each interview with participants and made field notes from each observation, then I transcribed all interviews verbatim. I then examined my transcripts and field notes to find recurring themes/patterns. Although I had some patterns in mind that I might expect to find (even before conducting the study), other patterns were unexpected and surprised me. I carefully documented all themes and patterns. From the data, I identified three types of identity mismatches and two types of identity work that occurred after losing a job. I also found mental health consequences that occurred when people were unable to successfully perform identity work. Further details about my research methodology, including data analysis, are contained in appendix A.

The upcoming chapters illustrate the interplay between job loss, identity, and mental health. First, in chapter 2, I briefly describe social psychological theories and concepts that are important to this study, and define basic sociological terms that are important to the experiences of the people in this book. Chapters 3 through 5 focus on the three types of distressing identity threats that occurred for people who lost their jobs. Chapter 3 introduces the first of these—a "feedback mismatch"—and explains that the way other people interact with us either helps us feel sure about who we are or leads us to question our identities. In chapter 4, I present the second identity threat—a "time mismatch"—which is when we feel like we are no longer the same person we used to be. This chapter also highlights the importance of social institutions and roles for time mismatches. Chapter 5 illustrates the third identity threat—a "status mismatch"—or the (perceived) incongruence between one's role (such as bank teller or executive) and at least one social status (such as gender, race, or age). This chapter also points out the importance of the subjective meaning people give to statuses, along with the strong influence of society's expectations on this meaning. For example, men in this study often used society's stereotypes of the "male breadwinner" to define what masculinity meant to them personally.

Chapters 6 through 8 focus on two types of identity work that people may perform in order to cope with identity threats, as well as what happens to people who are unable to successfully perform identity work. In chapter 6, I present the first of these types of identity work, namely "shifting" away from a work-related identity and instead emphasizing a non-work identity. This chapter draws attention to the value of having access to an available social institution (such as family) that can provide you with a role (such as mother) that fits what society expects for one of your statuses (for example, people generally approve of a woman putting most of her energy toward being a mother). Chapter 7 describes the second type of identity work—subjectively "sustaining" a work-related identity even though the individual is actually unemployed. Once again, I show that social institutions (such as job seekers' groups) and verifying feedback are critical to the ability to sustain. Chapter 8 portrays the extremely painful experience of "identity void"—or the loss of all sense of self— that can occur when shifting and sustaining are not viable options. I relate this back to low levels of involvement in non-work social institutions. Finally, in chapter 9, I summarize the practical and theoretical contributions of this book and place my findings within the sociological literature, with a special focus on job loss in historical context, cultural discourse and the meaning of work, and the role of social institutions and status in coping with job loss. I also recap the overall importance of identity for mental health after losing a job, as well as the relative weight of subjective and objective factors in this process.

2

Why Identity?

Imagine you just heard that your neighbor, John, lost his job. Like many people, the first thing that may pop into your mind is "What did he do wrong?" Because individualism is a strong American value (Williams 1965), we usually assume that bad things that happen to people are because of the choices they made or the ways they behaved. For example, you may assume that John did a poor job and was fired for his poor performance. When these situations are limited to a particular individual (or a few isolated individuals), are caused by the person's own behavior or character defects, and can only be remedied by his or her own actions, we categorize them as personal troubles (Mills 2000 [1959]).

However, let's say that the company John worked for was trying to cut costs, so it laid off 1,500 employees that day and John was one of them. It is unlikely that 1,500 people in the same company performed poorly enough to lose their jobs in one day. In this case, we cannot blame John (or the other 1,499 people) for losing their jobs, because it was not a result of their behavior. When many people at once are affected by a phenomenon (for example, when mass layoffs occur or unemployment rates go up sharply) and when the situation is not their fault, sociologists refer to this as a public issue (Mills 2000 [1959]). Public issues, unlike personal troubles, cannot be solved by each individual's own actions; instead, they require a structural solution—a change in the way society is set up or operates. For example, technology makes it possible for U.S. companies to globally outsource many jobs, that is, to base those jobs in non-U.S. countries (Sullivan 2004). If laws restricted the extent of global outsourcing, the U.S. unemployment rate might quickly decrease (assuming companies brought those jobs back to the United States).

Things that happen in the social structure, whether good or bad, filter down through their effects on social institutions to ultimately affect individuals.

For example, let's say the federal government (part of the U.S. social structure) decided that all colleges (a social institution) had to follow a new rule: students must earn a 98 percent in the class to get a letter grade of A. Through no fault of their own, most students (individuals)—even those who would have earned As before—would not earn As. There would be a nationwide drop in GPAs, and many individual students would become much more stressed out than they already are. So through no fault of their own, students' mental health nationwide would probably decline. In this case, mental health problems become a widespread public issue, not just a personal trouble (although they certainly can be troubling to the individual). Likewise, mental health became a public issue when many people lost their jobs during and after the Great Recession.

Because social structure can influence our mental health, many sociologists examine mental health from a structural perspective. One of the most prominent theoretical models taking a structural perspective is the Stress Process Model (Pearlin et al. 1981).

Stress and Mental Health as Processes

Losing a job—and the ways that we experience and react to that—is not a single event; rather, it is a process that takes place over time (Pearlin et al. 1981). The day you lose your job, which is a specific life event, is almost certainly difficult emotionally. However, as time progresses, the initial problems sparked by this life event may snowball and accelerate: sorrow may turn to depression; anger may trigger fights with loved ones; and, of course, financial difficulties can lead to property and personal losses. In other words, life events can produce chronic strains, or problems that continue to produce stress in their own right even after a discrete stressful life event is over (Pearlin 1999; Pearlin et al. 1981).

As the negative effects of losing your job multiply, things may become increasingly hard for you. Different people may try to cope with losing their jobs in different ways, and these ways may change over time. For example, perhaps at first Joe talks to his friends for support, but later he drowns his sorrows in alcohol. Alternately, Mandy may at first become more involved in her children's after-school activities, but later she may use most of her time to search vigorously for paid work. The stress process involved with losing a job may even begin while you are still employed. For example, you may "get a vibe" that your boss plans to fire you, or you may be told that layoffs are coming, and this can stress you out before the big event itself even happens.

The resources available to you help shape the stressful events to which you are exposed, how you cope with them, and how they affect you. Material resources, such as money, or clothes that are appropriate for an interview, may help you cope with being unemployed. But social and personal resources are also important. The Stress Process Model identifies several of these resources—self-esteem, mastery, and social support—as critical to our mental health (Pearlin et al. 1981). If you have relatively high self-esteem, you will be better able to manage stressful circumstances and your mental health may not suffer too terribly much after a negative life event (ibid.). Likewise, if your sense of mastery, or ability to manage your own life (Pearlin et al. 2007; Pearlin and Schooler 1978), is relatively high, you should also fare better when dealing with stress (Pearlin et al. 1981).

You also have better chances of successfully dealing with stress if you have lots of social support, or people in your life who encourage you, help you with money or other tangible items you need, or give you advice or information (Pearlin et al. 1981). Generally, having more resources helps protect you from ending up with poor mental health when stressful life events occur (Pearlin 1999; Pearlin et al. 1981; 2007).

Self-esteem, mastery, and social support can therefore be important to your coping strategies, another part of the Stress Process Model. Coping strategies are "cognitive and behavioral efforts to manage (master, reduce, or tolerate) a troubled person-environment relationship," and they help lower your distress (Folkman and Lazarus 1985, 152). For example, if you have failed your first statistics exam, but have high levels of self-esteem, mastery, and social support, you may think to yourself, "I'm usually a good student. I can find ways to study differently so I can do better on the next exam," and you may seek out friends, relatives, or professors who are especially good at helping you work through the material. So, although failing your first exam was a stressful life event and a little scary, you coped productively, aced the second exam, and got through the class without experiencing any major depression or anxiety. Alternately, if you failed that exam, but had little self-esteem, mastery, and social support, you might think, "I'm no good at math, so I really can't do anything about my grade," and you might not know people who have taken statistics or could be supportive. You will likely be very stressed out and fail the remaining exams.

The Stress Process Model highlights the social causes of mental health outcomes instead of individual causes (Pearlin 1989, 1999; Pearlin et al. 1981). It also features social statuses, which impact the kinds of stressful events or situations you may experience (Pearlin 1989, 1999). Social statuses are positions that have differing levels of prestige in mainstream society, such as socioeconomic class, race, or gender (Pearlin 1999). For example, mainstream society generally ranks men as being more competent than women; this stereotype reflects men's higher social status.

Social status influences your ability to cope with chronic strains by shaping access to resources (Pearlin 1989, 1999). For example, if a relatively poor waitress loses her job, she probably will not have savings to help cope with the ongoing money problems that several months of unemployment will produce. In contrast, a lawyer who loses her job is more financially secure, and would probably have sufficient savings to get through those months with minimal distress. In other words, the amount of coping resources that are available, and not just the job loss itself, may be a major cause of an unemployed person's mental health problems.

Social status also influences values, which affect the way you understand and experience stressful circumstances, thereby ultimately helping to shape mental health (Pearlin 1989). Your values, including what you believe to be important or desirable, contribute to whether a given event seems threatening to you. If you view a life event or chronic strain as a threat, it becomes stressful. One potential perceived threat is anything that could jeopardize your self-image or your identity (Pearlin 1989, 249), and when this kind of threat occurs, it feels stressful and is likely to harm mental health. Stress can involve achievements that do not match our aspirations (Pearlin 1999, 401), such as wanting to be a straight-A student but actually being a C student. This means chronic strains may involve mismatches between what you want and what is objectively true. If these mismatches involve one of your identities, then identity itself could conceivably produce a chronic strain.

Social statuses can become part of our identities (Pearlin 1999, 398; Simon 1997; Thoits 1985, 1986), and they influence how we interpret or understand our roles (or positions, such as manager or parent). For example, for a man (a status), the breadwinner role may be especially important (Townsend 2002). What a role means to us (especially in conjunction with losing or gaining the role) affects mental health (Tausig 1999). For example, if that same man who believes the meaning of manhood is to be a breadwinner loses his job, he may be very upset by being a stay-at-home parent while he is unemployed.

The connections between social status, the meaning of various roles and stressful events, and mental health suggest that identity threats may become "identity-based chronic strains" after you lose your job. Identity is not currently included as a component of the Stress Process Model. However, we could potentially better understand how life events affect mental health by examining identity-based chronic strains within a Stress Process Model framework. Doing so could be especially productive if we are examining life events that involve losing a role that was important to identity, such as a job.

Why Identity?

To get the most out of this book, it is important to understand the difference between identities and roles. Identity will refer to the "set of meanings one holds for oneself as an occupant of a particular role . . . group or category . . . or as a unique individual" (Burke and Harrod 2005, 360). Role will mean a position in society that has specific expectations and obligations attached to it (Merton 1957), such as a student or employee. This means that someone could be in, say, the role of student, but not necessarily "really" feel like a student (an identity). For example, Person 1 is in the student role and also feels like a student (has a student identity). Person 1 may think things like "I love my courses, and I enjoy learning new things. I really feel like I belong here," and may study hard, attend classes regularly, and make friends on campus. In contrast, Person 2, who is also in the student role, does not "really" feel like a student (does not have a student identity). Person 2 may think "I hate studying. I hate going to classes. I just don't feel like I belong here," and may stop going to classes altogether or even eventually drop out of school because being a student is not really "who they are."

The sociological perspective on identity asserts that we do not have one true identity or real self that is hardwired into us or exists throughout our lives. Instead, identities are more dynamic and fluid, and are really all about how well we "perform" them. In fact, Erving Goffman's concept of dramaturgy compares identity to playing a role on a stage and using "props," such as certain types of clothing, language, and so on to convince others that we are who we say we are. We are only "really" a particular identity while we are playing that role and interacting with others in it. A successful performance depends on others who react to us as though we really are the person we claim to be. In other words, all identity depends upon performances that convince others of who we are (Goffman 1959).

Roles are very important for your identities; many of your identities are based on roles (Stryker 1980). The more often you properly perform your role (that is, behave in the ways someone in that role is expected to behave), the stronger your identity involving that role will become (Burke 1991). Roles are usually embedded in social institutions (Stryker 1980), which are specific arrangements or groups of interdependent roles (MacKinnon and Heise 2010, 73) that provide organized ways of making things happen or getting things done. For example, family, church, the workplace, community organizations, and schools are social institutions. The interdependent roles in family would be, for instance, parent and child; to be a parent depends on your interactions with your child. The interdependent roles in the workplace might be boss and employee; to be a boss, you must have an employee who works for you.

Social institutions and the roles within them also help us understand our experiences, as well as what is expected of ourselves and of others (Stryker 1980). The more people we are connected to in a given social institution, and the deeper our connection to the people in it, the stronger our identities will be for that role (ibid.; Stryker and Burke 2000). For example, if you are a college student who has ten close friends, you will probably have a stronger student identity than a college student who has only two acquaintances.

Therefore, if you lose a role that was part of a social institution where you had many strong connections, your identity will probably be threatened. When you experience an identity threat or loss, it may harm your mental health (Thoits 1999). Overall, if you are involved in very few social institutions, you may not have many other available roles that you could emphasize as part of your identity after losing the other role. This could leave you to face the emotional impact of role loss head-on, which could increase distress.

For example, if Bob has children, is a volunteer at church, and coaches baseball, he might decide (if only temporarily) to redefine himself as a parent, parishioner, or coach. But if Bob was not involved with institutions other than work, he may have few available roles that could contribute to his identity after he loses his job. However, if he was involved with family, church, and the base-ball team, Bob could say "Well, I'm no longer an employee, but what really matters to me now is being a coach" (or a parent or a parishioner), and this could bolster his mental health.

Sociologists have firmly established the relationship between identity and mental health. (See, for example, Burke and Stets 2009; Higgins 1987; Thoits 1999.) Job loss is also related to mental health (Dooley 2003; Warr 1987), and identity may be a key factor in that relationship (Kalleberg 2009; Tausig 1999). Theorists who focus on work and occupations propose that work improves our mental health because it provides us with a clear and valued identity (Jahoda 1981, 1982; Warr 1987). This suggests it would be quite fruitful to give serious attention to how identity relates to mental health after job loss. It is no surprise, then, that several authors in the field (Ezzy 1993, 2001; Feldman 1996; Kalleberg 2009) have called for researchers to do so.

Identity Mismatches

Mismatches can occur between several aspects of your many identities, for example between role and status, or between who you wish to be and who you actually are. Identity mismatches help to explain mental health outcomes. (See, for example, Burke 1991, 1996; Higgins 1987; Marcussen 2006; and Thoits 1985, 1999.) They can harm mental health (Marcussen 2006), perhaps by directly decreasing self-esteem (see, for example, Stets and Harrod 2004) and mastery (Stets and Burke 2005).

Self-Discrepancy Theory (Higgins 1987) even links specific types of identity mismatches to explicit types of mental health problems (see, for example, Alexander and Higgins 1993). Identity mismatches can encompass the differ-ence between who you would like to be and who you actually are (an "aspiration discrepancy"), and this difference can lead to feelings of dejection, such as depression (Higgins 1987; Large and Marcussen 2000; Marcussen 2006). Another type of identity mismatch is between who you believe you should be and who you actually are (an "obligation discrepancy"). This leads to feelings of agitation, such as anxiety (Higgins 1987; Large and Marcussen 2000). Self-Discrepancy Theory lays a foundation for the idea that identity mismatches are important for mental health, and that other people and societal standards are important to this relationship. Therefore, other people's feedback about whether or not you are properly performing your role should relate to your identity and mental health. This is exactly what Peter Burke's (1991, 1996) work shows.

Feedback about Identity

Feedback from other people about your identities is important in order for you to be sure of who you are and for your mental health (Burke 1991; Burke and Stets 2009; Thoits 1999). We compare others' feedback to an identity standard, or our own behavioral expectations for ourselves in a specific role, to decide whether we measure up (Burke 1991). If we do not, we are likely to question our identity (for example, "Am I really cut out to be a student?") and to experience distress (Burke 1991, 1996). Generally, because we have been taught by society to understand what certain roles mean (Mead 1934), we tend to agree with mainstream society's views about what the proper behavior is for each role (Blumer 1962, 1969).

Identity Theory (Burke 1991, 1996; Burke and Stets 2009) proposes that if other people communicate in some way that you are not really the person you think you are or that you are doing a poor job in a role that is important to your identity, your mental health can suffer (Burke 1991; Burke and Stets 2009; Thoits 1999). For example, if you are an A student but fail an exam (a form of feedback from the professor), you may question whether you are really an A student and start to feel anxious or depressed. Additionally, if you monitor your own behavior and feel that it does not reflect the person you are trying to be, you will experience distress (Burke 1991, 1996; Burke and Stets 2009). For example, if you consider yourself a good basketball player, but make none of your thirty attempted shots in a game, you may question whether you really are a good basketball player even if no one says anything to you, and this will likely be distressing.

This happens for unemployed people, too. For example, unemployed working-class men said their wives stopped treating them like they were "workers" and instead treated them like disreputable unemployed people, by telling them they were no longer respectable and nagging them to get jobs (Willott and Griffin 2004). Similarly, unemployed Korean white-collar men said they lost authority and power in their households (Yang 2002). Both sets of men experienced distress because they were no longer treated as "men" or breadwinners (Willott and Griffin 2004; Yang 2002).

Social status can be important for obtaining feedback that verifies your identities. For example, higher (more privileged) statuses make it more likely that people will give you feedback supporting the idea that you are indeed the person you claim to be (Cast 2003; Cast, Stets, and Burke 1999). Additionally, when people believe there is a mismatch between your status and your role, they may interact with you in a way that threatens your identity, and this may harm your mental health (Burke 1996; Thoits 1985; 1991). For example, male homemakers might experience identity threats because the domestic role does not match up with cultural expectations for men (McDaniel 2003). For this reason, they might be subject to snide comments or disbelieving reactions when they tell people they are homemakers. In contrast, as Peggy A. Thoits (1985) suggests, identifying with roles that are consistent with what society expects for your status—such as being a male breadwinner (Townsend 2002)—may help you get feedback that confirms your identity.

Feedback that confirms you are the person you say you are is especially important for maintaining or establishing identity after losing a role. For example, feedback from other people that confirmed that injured runners were really still runners was critical to holding onto the runner identity (Hockey 2005). In contrast, when unemployed people labeled themselves as being "in transition," but others did not react in accepting, validating ways, unemployed people's distress increased (Baird 2010).

Identity Discrepancy Theory (Large and Marcussen 2000) combines Identity Theory's focus on feedback with Self-Discrepancy Theory's focus on identity mismatches. In short, Identity Discrepancy Theory proposes that when you get feedback from other people that indicates identity mismatches, or when you monitor your own behavior and find identity mismatches, your mental health will suffer (Large and Marcussen 2000; Marcussen 2006; Marcussen and Large 2003).

Time and Identity

We generally want our identities to feel consistent across time (Burke 1991, 1996; Swann 1983). We usually want some kind of continuity between who we were in the past and who we believe we will someday become (Ibarra and Barbulescu 2010). If you feel as though you are not the same person over time—like who you are has changed—you are likely to feel distressed (Burke 1996), whereas seeing yourself as the same person across time reduces distress (Hockey 2005; Iyer et al. 2009; Manzi et al. 2010).

But time-consistent identities are not the whole story. We also think about our identities as they relate to the past and the future (Markus and Nurius

1986). If you imagine a positive "possible self" or "future you," this improves your mood (Iyer et al. 2009; Manzi et al. 2010; Markus and Nurius 1986). Possible selves also help motivate you to become the person you hope to be, and when you believe it is possible to become the person you want to become (Markus and Nurius 1986) or when you identify with possible future roles (Iyer et al. 2009), your self-esteem increases (ibid.; Markus and Nurius 1986) and your mood becomes more positive (Markus and Nurius 1986). Herminia Ibarra and Roxana Barbulescu (2010) suggest that some people who are going through work-related transitions talk about their experience in terms of who they hope to become. If this is so, then people who lose their jobs could also think about who they will be in the future in order to cope with their loss and improve their mental health.

It is also possible that people can revert to past identities as a coping strategy. Sometimes when people lose their spouse roles (through divorce) (Duran-Aydintug 1995) or athlete roles (Drahota and Eitzen 1998; Hockey 2005; Stier 2007), they try to continue to say they are "still spouses" or "still athletes." Because having consistency in our identities boosts mental health (Burke 1991, 1996; Swann 1983), we would expect that, if people successfully convince themselves they are still the people they once were, their distress would lessen. Supporting this idea, Jennifer Tosti-Kharas (2012) showed that some people who lost their jobs tried to continue to identify with their old workplaces, and this improved their mental health.

Using Identity Work to Cope with Identity-Related Distress

When your distress comes from identity threats, it makes sense to try to manage identity in some way to reduce your distress. Sometimes people use identity work—the way "people construct and negotiate personal identities" (Snow and Anderson 1987, 1336)—to hold onto or repair their self-esteem and to reconcile what is actually true (for example, being unemployed) with their self-concept (for example, seeing yourself as "really still a manager"). For example, homeless people performed three types of identity work to deal with the stigmatizing nature of being homeless. They talked in ways that either: separated them from their actual homelessness; framed homelessness positively and welcomed the homeless identity; or embellished their past (ibid.).

People also perform identity work when other identities, such as those based on race (Khanna and Johnson 2010) or gender (Vaccaro, Schrock, and McCabe 2011), might create distress. Some authors have used the identity work concept to understand how people construct specific occupational identities (Pritchard and Symon 2011; Wrench and Garrett 2012) and to examine how older and disabled people manage being unemployed (Riach and Loretto 2009). If people's identities are threatened through identity mismatches after losing their jobs, it is reasonable to assume they may use identity work to try to cope with the distress these mismatches create.

What Does This Book Do and Why Is It Important?

Job Loss, Identity, and Mental Health illustrates the importance of including identity in models of distress and coping. The Stress Process Model makes major contributions to understanding mental health. However, it contains a gap; it does not fully explore identity, which we know is connected to mental health (Burke 1996; Higgins 1987; Pearlin 1989; Thoits 1983, 1986, 1999) and to our experience of stressful events (Pearlin 1989; Thoits 1999). It also does not directly address the importance of feedback or our internal processes, such as thoughts about who we are and the emotions associated with those thoughts. By including identity in models of the stress process, we can better understand mental health by detecting additional social psychological (as opposed to material) chronic strains, especially those that may occur after someone has lost a role (such as a job) on which a valued identity was based.

Many identity theories propose that mismatches can be detrimental to mental health. Identity mismatches may involve feedback from others who say you are not who you claim to be, or your own determination that this is the case as you monitor your behavior (Burke 1991, 1996; Burke and Stets 2009). They may also involve a lack of identity consistency across time (Burke 1991, 1996; Swann 1983) or between a role and a status (Burke 1996; Thoits 1985, 1991). However, many identity theories do not examine identity, stress, and mental health outcomes in terms of a process that occurs over time. They also do not give systematic attention to the interplay between time, status, and social institutions as people try to cope with stressful, identity-threatening events by performing identity work. In particular, combining the Stress Process Model's focus on social status, time, and coping with Identity Theory and Self-Discrepancy Theory's emphases on identity mismatches can provide powerful insight into how stresses and identity relate to mental health outcomes in real life.

Combining the two types of models could help us better understand our many identities (Stryker and Burke 2000), as well as how they might be used in identity work when one of those identities is threatened (for example, emphasizing an alternate role) (Simon 1997; Thoits 1995, 1999; Thompson and Bunderson 2001). Identity models that emphasize social structure (for example, focusing on social institutions and roles) complement models that focus mostly on internal processes (such as emotions and the meaning of identities) (Stryker and Burke 2000). In this book, I show that identity theories that focus on internal processes also work well with structural models of stress (not just structural identity theories), specifically the Stress Process Model. To date, most research has been conducted using either a structural or internal theoretical framework, so the theories remain largely disconnected from one another. This book takes a step toward examining productive connections between these two types of theories, and explores how using them together can uncover new information about the mental health process and identity change.

Preparing for What's Next

Losing a job can cause serious financial problems: you may fall behind on your mortgage, lose your home or small business, incur massive credit card debt, struggle to pay for your children's schooling expenses, and have your utilities turned off. Job loss may also lead to troubled family relationships: you may argue with a spouse or significant other, struggle with teenagers who are angry about their new lower standard of living, or you may even divorce. And losing your job can leave you with too much time on your hands, which can cause you to feel bored (Feldman and Turnley 1995), unproductive, and lacking purpose. But the psychological distress caused by job loss and other work-related problems goes beyond its effects on your finances and family.

Many of your identities are based on roles within social institutions (Stryker 1980), such as a job within a workplace, and work gives you a clear role (Warr 1987) on which you can base your identity. Work provides you with an idea of who you are—your identity (Jahoda 1981, 1982)—and work-related stresses are most harmful when they "threaten salient aspects of the self" (Warr 2005, 560). Unfortunately, this means that losing your job can harm your identity (Ezzy 2001; Lane 2011; Tausig 1999), which can lead to emotional distress (Cassidy 2001; Ezzy 2001; Sheeran and McCarthy 1992).

Job Loss, Identity, and Mental Health highlights three ways that work-related identity threats can create stress:

1. feedback mismatch: people no longer treat you like the person you believe you are (see, for example, Willott and Griffin 2004; Yang 2002);
2. time mismatch: you are no longer the person you were in the past (see, for example, McFadyen 1995; Warr 2005); and
3. status mismatch: who you are in terms of social status (for example, a male or a college-educated person) is threatened or does not match society's expectations for other parts of your identity. For example, you may think you are "too educated" for a specific job (see, for example, Feldman and Turnley 1995), or are no longer a "real man" if you are unemployed (Yang 2002).

These identity threats produce distress that is conceptually separate from that caused by other things, such as financial problems. Identity is central to the entire process of losing your job—before, during, and after the day your job actually ends. When losing your job threatens the idea of who you are, identity can become a source of stress and a chronic strain. You may be able to use identity work to cope with this threat, but your social statuses and the social institutions in which you are involved will affect the likelihood of your identity work being successful.

As you read the stories of people who lost their jobs, you may find yourself feeling sympathetic, sad, or compassionate. At other times, you might feel angry or even disgusted by what some of the people in this book say or do. Many different kinds of people lose their jobs. Not all of them are likable. Most have both good and bad qualities. When you read about the bad qualities, you may feel less sympathy for some of those people. I have chosen to include their stories because it is important to illustrate what losing a job is really like for real people—likeable, unlikeable, and those in between. In real life, people lose their jobs in many different ways and have diverse reactions to job loss.

The next three chapters (chapters 3, 4, and 5) focus mainly on the lives of three study participants—Charlie, Cindy, and Marsha—but they also contain briefer supplementary stories from other study participants.[1] They describe their backgrounds, former jobs, living situations, and families. They explain what happened and how they felt on the day they lost their jobs, as well as what happened in the days, weeks, and months that followed. They discuss how they experienced feedback, time, and status mismatches. Chapters 6, 7, and 8 continue to follow Charlie, Cindy, Marsha, and others to show how people use identity work to try to cope with the identity threats that arise from work-related problems.

The following chapter highlights how what other people tell you about who you are can clash with who you believe yourself to be, and how this can cause confusion and emotional suffering. It also details how individuals, social institutions (such as the workplace), and society-at-large are closely interconnected. Distress is not just caused by bad individual choices, but by public issues in the social structure (such as a recession) that affect many people at once. Charlie, Cindy, and several other people illustrate this with their stories.

3

"That's Not the Way
We Do It at Gentay"

Feedback Mismatches

Introducing Charlie: "It Just Really Sucked the Air Outta Me"

It has been three months and Charlie is still fuming.

At first, you cannot see this. Charlie seems calm and reasonable. He appears friendly, happy, and relaxed. He speaks freely, in even tones, without strong emotion. But as he continues, his words, tone of voice, and body language betray him. Something—hopelessness, resentment, or maybe anger—is bubbling just below the surface, and he is trying very hard to control himself, to not let it take him over. But his surface calm begins to crack as he discusses his past job and the day he was laid off by his boss, Cheryl.[1] Speaking in a sinister and angry voice, Charlie says:

> So clinical. So illegal. So precise. So antiseptic . . . [Charlie returns to a more normal tone of voice] That isn't the way you treat me. . . . And who do you think you are in your position treating anybody this way. . . . [Charlie whispers] I was made to feel like a criminal. . . . [Charlie stops whispering, but speaks quietly] That I can't forgive . . . I said, "Cheryl. Cheryl! Wow! You are incredibly cold. You're sitting here telling me that my services are no longer needed after twenty-four years, as if nothing's going on?" . . . But I thought to myself, you know what? You pushed me around for three years. You jerked my—I could use some language—you jerked my chain. You really insulted me by never coming to me and asking my opinion or my input. . . . And then you just sit there and you tell me I'm not a part of the future? . . . You unceremoniously dismissed me like an ordinary criminal?

Charlie, a white sixty-two-year-old man, wore a forest green flannel shirt, olive-colored slacks, and brown loafers when I first interviewed him.

His immaculately groomed short brown hair was graying at the temples, and his black wire-framed glasses highlighted the wrinkles around his eyes. Although he would have easily fit in at a middle-class office's "casual Friday," he gave a drab, generic impression.

Charlie lived with his wife, Janette, and their two preteen children, Monica and Michael. They owned a home in a highly desirable and trendy urban neighborhood, and they were maintaining about the same standard of living they had before Charlie lost his job. Charlie's former employer gave him a severance package worth six months of salary. This, along with his substantial investments, helped them avoid financial problems.[2] However, Janette, who had been employed part time when Charlie was still working, had returned to work full-time, so the family could keep getting health insurance. Charlie said he did not think Janette's increased work hours bothered her.

For most of the twenty-four years that Charlie had worked as a director of training at the national nonprofit Smith Organization, he had felt good about going to work each day. He enjoyed training other employees and clients, managing client relationships, supervising employees, traveling to conferences, and documenting organizational processes. Charlie, like others of his Baby Boomer generation, was in mid-career when educational credentials virtually guaranteed a good job. Charlie had even returned to school to earn two master's degrees, which probably solidified the job security typically expected by Baby Boomers (Sullivan 2004, 200) like Charlie. Like many Baby Boomers, he assumed that after years of paying his dues working in lower-level positions, he would be rewarded with a promotion (Lancaster and Stillman 2010, 89). Since early in his career at the Smith Organization, Charlie had aspired to become a vice president. When this position opened up in his organization, he applied. He did not get the job. Instead, the organization hired Cheryl—a woman fourteen years his junior—and she became his new boss.

Being denied a promotion to vice president was not simply disappointing; it threatened Charlie's identity, perhaps because Charlie already saw his job as a major part of who he was. Many of our identities are role identities, which are rooted in our roles (or positions, such as manager) within social institutions (such as the workplace) (Stryker 1980). These institutions are embedded within a larger social structure that has established specific ways to produce and exchange goods and services, communicate, and manage leadership and political processes (among other things). Each society's social structure (and culture) differs somewhat from those of other societies and creates behavioral guidelines and boundaries.

The overall social structure also lays the groundwork for the kinds of social institutions and roles that are important to us. For example, the U.S. social structure includes a capitalist economy in which we usually work for pay to make a living. Perhaps this is one reason that in the United States we tend to see our jobs as a major part of our identities (Jahoda 1981, 1982; Tausig 1999; Warr 1987), and why Charlie believed that his job had been "his life": "The Smith Organization was a huge chunk. . . . It was the longest I've been anywhere. I think it's sort of where I came into my own . . . became a professional man. . . . It was my life."

Over time, Charlie had begun to more clearly envision becoming a vice president. This served as a "future self" (Markus and Nurius 1986) that was extremely important to him. Believing it is possible to become who we want to be improves our mood (Iyer et al. 2009; Manzi et al. 2010; Markus and Nurius 1986) and our self-esteem (Iyer et al. 2009; Markus and Nurius 1986). But when the person we are does not match up with who we hope to be, we often become dejected (Higgins 1987; Large and Marcussen 2000; Marcussen 2006). Therefore, not getting the promotion shattered Charlie's emotional well-being. At age sixty-two, Charlie believed he had lost his last chance at having a "vice president" identity. The denied promotion served as feedback that he was not—and would never be—a vice president, and this started a downward spiral that Charlie could not reverse.

The denied promotion occurred several years before Charlie lost his job, but it threatened his employee identity even more than when he actually lost his job as director of training (three months before I first interviewed him): "[Losing the promotion] was a profound, profound paradigm shift. Because I thought earlier in my career that if I didn't retire as being a VP that my work life would have been a failure. . . . So when I didn't get that job, that was the point—not losing the job—that was the point when it just really sucked the air outta me."

Not receiving a promotion to vice president was a form of feedback that told Charlie he was not really headed toward the future self to which he had aspired. This may have also caused him to doubt his identity as a "good employee"; if he was not promoted, he must not be that good. He began to feel very distanced from his employee identity, and started to actively remove himself from it in his own mind and in his behavior. He described "drawing himself out of the picture" at one organizational meeting: "From a personal point of view, I had already disengaged. I had taken my heart and soul out of the process. That was really hard. . . . So I would sit in meetings . . . and I would be listening to other people—much inferior to myself, of course—drone on and I would draw this picture . . ." As I sit with Charlie he draws, one at a time, single small stick figures in a row moving toward the right side of the top of a piece of paper, each figure smaller than the previous one. ". . . of myself and I'd say, 'This is me with my ego. And this is me, taking myself out of this picture 'til I have . . . very little ego. [Charlie draws his initials on the page.] And this is just me sitting in this meeting."

Charlie was physically at the meeting but was literally drawing himself out of the picture. Although his employee identity was still important to him, knowing he would never become vice president weakened it. He started to disengage from his employee identity; he performed the duties of his job, but no longer went above and beyond what was expected of him: "I started sort of thinking that way as part of this process. I don't have to go to that meeting. It's optional. So I won't. Why? You know? Do I want to be seen as a player? For what?"

Charlie had begun to remove his identity from his job and acted accordingly by investing less energy in his work. This may have been one reason Cheryl decreased the amount of his raises, cutting them in half (to the minimum allowed by the organization) by the second year he worked for her.

During this time, Cheryl also called Charlie on the carpet for several policy violations. Cheryl reprimanded Charlie for allowing one of his subordinates to misrepresent her work hours on her time sheets. And when Charlie booked his travel arrangements for a conference without first getting permission, Cheryl told Charlie this was a policy violation and she did not allow him to go to the conference. She then held what Charlie called a "come-to-Jesus meeting" in which they reviewed the entire policy manual together.

Even though Charlie had distanced himself from his employee identity, he technically was still an employee, and could have reasonably expected to be treated as one. But Cheryl gave Charlie feedback that he was not properly performing his employee role, and when she disallowed his travel she even took away an opportunity for him to act like an employee.

These interactions between Charlie and Cheryl can be classified as what I call a feedback mismatch. We need feedback from others to confirm that we are who we say we are. Without this feedback for a specific role, we may stop identifying with it (Burke 1991, 1996), and may even leave the role altogether (Burke and Stets 2009, 147). Despite Charlie's own claim that he was disengaging from his employee identity, there was still some part of him that identified as a director of training. So when Cheryl treated Charlie in ways that told him he was not the director of training he thought he was, he experienced a feedback mismatch.

There was also a mismatch between the person Charlie had hoped to become—his "future self" as a vice president—and the ways others treated him. For example, when the hiring managers denied Charlie's promotion, they did not treat him as a (potential) vice president, and his new boss (the new vice president) treated him not as an equal, but as a subordinate. Even though Charlie technically was Cheryl's subordinate, he saw himself as the rightful vice president. The meanings we assign to identities are critical to our emotional reactions to potential identity threats (Burke and Stets 2009). Charlie's perceived identity combined with others' reactions to him produced a feedback mismatch in Charlie's mind, threatened his identity, and led to distress.

Charlie began to believe (correctly or not) that some of his subordinates were in league with Cheryl to get rid of him. One day, Charlie's anger came to a head when Stephanie, whom he directly supervised, disobeyed his instructions and challenged his authority as her boss. This created yet another feedback mismatch between the person Charlie believed himself to be (director/boss) and how Stephanie treated him (as an equal, someone she did not need to obey). Charlie reached the boiling point:

> We had a big dust-up. . . . [She] was totally insubordinate . . . I said [to Stephanie], "You can't do badges for this meeting because so-and-so is supposed to do those badges and we have to work within this process." And she wrote back and she goes, "She's no good. She doesn't do it right. They come back. They're wrong." . . . And I said, "If they're wrong, we'll talk to her boss." . . . I was controlling my employee. . . . I said, "You"— [Charlie taps on the table to simulate typing]—in capital letters on this email—I said, "YOU—WILL—NOT—DO—BADGES."

As Charlie struggled to control Stephanie (and to maintain his identity as a boss) he became so worried that she might disobey his orders that he discussed it with his wife that evening: "I said to my wife, 'If she does that . . . I'm taking those badges and I'm throwing them in the [trash] basket.' . . . And I walked in the next morning and she was doing badges. And my assistant came up to me and she goes, 'Charlie, Stephanie's doing badges and everybody's waiting to see what you're gonna do.'"

Charlie's peers had been watching closely as Stephanie challenged his boss identity. He may have felt a strong need to reestablish that he was Stephanie's boss, so he would not lose even more of his already threatened identity. Charlie took action:

> So I walked into [Stephanie's] office and very calmly said, "What are you doing?" And she goes, "I'm doing badges." I mean, it was just like a stick in the eye, and I said, "What did I tell you?" And she goes, "I have to do them for the success of the meeting." So in other words, [she's saying], "You're nobody. I'm doin' what I wanna do. You don't know what you're talking about." [She's saying] [Charlie puts his middle finger up] "to you."

Stephanie's behaviors told Charlie she did not see him as a boss—in fact, he was "nobody"—and so she would not follow his instructions. This feedback mismatch threatened Charlie's boss identity. Charlie had claimed that he was disengaging from his employee identity, but in reality his identity had been swinging back and forth like a pendulum. Although it was true that, at times, he intentionally disengaged from this identity, he now made a dramatic attempt to reassert it:

> I just took the badges and I just threw 'em in the basket. And she—and I didn't, you know, I said, [Charlie makes "monster" sounds] "Arrrrgggh arrrrgggh." I didn't, you know. I just said, "You're not doing them." She got all freaked out and she goes, "I'm calling one of the men down the hall." . . . So HR said to me . . . "Charlie, you shouldn't have done that. You should have just reminded her." . . . [Charlie whispers] [Stephanie] kept pushing and pushing and pushing and pushing. [Charlie speaks in a normal volume] So I thought a little drama, you know. . . . [Stephanie] went down the hall and said, [Charlie whispers in a high-pitched "little girl" voice] "Charlie was really, really mad and I was afraid and he threw the, the—and it ripped the plastic and I, in the, in the, in the basket."3

Charlie was so angry that Stephanie had challenged his boss identity that he had blown up. This behavior, along with some of Charlie's other reactions to work-related identity threats, led to multiple reprimands, additional feedback that he was not a good employee, and ultimately to probation and dismissal.

The "badges" fiasco and Charlie's violations of company policy may have established him as an unfit employee in Cheryl's eyes.4 But Charlie's admitted disengagement from his job also contributed to Cheryl's decision to fire him.5 When she put him on probation, she highlighted Charlie's lack of commitment to his job: "[She] said I was checked out. . . . She said I wasn't engaging with the members and I wasn't engaging with the staff. . . . She said, 'You're just not engaged.'"

When others' feedback contradicts the person we believe ourselves to be, we begin to lose that identity and suffer emotionally (Burke 1991, 1996). Charlie began to lose his employee identity when he was denied a promotion and was repeatedly reprimanded. Both of these forms of feedback told Charlie he was not a good employee.

Even though Charlie may have brought some of his problems on himself and was conflicted about his employee identity, he still experienced the ways others treated him as identity threats. During his final year at the Smith Organization these threats became like "torture," to the point where he claimed he had not cared if he was going to lose his job: "I really didn't wonder [about being laid off] for that whole year. I was just unhappy. You know . . . when one is tortured . . ."

Unfortunately, though, he did care. That final, ultimate message to Charlie that he was no longer an employee came when he was called to his boss's office and laid off:

> It was just a day like any other day . . . I got this email: "Please come down to my office at three o'clock." . . . So it was about ten to three and I thought, "Oh, this is not good." So I went to the bathroom and I just

kinda [Charlie sniffs] did some deep breathing exercises and went into the office and there was the head of HR and there was my boss. "Close the door please." Both of 'em had folders. Now I thought two things: either they're re-orging and I'm going to be reporting to somebody else, or they're eliminating the snake [his subordinate], or this is not good for me. . . . So very officiously . . . [Cheryl] goes [Charlie mimics his boss's clipped, formal voice, just above a whisper, using an exaggerated falsetto] "As you know, Janet is doing a reorganization of the organization and there's going to be some fundamental changes." . . . Which I didn't know. And she said, "So there'll be big changes in [the department] and you will not be part of that process. You will not be a part of the future of the Smith Organization." And I said, "What are you saying?" And she said, "Your services are terminated as of today." [Charlie whispers] I just sat there. And I looked at her. I said [Charlie speaks in a normal volume] "Wow. You are cold."

Just after he lost his job, Charlie went back to his desk and gathered his personal items. He felt a whirlwind of conflicting emotions: "I wasn't crying or anything. . . . You just walk around and you're like 'Ummmm, okay. I'll take my clock. . . . What just happened?' . . . I look at the [termination] folder and I think maybe I should read the folder. Maybe I should march back in there. . . . [I felt] shock. And dismay. But in a weird kind of way, relief?"

People are often ambivalent about losing their jobs (see, for example, Ezzy 2001, 59–61; K'Meyer and Hart 2009, 98), and may even frame their feelings about it differently at different times (Ezzy 2001). Charlie showed his ambivalence by describing his experience as relief, dismay, and torture, and by alternately strongly identifying and dis-identifying with his job.

Charlie's initial shock and dismay later turned into bitterness and anger. He believed his boss had been "jerking his chain" all along. Being laid off gave Charlie the ultimate feedback about just how "bad" an employee he was—he was so bad that he was now not allowed to be an employee. He was relieved that the conflict with his coworkers was over, and that he would no longer experience feedback mismatches at work. Nevertheless, losing his job was still very hard for him, partially because of the effect it had on who he was.

Feedback mismatches, and the anxiety and anger they produced in Charlie, had occurred repeatedly for three years before he actually lost his job. Charlie's roles as boss, director of training, and (potentially) vice president had been very important to his idea of who he was. But he was denied a promotion to vice president; his subordinate, Stephanie, refused to follow his orders; and his boss repeatedly reprimanded him, lowered the amount of his raises, put him on probation, and ultimately fired him.

Charlie had become increasingly disengaged from his job after he did not get the promotion he wanted. But now he was officially cut off from his former work environment and workplace identities. He would struggle to answer the question "Who am I now?" because he felt as though he was becoming a different person than he had been in the past (see chapter 4), and he was also troubled by feeling less like a man (see chapter 5).

Introducing Cindy: "I Was No Longer a Top-like Salesperson"

Two-and-one-half months before I spoke with Cindy, a friendly and optimistic white sixty-two-year-old former account executive, she had lost her job at a national travel industry chain where she had worked for eight years and had been an award-winning employee. As with Charlie, the threats to Cindy's identity were triggered while she was still employed, when her boss gave her feedback that she was no longer a "good" employee. Like Charlie, Cindy's employee identity was very important to her and she experienced feedback mismatches from interactions with her new boss. But, unlike Charlie, Cindy was not dissatisfied with her position at work and she did not disengage from her job.

Cindy's story began with a large-scale (or macro-level) phenomenon—forty years of an increasingly global economy. Global corporate competition has made it much more common for workplaces (meso-level social institutions) to merge with other companies, restructure their workforces, and lay off employees in an effort to maximize profit (Kalleberg 2009). These meso-level changes at Cindy's workplace, Gentay Travel, made her an individual (or micro-level) casualty of the global economy. A company merger ultimately led Cindy to lose her job, question her own mind, and become confused about her identity.[6]

Cindy lived in a quiet neighborhood lined with large, old trees and small flower gardens, just off of a busy main street. Cindy and her husband, Peter, who was ten years her senior and was beginning a second, part-time career in sales, owned a modest 1,500-square-foot townhome, which contrasted with the "old money" mansions in the neighborhood. Cindy's severance package, Peter's retirement funds, and their savings helped them retain their upper-middle-class standard of living in the face of Cindy's unemployment.

As I entered Cindy's home, she welcomed me warmly, offered me tea, and gave me a tour of their newly remodeled kitchen, complete with dark granite countertops and light-colored, smoothly polished wood cabinets. She told me to "ignore the dirty dishes in the sink," then bemoaned the thought of their finances becoming strained to the point where they would possibly have to give up their cleaning lady.

Cindy sported a red v-neck T-shirt, loose-fitting black slacks, and several trendy chunky gold and silver braided rings, and her brown oval-shaped glasses framed her lively bright blue eyes. Her short, feathered reddish-brown hair was graying a little, but overall she gave a vibrant impression.

She escorted me into her stylish living room, which swam in creamy earth tones and featured Brazilian cherry hardwood floors. Modern art paintings and sculpture were prominently displayed throughout the room. We sat in comfortable beige-orange leather swivel chairs beside a window, near several tall leafy indoor plants. Cindy was relaxed and talkative as she told me her story.

Cindy had once loved her job and the company she worked for. She loved her clients, some of whom she described as "characters," and she knew they trusted her. She usually worked autonomously from home and had guidance from supportive managers when she needed it. On an average day, she spoke with clients by phone to arrange events and travel plans, and helped troubleshoot any problems clients might have. She worked on commission, earned a high salary, and was her family's primary breadwinner. She described her work relationships in glowing terms: "It was very positive because we were all in it together. It was not a top-down kind of thing. It was very collaborative . . . I had such a wonderful relationship with all the people I worked with."

Before the merger, most of Cindy's clients were nonprofit groups, including fraternal organizations, religious groups, and the military. She had recruited her own clients over an eight-year period, had invested in them, and cared about them deeply. Cindy's mood ran high when her clients told her that she had done a good job: "[I felt happiest] when I did have a relationship with a customer that was positive and they would thank me for all I had done. If there was a problem, I was able to help resolve their problems. That made me feel great."

Positive feedback from coworkers about her job performance also left Cindy feeling good about who she believed she was—a top-notch account executive:

Sometimes my interactions with some of my colleagues [were] just delightful. . . . One of them called me up one day and . . . there was a certain situation with another colleague and she said, "I just wanna know what you think about this." . . . I told her just to cool it, but in a very, very nice way. . . . And she goes, "You know what? I knew that if I spoke to you, you would make me see it in the right way." . . . I felt like she and a lot of my colleagues just really respected me. . . . Those situations made me feel really good. . . . I really excelled at my job . . . and I won all kinds of awards. . . . I've always worked. . . . I was always identified with [travel]. . . . I've always been so consumed by my job and it was everything, and part of my identity.

Unfortunately, a potentially ominous future hovered over the company. Cindy had known for three years that the company planned a merger. When it occurred, Cindy had to compete with other job seekers and had to interview to try to keep her own job. But Cindy was not selected to keep her position. She was demoted, and even though the duties of her new job within the company were very similar to those in her old job, it paid only half as much.

At first, Cindy held on to her executive identity even after her demotion. In fact, she enjoyed her job so much that she chose to stay with the company despite the lower pay and rank, and she anticipated continuing to do the job she loved until the end of her career. But after the company's merger, Cindy was assigned a new boss, Lisa, who was about half her age. Lisa restructured the way in which clients were assigned to account executives. This meant that the clients Cindy herself had recruited long ago were transferred to another person's oversight, and Cindy was told that the clients were "not hers." As her work was taken from her, she had fewer opportunities to perform the work-related identity she had been used to. This may have lessened her feeling of being a Gentay executive: "Bit by bit, my accounts were taken away from me. The ones I had found and built up were given to other people. And I bought into the whole stupid thing . . . that these were quote 'Gentay's' accounts, not mine. Which was horseshit [Cindy laughs] looking back on it, because my clients weren't served by the change at all."

It became hard for Cindy to perform her occupational role. Her responsibilities had not changed, despite the change in official job title. However, the specific ways in which she was required to perform these responsibilities had changed. Lisa gave Cindy much less autonomy in her job. Now, instead of working directly with her brand-new clients, Cindy was required to start her work by talking to travel industry representatives about rates they would charge on various dates, and then find a client who fit those parameters. All the while, Cindy had to bounce back and forth between multiple travel industry representatives to gain clearance for each deal:

> [They] would say they need business on such-and-such a dates. I'd go out and find something and then . . . because of the way the system was set up . . . somebody in a cubicle in [a separate location] would say "No. It doesn't fit the [rate] parameters." So I would then have to call the person. And then I'd have to go talk to the . . . revenue manager. And then I'd have to go back . . . and say, "They're tellin' me no. Do you want this or not?" It was such a rigmarole to really do your job. I could always manage it before, but in this new situation I just could not come to grips with it or to make it work.

The policies, procedures, and performance quotas that had been put into place also changed from week to week. Cindy responded with skepticism and confusion:

> The teamwork in the new position felt very contrived. . . . There were all these new systems and ways of doing things that were . . . [Cindy sighs]. It almost seemed like busy work, and it would change. You'd do it one way one week and then they'd say, "Oh, you know what? We're gonna do it differently. Now let's do it another way." . . . The whole concept of how I had been trained for all these years with Gentay. . . . The whole system was so turned on its head.

The sense of teamwork she had loved so much was now gone, along with the clear and consistent expectations for how she would be evaluated. Success was no longer measured in terms of client satisfaction. The new evaluation system instead involved primarily numerical measurements that mostly focused on volume, such as the number of contacts made. And to make matters more complicated, the new multidimensional evaluation plan meant Cindy could sometimes "fail" on some performance dimensions while receiving bonuses for exceeding in others. Perhaps worst of all for Cindy, the new ways of doing the work seemed to leave her beloved clients dissatisfied.

Cindy thought the performance criteria set by the company were impossible to meet, but when she saw her colleagues apparently meeting them with ease, she blamed herself. She thought that surely this was evidence that she was an incompetent failure:

> [Lisa] gave me a list of things to do and it was impossible. There was no way any one handler could accomplish all these things and still keep up all of the bookings. . . . You had to do so many calls. And [Lisa] would question everything. "Well, that's not really a call . . ." I really felt my confidence starting to erode then because I just couldn't achieve what I had been achieving before. . . . And [yet, in the past] I had had such a stellar career.

The negative feedback Cindy's superiors gave her affected more than just her feelings about how well she performed; it changed her thoughts about who she was, just as Identity Theory predicts (Burke 1991, 1996). Cindy's bosses gave her feedback that she was not a "good executive" because she could not meet their expectations. This caused a feedback mismatch between Cindy's "award-winning account executive" identity and the "bad employee" identity her bosses' feedback implied.

When I asked Cindy to describe an instance that stood out for her of when her boss gave her feedback, she told me about a visit to a client that became a dreadful experience of exclusion from "the Gentay crew." Lisa told Cindy she should bring cookies along with her when they went together to visit a dissatisfied client. Cindy arrived with cookies in hand, ready to meet her client. But Lisa decided the cookies were inadequate and did not represent how "Gentay people" did things: "So I went into this one client that I knew that was having problems with us. [Lisa] went with me. I didn't have time to do this elaborate wrapping so I went to a grocery store and I bought some cookies. . . . And afterward she criticized me because they weren't good cookies. . . . [She said] [Cindy uses a snippy tone] 'That's not the way we do it at Gentay.'"

Lisa sent a clear message to Cindy that day: You did it this way. We at Gentay do it this other way. Therefore, you are not a "good" Gentay employee. Feedback mismatches create distress, and when they occur frequently enough they can lead to serious mental health problems. This is what happened to Cindy. One early sign of future debilitating mental health problems was Cindy's severe anxiety at the very thought of meeting with Lisa: "Any time I had a one-on-one [with Lisa], I knew I was gonna get beaten up. The doctor kept prescribing very mild anti-anxiety medication and so I found out that there was anxiety and there was *anxiety*. And whenever I had to meet with [Lisa] I had the pills with me and I had to take one—and full strength—because I just couldn't deal with her."

As time went on, things worsened for Cindy: "[Lisa] said something like, 'That's not working for you. I think you should be in something else.' And I felt like, here she had written me up twice. . . . I was more and more stressed. I was depressed. My body hurt. . . . Anxious, I guess, is the word. . . . I just . . . had such terrible feelings of self-doubt. . . . I felt that . . . something had happened to me, that I was no longer a top-like salesperson."[7]

Experiencing anxiety (Hanisch 1999) and depression (Dooley 2003; Hanisch 1999; Woo and Postolache 2009) is common after losing a job, but many of the people I spoke with said that they became anxious and depressed while they were still employed. However, reverse causation—mental health problems that led to people losing their jobs—is unlikely because these symptoms typically only occurred after new bosses told them they were not the person they thought they were. Although some people had experienced mental health problems throughout their lives, this did not appear to cause them to lose their jobs.

For example, Cindy was frank with me about her long history of depression. She had taken medication for many years, and attributed periods of depression to specific life transitions (which can relate to identity changes). She also told me she tended toward self-blame. Although these tendencies predated the merger and her new boss, they may have strengthened or made more salient the effect of the feedback she received. Nevertheless, despite her depression history, Cindy had typically been a top performer and was usually happy at her job until the merger and feedback mismatches occurred.

Evaluative messages ("How good am I?") and identity messages ("Who am I?") may co-occur, but they are conceptually separate. It was not just criticism itself that caused distress, but rather its effect on identity. When you feel like you are not the person you would ideally like to be, you are likely to experience depression (Higgins 1987; Large and Marcussen 2000; Marcussen 2006). When you feel like you are not the person you believe you should be, you may feel anxious (Higgins 1987; Large and Marcussen 2000). Feedback can trigger these thoughts about identity, which in turn can create distress (Burke 1991, 1996).

Over time, all the messages Cindy got from her bosses—the reprimands, the suggestions to take a different job, being told she was not "one of us"—had added up. She had descended into despair, anxiety, and physical illness because others told her she was not the "top-like salesperson" she had believed she was.

Being told that you are doing a bad job is always hard to take. It can make you angry and insecure, and can cause your self-esteem to plummet. But once again, feedback mismatches are about more than just being told you are not good enough; they are about being told you are not the person you think you are. For example, Cindy told me the hardest part of losing her job was: "Oh, I think your sense of self. . . . I always was identified as being in the [travel] industry. . . . If I decide I wanna go work for Jules's Grocery Store or drive a school bus . . . that'll get me through, that'll take the edge off of things financially and timewise, but what else am I gonna do? . . . What can I do to make myself feel valued again? . . . Who am I and what am I gonna do is like the big, big, big thing."

Cindy underscored her lost "sense of self." If she was not a high-performing account executive, then who was she? Cindy turned her identity toward something about which she was certain: she was a sixty-two-year-old woman. And she had a family history of Alzheimer's disease.

> [My boss's boss] said, "You just don't seem to get it." . . . It was horrible. That's when I thought, "Maybe there's something wrong with me." . . . I had this family history of Alzheimer's . . . and I thought, "Maybe I am having . . . early signs of dementia." . . . So I went through a series of tests. . . . I had this huge document that shows all the results and everything. And the result was no, I didn't . . . [but I was] somewhat disbelieving.

Cindy's age was another part of who she was, and she used it to help her explain the problems she had had in the workplace. In the United States, people who are "old" are often expected to be sick (Cruikshank 2013) or have memory problems (Ryan 1992). Older people often internalize these ageist stereotypes

(Cruikshank 2013; Krekula 2009) and may even conform to them as they age (Krekula 2009). For example, older adults who were reminded of their age before taking a word recall test performed more poorly than those who were not reminded, and this was partially explained by adopting the expectations of an "old" identity (O'Brien and Hummert 2006).

Similarly, Cindy believed that "to be old" could also mean "to have memory problems." She started to question herself and her mental health. She tentatively began to replace her "award-winning account executive" identity with a new identity based on a combination of her age and her bosses' feedback—"potential dementia patient." And even when brain scans and medical tests proved her wrong, at first she did not believe the results. It took time, but eventually as Cindy reviewed the results, which included many above-average scores, it sunk in that she was not a dementia patient, and she stopped thinking of herself that way. However, Cindy was still without a solid identity as an account executive, and she continued to be very distressed.

The more Lisa told Cindy she did not belong in her job, told her she was a poor employee, and formally reprimanded her, the more feedback mismatches Cindy experienced and the deeper her depression became. She also grew more depressed as she compared herself with younger coworkers who seemed to be meeting Lisa's demands. Her anxiety and depression made it hard to concentrate and to perform well in her job. Finally, about one year after Lisa became Cindy's boss, Lisa indicated to Cindy that she would be fired if she did not meet Lisa's demands. At this point, Cindy's depression skyrocketed and she went to a psychiatrist for treatment. Although Cindy tells me she "wasn't at a point where I had to be hospitalized," her psychiatrist determined that her condition was so severe that she should combine her accrued paid vacation time with paid disability leave to focus on treatment and recovery from anxiety and depression. She did so for one and a half months.

Cindy also hired a lawyer, and with his guidance, Cindy resigned and negotiated a severance package that gave her what she referred to as "a financial cushion" in exchange for agreeing that she would never work at Gentay again.[8] Although technically she left voluntarily, she saw losing her job and her valued account executive identity as unavoidable, and believed that she really had no choice because of the way the job was affecting her mental health. "Voluntary" resignations after months of feedback mismatches were common for the people who spoke with me.

Cindy had believed the bosses' expectations and performance criteria were impossible to meet, and she was eventually proven correct. After she lost her job, a few former coworkers confided to her that they had fudged their numbers to make it look like they had met the criteria. Unfortunately, while she was still employed, Cindy's failure to meet Lisa's performance criteria left Cindy believing she was no longer a "good" Gentay executive. She also began to believe that she was too old to be a travel executive, and this belief stuck with her as she searched for a new job (see chapter 5). In chapter 8, Cindy describes how losing her executive identity meant she no longer knew who she really was, which made her very tense and depressed.

Common Themes in Feedback Mismatches

Feedback mismatches often: (1) occurred when people were still working, after they got a new boss; (2) were exacerbated when job-related tasks were taken away; and (3) occurred when people monitored themselves, after first receiving a boss's identity-threatening feedback.

Feedback Mismatches Occurred While Still Working

Feedback mismatches commonly occurred while people were still employed (not after losing their jobs), and were often triggered by the arrival of a new boss who gave them direct feedback that they were not the employees they had thought they were. Most of Charlie's and Cindy's feedback mismatch experiences and much of their identity-related distress occurred when they got new bosses while they were still employed. Another example is Charlotte, a forty-one-year-old white woman who had held a strong identity as a nonprofit organization's chief financial officer (CFO) when she worked for her previous boss, Rod. But she began to doubt her CFO identity when her new boss, Shannon, repeatedly told her she was not a good CFO:

> [Previously] I was told [by Rod] that I was good at that job and I felt that I was good at that job. . . . [Shannon] would say, "This sucks. This sucks. This sucks," and I would be devastated. . . . The worst would be when I would send her an email or communicate something to her that I thought was great. Like, "Here. I thought of this and it's this creative use of money. . . ." So I would actually think I was hitting it and what I would get back was "Well, that's just the stupidest thing I've ever heard."

Shannon had even specified that Charlotte did not have enough "vision" to be a CFO and that she was really better at just following orders: "[Shannon] just was not gonna give me an atta-boy. . . . She always took great pains to tell me that I was good at checking off boxes and that if someone gave me a list of things to do, that I could do those. . . . That I was an executer. I wasn't a visionary."

Feedback mismatches were distressing to Charlie, Charlotte, and others, just as Identity Theory suggests (Burke 1991, 1996). At times they were so painful that some people compared them to torture (see Charlie's quote earlier in this chapter) or abuse. For example, Charlotte described her emotional reactions to feedback mismatches in terms of an abusive relationship:

> It was terrible. . . . It was a very tearful thing. . . . I was exhausted. . . . It was like almost an abusive relationship. . . . She would, at the last second, throw me an "atta-boy" and . . . I would take her back in a second. . . . She would [Charlotte laughs] be so awful to me. . . . I thought that I had failed. . . . And then she would bring me flowers and say "I'll never do it again. . . ." It would be like when women are in relationships and then "Oh, I promise I'll never do it [again]. I love you so much."

Similarly, feedback from Minnie's boss, Haylee, triggered a feedback mismatch while Minnie was still working. Minnie, a sixty-three-year-old white woman, who had worked for about a year and a half as a periodical editor, lost her job two months before I interviewed her. Haylee insisted that Minnie should use a computer to do certain tasks instead of using hard copies and Post-it notes, so she had essentially already put Minnie "on notice" that she was not properly performing her editor's role. Then, when Minnie made three relatively minor errors, Haylee indicated that Minnie was such a poor editor, someone else would have to check her work: "[Haylee] said . . . 'I can't be responsible for your work as well as my work. I don't wanna have to go behind you [and] check you, have somebody else goin' behind you. And there can't be any more mistakes.'"

When Minnie made a fourth mistake, Haylee again gave her feedback that she was not a good editor and took her to Human Resources to arrange for her exit: "[Haylee] made a couple of comments . . . that she just didn't feel that she could have confidence in my work and that she didn't know how that could be changed. . . . She said 'We need to go to [Human Resources]. . . . This just isn't working for me. . . . We've already assigned all the articles for the next issue.' That really did confirm that she didn't trust me to do the work." These feedback mismatches led to "a lot of depression. I felt like I had failed. I'd never failed at a job before, and that's been really hard to deal with."

As with Charlotte, Minnie's feedback mismatch affected her occupational identity and was highly distressing. When I asked what had been the hardest part of losing her job, she paused thoughtfully, then replied in terms of her employee identity: "I think doubting myself. . . . Having come to doubt myself and to feel . . . uncertain about my ability, not just as an editor but as an effective worker. . . . And I guess that's the part of it that has to do with relating to my boss."

New bosses often meant new feedback about identities. Feedback that contradicted what people believed about their identities created identity confusion and distress. These feedback mismatches often led people to feel like their employee identities were threatened even before they lost their jobs. In fact, these threats occurred while they were still working.

Feedback Mismatches Got Worse When Job-Related Tasks Were Taken Away

Behaving in ways that are expected for our roles helps solidify the identities associated with those roles (Burke 1991; Burke and Stets 2009). So if we are not allowed or able to pursue activities and behaviors that are usually expected for a specific role, it becomes very hard to hold on to that identity (Burke 1991). For example, if a professor is on leave for a semester and is not teaching, he or she may feel less like a professor.

When bosses took away opportunities to perform employee responsibilities (such as when Charlie's boss did not allow him to travel to a conference), this heightened existing identity threats by shutting off potential behaviors that could help them feel like employees. Charlotte's CFO identity was further endangered once she was told she would soon lose her CFO title and be reassigned to "special projects": "Ultimately, [Shannon] decided to offer me a special projects job. She was gonna get a new CFO. . . . I knew that I was losing these responsibilities. . . . There were lots of tears on Sunday. . . . Having to go to bed at eight 'cause I was just so depressed I couldn't stay up on Sunday nights."

Charlotte had struggled in vain to meet Shannon's expectations of what being a CFO meant. She could not reconcile her CFO identity with Shannon's feedback that she was really a "special projects" employee, nor with the fact that she was about to lose her CFO responsibilities, so she (like Cindy) reluctantly decided to "voluntarily" resign. Ironically, part of this decision was based on an attempt to hold onto her CFO identity: "I said, 'I'm not gonna take that because that's not my job. That's not what I was trained for . . . I am a CFO. I'm the CFO here. That's my job. Let's negotiate my exit.' And that's what we did."

Minnie was also barred from her job responsibilities while she was still employed. After fearing that she would be fired, she grudgingly resigned. At that point, her bosses allowed her to remain at her workplace for one more month to search for jobs, but she was not allowed to do editing work during that time. In the past, Minnie had felt like she was part of a workplace community: "What I always used to feel like in my other jobs [was] that I was fully part of the organization and the group . . . a valuable part of the workforce." But now her lack of job-related tasks, along with the feedback Minnie got from Haylee, led her to feel confused about her identity even though technically she was still employed: "It was a weird month. . . . At the staff meetings, they were talking about things that were gonna happen after I was gone. . . . I really sort of felt like a ghost. . . . I wasn't gonna be part of things any longer. . . . Like I wasn't really a part of this, but I wasn't part of anything else."

Sheldon Stryker (1980) emphasizes that being in roles is important for our identities. But as the examples of Charlie, Charlotte, and Minnie demonstrate, simply being in the role is not enough. We need opportunities to perform the behaviors associated with the role, or we may lose the corresponding identities and suffer emotional pain from that loss (Burke 1991, 1996).

People Also Produced Feedback Mismatches by Monitoring Themselves

When others tell us directly that we are not who we think we are, we begin to question and eventually lose that identity (Burke 1991, 1996). But we also determine who we are by monitoring our own behavior to ensure we are properly performing our roles; if we are not, we often try to adjust those behaviors to better meet role expectations. If we are successful, the identity in question gets stronger (Burke 1991; Burke and Stets 2009). For example, if a professor gave a poor lecture, he or she might try to prepare a better lecture for the next class, and by doing so would strengthen his or her professor identity. However, if we are unsuccessful in adjusting our behavior, we often start to dis-identify with (Burke 1991; Burke and Stets 2009) or even leave the role (Burke and Stets 2009). This is what happened with Charlotte.

Charlotte decided that, given her boss's feedback, she had misidentified what being a CFO meant. Initially, when Shannon told Charlotte she was not behaving like a CFO, Charlotte tried to adjust her behavior. Shannon had asked Charlotte to focus on cost-cutting initiatives, and Charlotte tried to do so. But even then, Shannon kept telling Charlotte that she was not cut out to be a CFO. As Charlotte monitored her own behaviors, she adopted Shannon's definition of CFO and decided she could not live up to those expectations. Therefore, Charlotte ultimately decided she was "not that person" (not a CFO), claimed she did not really want to be a CFO anyway, and distanced herself from that identity:

> I think that ultimately why I wasn't successful there was that what I thought being a CFO meant was different from what [Shannon] thought. . . . At first I thought I couldn't be who she wanted me to be and I think at the end I realized that I didn't want to be that person. . . . I don't want that job anymore. . . . I don't think of myself as that person because I actually think that [Shannon's] idea of a CFO . . . that's actually the correct one.

Charlotte eventually resigned after being told she would soon lose her CFO position and would work "special projects" instead. Her resignation reflected walking the fine line of her desire to maintain some sort of CFO identity while removing herself from the feedback that would tell her she was not one. Like Charlie, Charlotte was ambivalent about her employee identity. She still wanted

CFO as one of her identities but was being told she was not a CFO, and this distressed her greatly.

Minnie was never explicitly fired or asked to resign, but she did so after Haylee and a Human Resources representative hinted that she would likely be fired if she did not resign. Minnie had tried (unsuccessfully) to negotiate a probationary improvement period. Being told she was not the editor she thought she was left her anxious and depressed, so she resigned. Her attempts to stay, her sorrow at not being allowed to work during her final month of employment, and her comments about feeling "like a ghost" show that resignation was the better of the two identity-threatening options: stay and be told she was not the person she thought she was (and be fired), or leave and lose that negative feedback, but also the role on which her editor identity was based.

To some degree, these supposedly "voluntary" resignations are instances of abandoning the roles associated with threatened work-related identities. Often despite people's best efforts to behave in the ways their bosses expected, they were still told they were not the people they thought they were. This was stressful, and leaving these roles helped alleviate the mismatch and the distress to some degree, as Burke's (1991, 1996) Identity Theory might predict.

The effects of feedback mismatches could last even after people lost their jobs and could affect job search behavior. For example, Shannon's comment that Charlotte was not a leader but rather someone who could execute a visionary's commands seeped into her identity during her job search:

> I had had an informational interview with someone who asked me what I was looking for, and I said, "I wanna be someone's number two. I wanna be someone's right hand . . . I want someone else to have the vision . . . because I don't have any vision. I'm not a leader. I'm a doer." And she said to me, "My God . . . How could you even say that?" And I said, "Well, because that's what Shannon told me."

Feedback mismatches affected Minnie's job search, too. Even though Minnie could tell herself intellectually that she was a good editor, the feedback mismatch regarding her editor identity continued to affect her emotionally. It had eroded her confidence and made her worry about interviews: "This experience has really kinda rocked me. . . . I'm still really worrying about interviews, because I'm afraid. I don't have a lot of confidence in myself right now even though I know again that I'm a really, really good editor. I guess I don't have a lot of confidence in myself as a performer right now."

Feedback mismatches often started while people were still working, after they got new bosses who told them they were not the employees they had thought they were. The effects of feedback mismatches were compounded when bosses took away titles, tasks, or other opportunities for them to enact their occupational identities. And although people tried to behave in a way that emulated how their bosses defined their roles, they often did not succeed. As they monitored their own behavior, they became more convinced that they were not who they thought they were, and dis-identified with their jobs to some degree, experiencing much ambivalence along the way. The effects of feedback mismatches were potent, long-lasting, and sometimes even affected people's job searches months later.

Summing Up

Charlie, Cindy, and others suffered from the experience of feedback mismatches. Many of these feedback mismatches originated from meso-level workplace management changes, which were triggered by macro-level changes in the economy. Ultimately, the effects of the macro- and meso-level changes filtered down to affect individuals at the micro level. For example, the Great Recession of 2007–2009 was a macro-level economic problem that may have increased financial pressure on companies. Gentay's meso-level reaction was to try to cut costs by merging with another company and laying off or reassigning employees to new positions with lower pay. These layoffs that are so common today were largely unexpected by Baby Boomers (and probably older members of Generation X) that had grown up in an historical era in which a college degree would pretty much guarantee employment (Dudley 1997 [1994], 181). Therefore, workplace changes such as mergers and layoffs could be exceptionally upsetting. Cindy was reassigned and given a different boss as a result of the merger. Her new boss's feedback threatened her identity and she experienced extreme distress—a micro-level phenomenon.

Identity is important in the stress process. When people experience a feedback mismatch, identity threats become a chronic strain that leads to distress. Although distress after losing a job may come from a variety of other factors, including limited finances (Newman 1999 [1988]), problems with significant others (Willott and Griffin 2004; Yang 2002), or boredom from not having enough to do (Feldman and Turnley 1995), identity threats are sources of stress that are conceptually separate from these problems, and are important in their own right.

For Charlie, Cindy, Charlotte, and Minnie, the feedback they received at work did not match the ways in which they had identified themselves. For many years, Cindy saw herself as an award-winning travel executive, but her new bosses repeatedly told her that she was not one. Over time, she began to believe it herself and ultimately decided that she could no longer be a travel executive, and that she might even "really" be a potential dementia patient. Charlie had identified as a director of training in line to become a vice president.

But Charlie's subordinate challenged his authority, and his bosses denied him the promotion he had dreamed of, repeatedly reprimanded him, and ultimately fired him. Each of these interactions pushed Charlie further away from his director identity. All of the people in this chapter suffered from the feedback mismatches they experienced. They felt anxious, angry and, at times, despondent because they were being told they were not the people they believed they were, and started to believe this about themselves.

The feedback mismatch process often began while people were still employed. Bosses' and coworkers' words and actions triggered feedback mismatches—identity-related processes that often took time to manifest in full-blown distress. Sometimes it took months or even years to feel the full effects of these mismatches. Identity can strongly contribute to stress, so including identity more explicitly in the Stress Process Model could help us better understand those stressful experiences.

Sometimes when people have trouble with bosses or coworkers, or when they lose their jobs, their identities are challenged in a second way. A question arises: Who am I now? Although people may make many changes in their lives, it is usually disturbing to feel like, overall, they are not the same people across time (Burke 1991, 1996; Swann 1983). As Charlie struggled over his identity at work and after he lost his job, he no longer felt like the same person he used to be; in other words, he did not feel like he was the same person across time. He began to experience another type of identity mismatch described in chapter 4—a time mismatch.

4

"I Wasn't the Same Person"

Time Mismatches

Chapter 3 focused on feedback mismatches. When Charlie's, Cindy's, and others' ideas about who they were differed from how other people treated them, they became distressed. This chapter centers on another kind of mismatch that can occur after losing your job—a time mismatch. A time mismatch means you feel like you are no longer the person you were in the past; you have become a new or different person or are confused about who you are compared to who you once were. Time mismatches can be very stressful because they deprive us of a consistent identity (Burke 1996; Swann 1983).

At the beginning of this chapter, Charlie explains what time mismatches were like for him, both while he was still at his old job and after he was laid off. Then a new person, Marsha, describes the time mismatches she experienced after losing her job, and expresses how her perception of identity and her mood fluctuated depending on whether she was doing activities similar to her old job. This chapter also includes several brief quotes by other study participants to help illustrate the main themes surrounding time mismatches.

Although Charlie and Cindy were both central to chapter 3, Cindy plays a smaller role in this chapter. (Her story will reemerge in detail in chapter 5 and briefly in chapter 8.) To keep the main points easy to follow, most chapters focus primarily on two people's stories and contain shorter supplementary quotes from other study participants. Cindy described her time mismatches in less detail than Marsha did, so I chose to highlight Marsha more prominently than Cindy in this chapter.

Charlie's Time Mismatch

Charlie's work-related identities had slowly been deteriorating even while he was still employed. First, the "future self" he had long hoped to become—vice president—was denied him. He was so dismayed that he began to purposely disengage from his employee identity. He no longer felt like a Smith Organization employee, but he did not strongly connect with any other roles that could give him a new identity. Second, his employee and boss identities were threatened by his boss's and subordinate's feedback, which told him he was not a good director of training. Third, he was forced to vacate his director position on the day he was laid off. Consistent with Identity Theory (Burke 1991, 1996), the mismatch between Charlie's definition of who he was and others' feedback about his identity made him depressed, anxious, and angry.

But Charlie also experienced another kind of identity challenge: he believed that who he was had changed over time, that he was no longer the same person he had been in the past. Like Sheldon Stryker (1980), Charlie believed that people acquire their identities from roles, many of which occur sequentially in our lives, such as moving from high school student to college student to professional employee. After losing his job, Charlie had no new work-related role, and had trouble figuring out who he was. This time mismatch ultimately caused him great anguish.

Charlie's role as a director of training had lasted for a very long time, made up a substantial part of his daily routine, and had become a big part of his identity: "[My Smith Organization job] . . . was my life. . . . It afforded me an opportunity to really develop and to see the world and meet a tremendous amount of people and . . . expand my worldview."

Interestingly, even though Charlie's time mismatch distressed him, he objectively described his belief that identities are temporary—that they change over time and occur in various "chunks," each of which depends on an institutional role: "Wherever you are will just be a part of your life. . . . Here's four years for high school and here's four years for college. Here's my first teaching job. . . . You know, chunk, chunk, chunk. Well, the Smith Organization was a huge chunk."

Charlie said these "chunks" were bounded by "bookends." Entering and exiting a role within a social institution (such as a student within a college) created a beginning and end to the identity associated with that role (Stryker 1980). So once Charlie's involvement in the Smith Organization ended, the identities that were based there (director and employee) "died":

[The Smith Organization is] the most recent huge chunk of my life. . . . But . . . it has bookends. . . . When my dad died, the family priest . . . said, "When a person dies and when you have the funeral . . . you can for the first time . . . talk about that person's life . . . because there's a bookend." . . . The day I walked out the door, that was the bookend. Doesn't mean that you're not still sort of living in the afterglow of that as you make your adjustments. . . . But it didn't take me very long to actually be glad that that part of my life was over and . . . I could put a bookend on it.

Charlie used death metaphors to describe what happened to his work-related identities. But, like some other people who have lost jobs (K'Meyer and Hart 2009) or other roles (Thoits 1995), he had mixed feelings about the end of these roles and identities. He claimed he was glad his employee identity had finally ended and said that in some ways losing that identity was a relief. However, he also noted that the "afterglow" of that identity still lingered; he had a hard time completely separating himself from it.

Several study participants described lost work-related identities by using metaphors for transformation and transition, uncertainty, and death, comparing job loss to being "like a ghost" or "like someone died." Similarly, Charlie described his identity transformation as taking himself "out of the picture" and being "at sea" with his identity (or uncertain about who he was). He referred to his former employee identity as separate from the present time ("bookends") and as being dead (discussing job loss by using a funeral metaphor).

Often, one aspect of the self must first die to allow a new self to fully emerge. Charlie described the idea that the "old me" had died and that he was no longer the same person anymore. Feeling unsure of who we are disturbs us (Ebaugh 1988), so unemployed people may become fixated on hopes of returning to their old job or may try to hold on to their occupational identities (Fraher and Gabriel 2014; Gabriel, Gray, and Goregaokar 2013). For example, Charlie's job had been so central to his daily (and weekend) routine that three months after losing his job he still thought about what he would be doing on a Saturday if he had remained the director of training, and said that as he reflected on this he felt like he was mourning: "I was there for twenty-four years. So I can't help but think, 'Today is Saturday. We'd be doing registration. The speaker would be coming in. I'd be taking them out to dinner.' . . . It's kind of painful and on another level it's such a terrific relief. But it was just like . . . mourning."

Lorna, a fifty-one-year-old African American woman, also compared who she was now to who she used to be. Lorna had worked for twenty-eight years in the broadcast music and entertainment industry, most recently as a supervisor, and was laid off six months before I first interviewed her. Like Charlie, she experienced a time mismatch and thought about her identity in terms of loss: "I think not bein' at JCC, [I] kinda lost my whole music identity. . . . [I'm] sometimes depressed because I'm used to bein' in broadcasting. . . . It made me somebody important. . . . Now I don't have it anymore. . . . So that kinda hurts. It hurts. . . . Now it's all gone."

Like Lorna, who believed that without a job her identity was "gone," Charlie also thought that losing his job—which had existed between the "bookends" of his director role—meant that part of his identity was "over": "Every day I sort of construct my life. . . . [In my past job] from November to May [Charlie chuckles], I'm this expert. But that's what it is; it has bookends. It's over. It's done. . . . That part of my life was over."

Losing a job can make you feel like you are no longer who you used to be (Cottle 2001, 276). For example, some former professionals who lost their jobs no longer felt like the middle-class people they once were, and instead saw themselves as being in limbo between two identities (Newman 1999 [1988], 91). When Charlie lost his job, he no longer felt like the same person anymore. Exiting the workplace and losing the role associated with it produced distressing time mismatches for Charlie and Lorna. But identity change is a process. Remember that Charlie's identity change process actually began while he was still working, when he did not receive the promotion he wanted:

> I wasn't the same person from the day that I didn't get that VP position. That was a profound and fundamental change for me. . . . Because I thought earlier in my career that if I didn't retire as being a VP that my work life would have been a failure. . . . I had taken my heart and soul out of the process. That was really hard. . . . [I thought] "I have no future at this place. . . . It is so painful to not be a part of the process that I need to move on. And so what does that look like?" . . . It was really a very depressing process.

When one's progress toward career goals is suddenly blocked, comparing past and present work experiences can harm mental health (Warr 2005). This suggests that thoughts about work identities that are not consistent over time can be distressing even for people who are still employed. Cindy described a similar experience—no longer being a top salesperson—that was initially triggered by a feedback mismatch when she was still employed (as described in chapter 3): "[Lisa] said something like, 'That's not working for you. I think you should be in something else.' And I felt like, here she had written me up twice. . . . I was more and more stressed. I was depressed. My body hurt. . . . Anxious, I guess, is the word. . . . I just had such terrible feelings of self-doubt. . . . I felt that . . . something had happened to me, that I was no longer a top-like salesperson."

As noted in chapter 3, Charlotte, the former CFO, showed this same pattern. In her case, she was disturbed by feeling like her identity was at risk of changing during her employment. You may recall that in chapter 3, she said: "What I thought being a CFO meant was different from what the current executive director thought. . . . She just had a different idea. . . . At first I thought I couldn't be who she wanted me to be and I think at the end I realized that I didn't want to be that person. . . . I don't think that's me and I don't want to be that person. . . . It just was never gonna work."

Charlie's, Cindy's, and Charlotte's experiences of lost or threatened workplace identities, even while they were still employed, shows that although institutional roles can be important for identity (Stryker 1980), simply being in one does not guarantee your identity. Rather, feedback about whether you are the person you think you are is critical to how you experience identity (Burke 1991,

1996). However, once you lose the role, you no longer even have the structure to support your former identity, so a time mismatch becomes virtually unavoidable.

We tend to resist major identity changes and prefer to feel that who we are has stayed the same over time (Stets and Burke 2014; Swann 1983). Some people who lose their jobs seem to be able to easily hang on to their work-related identities if they were part of a childhood dream (Fraher and Gabriel 2014). Other unemployed people may simply try to tell themselves that they are still the employees they used to be (Newman 1999 [1988], 90). However, many people lose their professional identities when they lose jobs (Castel, Minondo-Kaghad, and Lacassagne 2013), and simply telling yourself you have not changed rarely works (Newman 1999 [1988], 91).

Keeping these "past selves" (Markus and Nurius 1986) consistent with our current identities may be essential to effectively coping with identity-related distress after losing a job. Perhaps this is why unemployment counseling literature recommends coping strategies that help maintain some sort of consistent identity. For example, counselors are urged to emphasize unemployed people's existing skills or personal qualities (Amundson 1994), and support groups often encourage unemployed people to keep dressing as if they are going to work, even when they are at home (Garrett-Peters 2009, 555–556). Philippe Castel et al. (2013, 361) have even suggested that identity consistency is so important that counselors may need to help unemployed professionals "reanimate" their work-related identities before they can successfully find new jobs.

When identities vanished or were threatened, Charlie, Cindy, and others thought about how to replace or regain those identities. The pain associated with identity change may be especially profound if we have involuntarily and suddenly lost a treasured identity (Bennett 2010; Drahota and Eitzen 1998; Duran-Aydintug 1995), because we are not ready to change, have little time in which to prepare psychologically for a new role, or do not have a chance to practice acting as expected for the new role (Blau 1973; Duran-Aydintug 1995). The "death" of Charlie's work-related identities left him feeling depressed, confused, and lost. His idea of who he was had vanished. Even as he recognized who he had once been, his words indicated that he knew he could not go back to being "Charlie, director of training": "The past is the past. It is there. . . . It's kinda like Chernobyl. You seal it in concrete and it's there. You look at the best of it and you just seal it off and you just move on."

But if he was no longer an employee, who was he or who would he become now? Like a pop star who had gone several years without a Top 40 hit, he was immersed in how to remake himself. Charlie tried to think about his identity in terms of a transformation and rebirth. After he lost his job, Charlie felt that he needed to "refocus" and shift into becoming a new and different person than he had been before. But he floundered as he tried to negotiate this new identity.

At first, Charlie, like several other people who lost their jobs, experienced what I call the "just me" phenomenon, in which people said they were "just Charlie" or "just Cindy," and tried to find an identity that did not depend on holding specific roles: "I just became Charlie Duncan . . . as opposed to . . . executive. . . . I tried to say I am not my job. I am who you see sitting here today. Unvarnished. A good [Charlie whispers] guy, talented guy. I do a lotta different things. Don't need a job to be that guy."

Charlie was trying to work it out. He said he no longer needed to be an executive and wanted to be "just Charlie." But this did not completely work because, as Charlie insightfully recognized, institutional roles are often critical to identity: "[You have] your identity from who you are in relation to other people—your family, your job, your community, your church. . . . [My former job orientation] is . . . dead and gone. . . . I tried to . . . refocus either toward retirement or toward a second career or a different future or more time with family or hobbies. . . . It was really a difficult transition. . . . I do a lotta stuff, but I don't really have a passion for it."

If unemployed people can redefine themselves as retirees (Schöb 2013) or can enter a new role by moving into a new career (Fraher and Gabriel 2014; Gabriel et al. 2013), they feel better about themselves. Unfortunately, Charlie was unable to do either of these things. Had he been able to shift his identity emphasis to another role, this could have benefitted his mental health; however, he believed roles involving retirement, family, or hobbies were inadequate focal points for his identity: "There wasn't a new high. There wasn't a new interest. There wasn't a new direction. There wasn't a new sense of self-esteem. . . . I feel sort of at sea? . . . There's sort of a hangover from your work life."

Similarly, the first time I interviewed Lorna, she said that the mother identity was an insufficient replacement for her work identity and that, on its own, it left her unhappy: "Bein' a mom and a housewife type thing . . . it keeps me busy but it doesn't make me happy. It's not what I really wanna do. . . . It's not me."

Charlie's and Lorna's identities remained in limbo. Charlie posed the question that would continue to consume his thoughts for some time: "I think I'm coming to a new identity. I guess the word I wanna use is I wanna be authentic. So what do I want that story to be?"

Ultimately, Charlie tried to center his identity in other roles that he held, such as father, husband, and parishioner. But he was unsuccessful. In contrast, in chapter 6, Charlotte, Lorna, and a man named Marcus describe how (over time) they successfully shifted their energy into identities based on roles that were separate from paid employment, making mother or volunteer basketball coach into primary identities. Doing this made them feel better, even though they had not found new jobs. However, Charlie did not think that being a dad, husband, or parishioner was "manly" enough. This made it hard for him to accept these as identities. (See chapters 5 and 8 for a full explanation.) Charlie could not remain the same person he had been before. But he could not shift to become someone new. Without some idea of who he was, Charlie descended into a very depressing and worrisome lack of all sense of self—identity void (see chapter 8).

Ever since Charlie was denied a valued promotion, he no longer felt like the same person. Marsha also experienced a time mismatch that made her feel depressed and anxious, but her experience of it was somewhat different from Charlie's experience. Marsha's story is also a good example of how identity-related distress is separate from (and happens in addition to) distress caused by financial and family problems after losing a job.

Introducing Marsha: Public Safety Manager

Marsha was looking forward to taking her kids to the county fair. She sat in her car outside of her ex-husband Hank's house and waited for her children to finish their visit. As she waited, Hank's new wife approached the car with official-looking papers. She handed these to Marsha through the car window, then walked away. Marsha slowly examined the court documents that had begun a custody battle. She had already lost her job; now she could lose custody of her son.

Two weeks later, when Marsha dropped off her kids for another visit with their father, she got out of her car and walked onto Hank's porch to confront him: "I said, 'How could you do this to me?' And he was like, 'Well, you're gonna lose everything soon anyway. [Our son] might as well have a stable place to live.' . . . It was devastating."

It was just two weeks before Christmas—and five-and-a-half months after losing her job—when Marsha told me this story. Her frustration and upset about losing her job was already overwhelming; now she feared she could lose her home and custody of her son. Additionally, at times she experienced time mismatches and felt as though she had lost an important identity—public safety manager. But things had not always been like this.

Five-and-a-half months earlier, Marsha still had a job. She had struggled to make ends meet, but she certainly had not been on the edge of losing every-thing. Marsha, a divorced white forty-one-year-old woman, lived with her twelve-year-old son Erik and her eighteen-year-old daughter Tenille, who attended community college. Marsha and Hank shared custody of Erik, who lived with Marsha most of the time.

Marsha was the least affluent participant with whom I spoke. She had taken college courses but lacked a degree; this limited her earnings. It had been hard for Marsha to earn enough money to keep her family out of poverty, but she had done it. She owned the run-down home where she lived with her kids and she owned one antiquated car that she shared with Tenille.

Even before Marsha lost her job, she had struggled financially. She had had ongoing trouble paying household bills. She had incurred a lot of credit card debt just trying to pay for basic needs as a single parent, and she had filed for bankruptcy while she was still employed. Hank paid child support, but usually balked at spending money on basics for the children, such as a new pair of shoes. Despite the many challenges Marsha faced, she tried to stay positive and be a good person. She had a good relationship with her children, and was proud of her Christian ethic, as well as her ability to financially support her family, which she said established her as a "good woman."

Marsha had worked full-time as a public school safety and security manager for the past three years. On a typical day, she conducted security patrols, worked with vendors, managed other officers, and ensured that safety regulations were met. She was proud of her job, enjoyed the autonomy she had in her position, and cherished the responsibility she had for keeping others safe. Her job was a big part of who she was; to lose it could potentially create a time mismatch in which she would no longer feel like the same person she had been.

I first met Marsha at the local unemployment office, one month after she had lost her job. She was attending a workshop on applying for government jobs. The office was housed in a stark, imposing three-story brick government building that also contained courtrooms and child protective services. As I entered the building, I felt like a suspect as I experienced what Marsha and other job seekers went through every time they requested services. I was scanned with a metal detector. Security guards checked my driver's license. I was visually inspected (with suspicion) from head to toe. Next, I crowded into a tiny, antiquated, and painstakingly slow elevator with several other people and eventually arrived on the second floor where the unemployment office was located.

Marsha and I sat at a small round table in an empty office. Her dark brown shoulder-length hair spiraled loosely around her face. She wore brick red lipstick. Dressed in a black short-sleeved soft cotton shirt and khaki slacks, she gave the impression of a polished, quietly self-assured woman. I closed the door and she started to tell me the kinds of things she had done during a typical day at work:

> General security patrols, plus I managed other officers. I maintained and worked with vendors to maintain the security systems. . . . I did public relations. . . . I set up anything that had to do with emergency management, security, or public safety for the facility, including . . . accessing camera systems, operating security codes, handling population problems . . . liaison with local law enforcement and fire and rescue . . . making sure that there weren't any building code violations, making sure MSDS standards were met . . . checkin' first aid kits, making sure that the paperwork is all done. . . . It was a field that I wanted to grow in.

Unfortunately, Marsha's enjoyment of her work had been curbed by problems she had had with Chuck, a disgruntled subordinate of hers. According to Marsha, Chuck had resented taking orders from her and had even tried to set her up to get her into trouble: "He believed that he was more experienced and should have my position, primarily because I made more money, so . . . he would do things like he'd start a conversation about his girlfriend and I'd say something about my boyfriend and then he would . . . go to [my boss] and say that I'm talking about my personal life."

Marsha had had two bosses during the time she worked at the school. She enjoyed a respectful and productive working relationship with her first boss, Jenay. Before Jenay left her position, she told Marsha that she knew Chuck was causing problems for her, and warned Marsha that he might be baiting her to try to get her into trouble. This compassionate and reinforcing communication may have strengthened Marsha's identity as a "good employee."

Unfortunately, Marsha's relationship with her new boss, Samantha, became hostile just two weeks after Samantha arrived. Marsha had responded in person to a problem in the school's parking lot. As policy required her to do, Marsha called Samantha from the site to inform her of the incident and completed all required reports. But Samantha neglected to take the next steps she should have taken after she was notified. She then blamed Marsha, claiming that Marsha had never called her. Samantha demanded that Marsha sign disciplinary paperwork that would place the blame firmly on Marsha, but Marsha refused and fought back: "I said, 'I will not sign a reprimand for that because it's inappropriate. . . . I did what I was supposed to do.' . . . And [Samantha] said, 'Well, I can tell you right now that I will keep documentation that will not allow you to stay in your position, so don't mess with me.'"

Samantha was angry about Marsha's refusal to take the blame for something she did not do, and Samantha sought revenge at every turn. She refused to allow Marsha to buy women's uniforms or uniforms in her size, criticized Marsha's leave requests, and joined forces with Chuck and another employee who made false claims against Marsha. After six months of reprisals, Marsha filed a harassment complaint against Samantha. Six months later, Marsha was suddenly called into a meeting and given an upsetting (and likely retaliatory and illegal) ultimatum—resign immediately with a three-month severance package and drop the harassment complaint or be fired:

> I was called into a room for a meeting. . . . They brought a sheriff's officer. . . . [Samantha] gave me a list of things she had accumulated over the last year and . . . [Marsha takes a long pause] 90 percent of it never happened. . . . They told me I had two choices. I could either resign at this moment and collect severance or I would be fired. I asked what the

precipitating event was and she was just snide. . . . She was like [Marsha speaks in a snippy tone], "I think you know why."

Samantha told Marsha she must sign paperwork on the spot indicating her decision. After she signed, Marsha went to her office to remove her personal belongings and a tense situation arose between her and Samantha:

> I went to my office and collected up my things. . . . [Samantha] came in at one point—she was out with the sheriff's officer. . . . She waited till the HR lady left. . . . She came in with the officer and she says [Marsha uses an angry, snarling voice] "You're not allowed to take anything that belongs to [the school]." . . . I said, "These are my things." . . . I had worked there for three years. I had all kinds of training materials and my Rolodex and all kinds of stuff and so I packed it all into a box. . . . And when I told her that she said [Marsha uses a hostile, threatening voice] "You got five minutes." She was trying to goad me into a fight so that the officer would have to intervene.

Although technically Marsha resigned "voluntarily," she had actually just been fired. Her immediate reaction was shock, humiliation, and concern for her children: "I was upset. I was thinking of my children. Having a place to live. I was sort of shocked. . . . At first you always feel like was there anything I could have done to prevent things from being like this? . . . The process was antagonizing and humiliating."

But the stresses Marsha experienced after losing her job went beyond her potential financial problems and struck at her identity. One month after she lost her job, Marsha thought back to that unfortunate day. She told me she was proud that she had conducted herself with dignity when they fired her. She then linked this to her concern that she could possibly lose "who she was," and noted her conscious decision to try to make sure that who she was stayed the same: "In the end . . . sometimes all you have is your integrity. . . . They took a lot from me . . . my reputation. . . . You can't let someone take who you are."

Despite Marsha's intention and efforts to not let others take her identity, she worried that it could happen. Marsha had performed specific tasks and had interacted with the same people each day at her job for three years. Part of working in the field of security was related to how strongly she valued community: "I really cared about a lot of the kids that went [to the school] and a lot of employees that worked there. . . . I like to work for companies that are community-minded. . . . It's just who I am."

After losing her job, Marsha still saw herself as someone who cared about community. In her old job, Marsha had been able to perform the part of her identity that valued community and others' safety, so being a public safety employee had been central to her idea of who she was. However, in order to sustain an identity, it is important to be able to perform the behaviors associated with it (Burke 1991). After losing her job it was hard for Marsha to consistently feel like she was still a public-safety-oriented person because she had no way to perform the tasks that showed herself and others who she was.

At both of my interviews with Marsha (one month and five and a half months after losing her job), Marsha claimed to still know who she was since she lost her job, but also said she was confused and ambivalent about her identity, and this troubled her. Marsha emphasized how hard it was to lose her public safety identity: "I'm a very service-oriented person. . . . It's hard not to . . . view the world from someone who is into safety and security and that kind of thing. It's no longer any of my business if people are being safe. . . . That's very tough. . . . I've always been that person, the one to stop in an accident, the one to report an accident. . . . I would love to work in my field. . . . It's hard not to be that person anymore."

Time mismatches could even be upsetting enough to lead someone to leave a job. As noted in chapter 3, when Charlotte's boss told her she would replace her with a new CFO and move Charlotte to a "special projects" position, she experienced a time mismatch that was disturbing enough for her to resign: "I said, 'I'm not gonna take that [job] because that's not my job. That's not I was trained for. I am a CFO. I'm the CFO here. That's my job. Let's negotiate my exit.' And that's what we did."

Cindy also said she felt like someone different after she lost her job. As noted in chapter 3, when I asked her what the hardest part of losing her job was, she reflected on her potential future employment options and replied: "Oh, I think your sense of self. . . . I always was identified as being in the [travel] industry. . . . If I decide I wanna go work for Jules's Grocery Store or drive a school bus . . . that'll get me through, that'll take the edge off of things financially and timewise, but what else am I gonna do? . . . What can I do to make myself feel valued again? . . . Who am I and what am I gonna do is like the big, big, big thing."

Marsha had no choice about keeping her job or staying with her employer. In her case, actually losing her job led to a time mismatch. Regardless of what triggered time mismatches and the amount of choice involved in leaving the role, when time mismatches occurred they were very stressful. Charlotte did not have to lose her job to experience a time mismatch. But she could not reconcile her CFO identity with an impending, different identity: "special projects employee." To avoid the discomfort associated with this potential new identity, she left before entering the "special projects employee" role. And Cindy's self-esteem decreased because, after losing her job, she could not see how any of her potential future jobs could be consistent with the travel executive identity she had held for so many years. Cindy clarified that it was not too little money or too much free time that bothered her; it was no longer having her valued identity.

Simply keeping busy with a different type of job would "take the edge off finan-cially and timewise," but would not restore her identity. Losing your job can be stressful because of financial problems, not having enough to do (Creed and Bartrum 2008), or loss of structure in your life (Garrett-Peters 2009). But because work is often a strong part of our identities (Jahoda 1981, 1982; Tausig 2009; Warr 1987), jobs that only filled time or made money would not have reduced Cindy's identity-related distress. It may be that when identity is threat-ened, only identity-based coping strategies can repair the damage.

When someone suffers financial devastation after losing a job, it is often easy to ignore the less tangible things that cause stress. Often for good reason, we focus on the very real depression, anxiety, and frustration that result directly from not having enough money to buy basic necessities or to maintain a cer-tain, usual lifestyle (see K'Meyer and Hart 2009 and Newman 1999 [1988] as examples). We tend to try to find "the cause" of emotional problems. But stress can come from several sources at the same time. When we only focus on mate-rial issues, we can inadvertently miss the less visible causes of emotional pain. This leaves us without a full understanding of what unemployed people are going through, and limits the ways that individuals and society might best help them.

It was not just the very real financial strain that was hard for Marsha. It was also a lack of identity consistency (Stets and Burke 2014; Swann 1983)—or "not being that person anymore"—that occurred after she lost an important role on which part of her identity was based. So could activities similar to her old job help her feel like she was still the same person as before?

Marsha's thoughts and feelings about her identity fluctuated depending on whether she was involved in other public safety-oriented roles. For example, although losing her job certainly bothered her, her distress did not become severe until about two weeks later, after she was no longer doing activities similar to her old job: "I would say that I've probably been depressed. . . . [Recently] I spent probably three days in bed probably just not motivated to go do anything. . . . At the time of the . . . forced resignation I was in the middle of an EMT class. . . . That was good because it gave me a transition. . . . It was like I was still working. And then once I was out of [the EMT class] the first week, I really didn't know what I was gonna do."

Marsha said the EMT class made her feel like she was "still working" and that this was good for her mood. Participating in a role similar to her former public safety job had allowed Marsha to engage in activities similar to those she had previously done in her job. Being in the EMT class had helped her feel like her employee identity had not changed, even though she had lost her job. But two weeks later, once the EMT class ended, so did the feeling of "still working." At that point, she no longer felt like an employee, and began to feel so depressed that she struggled to get out of bed.

Although Marsha said that some of the relief she experienced from the EMT class came from staying busy, she did not describe it only in those terms; rather, she emphasized that the most important thing was how it helped her sustain her public safety worker identity. (See chapter 7 for a full treatment of this "sustaining" phenomenon.) She told me she that if she did not participate in public-safety-related activities then she would not feel like the person she had always been: "It's just not me, being forced to be somethin' that I'm not. . . . It's kind of a sickening feeling. Leaves a bad taste in your mouth. . . . It's not a skin I'm comfortable in."

Becoming involved in a new role similar to the one we lost may help sustain identity and relieve our suffering (see, for example, Lane 2011; Sharone 2013a). But once those substitute roles end, our distress usually returns. Chapter 7 shows that Marsha's identity and distress level did not change over time in a linear fashion, as previous theorists (Eisenberg and Lazarsfeld 1938; Kelvin and Jarrett 1985) have proposed. Instead, her distress level varied depending on whether she was able to "perform" a public safety identity through inhabiting other roles that were like her old job (such as EMT student). These findings support work theories that emphasize the importance of identity (Jahoda 1981, 1982; Tausig 2009; Warr 1987), especially in light of the other potential reasons Marsha had for feeling depressed and anxious: a dire financial situation; the stigma of being on public assistance; a child custody battle; and the anniversary of her father's death.

Comparing and Contrasting Charlie and Marsha

Charlie's and Marsha's employee identities were threatened by time mismatches. They both felt depressed and anxious from these mismatches. But in some ways their experiences were very different. For example, Marsha's time mismatches and distress came and went, but Charlie's persisted. And Marsha at times found ways to feel as though who she was had not changed, while Charlie (as well as Lorna, Cindy, and Charlotte) did not.

Why were these issues so different for Charlie and Marsha? In part it was because of the other (non-occupational) roles each held before their employee identities were jeopardized. Given that roles in established social institutions are critical to identity (Stryker 1980), if you are already in at least one other role that is similar to what you did in your old job, it can help pave the way for identity stability (see, for example, Lane 2011; Sharone 2013a) and the emotional well-being that accompanies that stability (Burke 1996; Swann 1983).

For example, when Charlie's employee identity was challenged, he (like Lorna, Cindy, and Charlotte) was not involved in any other roles that were similar to his occupation. Even though he remained employed for a while, he had been getting feedback that told him he was not really an employee. This feedback, combined with the lack of other roles that were similar to his job, made it extremely hard to sustain his employee identity. Therefore, he experienced relentless time mismatches that produced consistently high distress levels. In contrast, even though Marsha had lost her job, her easy access to roles that were similar to her public safety manager job (such as EMT student) helped her sustain her employee identity, and she only became distressed when she was not participating in one of these similar roles.

There were some other differences between Charlie's and Marsha's time mismatch experiences. Charlie (like Cindy and Charlotte) experienced time mismatches while still employed. He also had mixed feelings about whether or not he wanted to keep his employee identity, and sometimes he even intentionally distanced himself from it. Marsha only experienced time mismatches after she lost her job, and she was very certain that she wanted to keep her public safety employee identity and did not distance herself from it.

Charlie's reactions may have been partially due to the great length of time he had been with his organization, the plethora of negative feedback from his colleagues about his job performance, and the absence of any feedback that he was a good (or even mediocre) employee. If he had had this, it could have countered the identity-challenging messages. Even though Marsha got some feedback at work that threatened her employee identity, she had also gotten feedback from her former boss just before she left warning her that she was not at fault; rather, it was her subordinate. She may have maintained the idea that she was a good employee throughout her difficult experiences on the job, and this may have counteracted the negative feedback she received later. So, although all of the people quoted in this chapter had bad experiences while employed, Marsha's identity (unlike the other people's identities) was not challenged until after she actually lost her job and after her EMT class ended.

Charlie (unlike Marsha) began to distance himself from his position as director of training and from the organization. But it was hard for him to completely commit to abandoning his work-related identity. After twenty-four years at the Smith Organization, he had no idea of who else he could be. He had not yet found an alternate identity that he thought was substantial enough to invest in. Like Cindy, Charlotte, and Lorna, he could not sustain his occupational identity, but he could not yet replace it either, as Lorna and Charlotte would ultimately do (see chapter 6).

Although Charlie periodically tried to find ways to sustain his identity as a Smith Organization employee (see chapter 8), he did not succeed because he had no one telling him that he was a good employee, and he had no other roles similar to his old position. Therefore, he moved back and forth between pushing his employee identity away and trying to temporarily embrace it again, which caused a great deal of distress.

Marsha did not experience a time mismatch until after she had both lost her job and completed her EMT class. She had no need to shift to another identity because she was able to sustain her public safety identity by participating in roles similar to the job she had lost. This gave her a way to still behave like the public-safety-focused person she had been in her job and to feel like she was "still working." Feeling like her identity was consistent helped Marsha keep at least some negative emotions at bay. So even though she was very upset about losing her job, she did not become seriously depressed until her EMT class ended.

Although Amy L. Fraher and Yiannis Gabriel (2014) suggest that we do not necessarily need roles similar to the job we have lost in order to hold on to our occupational identities, other research (Lane 2011; Sharone 2013a; Stier 2007) supports the idea that having these kinds of roles available helps sustain work-related identities. Our connections to social institutions, such as the workplace, often link us to specific roles, such as employee. As Charlie mentioned, these roles often provide a strong base for our identities (Stryker 1980). Without these roles, it may be hard to pinpoint who you are, leaving you "at sea" in your identity. Marsha felt better when she engaged in roles that were similar to her old job, then became more depressed when those roles ended.

Roles similar to lost jobs are important to sustaining work-related identities. Unemployed technology professionals sustained their occupational identities by reframing their freelancing and contract-seeking activities as "entrepreneurship" (Lane 2011), thus giving them a sense of continuous identities as professionals. Similarly, access to job seekers' networking groups provided pseudo-professional roles that helped unemployed professionals sustain their occupational identities and reduce their distress (Lane 2011; Sharone 2013a). Chapter 7 presents a detailed discussion of these authors' findings, along with specific ways job-seeker groups did or did not help my study participants sustain their identities.

Because of the connection between roles and identities, it makes sense that Charlie's attempts at being "just Charlie" (without a job title or role) did not give him a new sense of who he was after he lost his job, and left him feeling distressed and empty. As chapter 8 will demonstrate, Charlie may have been confused about who he was, but he was clear about two things: (1) like many unemployed people (McFadyen 1995; Schöb 2013; Wahl, Pollai, and Kirchler 2013), he did not want to adopt a stigmatizing identity as an unemployed person; and (2) he was not ready for an identity as a retired person.

Stress can result from a process, not just from a specific event at one point in time (Pearlin et al. 1981). In several ways, time affects how stressed out we feel, including thoughts about who we once were or could someday become (Markus and Nurius 1986) and feeling like we have lost consistency in who we are (Stets and Burke 2014; Swann 1983). Losing a job, in itself, does not necessarily determine how stressed people become. Rather, over time, people may flexibly and creatively manage how losing a job affects their identities (Gabriel et al. 2013). The stories that were presented in this chapter build on this idea by showing that as circumstances change (for example, gaining or losing access to roles that help sustain work-related identities), our experience of distress may change as well.

So far, you have read about how losing your job can threaten your identity in two ways—feedback mismatch and time mismatch. Charlie, Cindy, and others experienced feedback mismatches when they received feedback from others that they were not the people they thought they were, which made them feel depressed, anxious, and angry. Marsha, Charlie, and others experienced time mismatches, and felt anguished, confused, anxious, and depressed because they felt that they were no longer the same people they had been in the past.

The next chapter describes how losing your job can challenge your identity in a third way—by producing what I call a status mismatch. A status mismatch can make you feel like you are not a good man or woman, or not a good "thirty-year-old," or not a good "college-educated" person. Gender, age, education level, and race are statuses—or ranked characteristics—that often become part of our identities. Losing your job can challenge these status-based identities and cause distress.

5

"Me Caveman . . . I Club Deer"

Status Mismatches

Your age, gender, education level, and other statuses can influence your thoughts about who you are (Pearlin 1999) and what is possible. If you are a scientifically talented young woman, for example, you may still find yourself thinking that you are not good at science, and you may avoid a career as a scientist simply because you are not a man (Lee 1998).

The meanings of these various statuses—being young or old, a man or a woman, and so on—are strongly influenced by society (Blumer 1962, 1969) and are important to mental health (Simon 1997). These meanings often become part of people's identities (Pearlin 1999).

Mainstream society values some statuses over others (for example, being white comes with more privileges than does being black) and puts forth the idea that some statuses do not "go with" other statuses and roles (such as being a doctor and being black). When others communicate mixed messages about our supposed mismatches, we may feel angry and hurt (Thoits 1985). But the people you will read about in this chapter show that mismatches need not always involve a devalued identity in order to be distressing. Rather, when expectations for one identity simply differ from what is expected for another identity, you can experience a status mismatch. In this chapter, Skip, Cindy, Charlie, and others will explain how three types of status mismatches lead to distress, a constrained job search, and even to abandoning a treasured identity.

No Longer Breadwinners, No Longer Men: Gender-Based Status Mismatches

Different social statuses can expose people to different kinds of stress (Pearlin 1999). Research on social status and stress generally centers on the simple existence of a status. For example, the objective fact of being male can make it more likely that you will be exposed to the front lines in war. However, the subjective side of status—what status means and how it can become part of identity—is also important to stress and mental health (Simon 1997).

Employment and breadwinning are often central to men's identities (Townsend 2002); most research shows that when men lose their jobs, they feel like they have lost their manhood (Cottle 2001; Newman 1999 [1988]; Nixon 2006).[1] Charlie, for example, believed that because he was a man, society expected him to work for a living and be his family's main breadwinner. But now he was unemployed, and an unemployed person does not work or earn a paycheck. This led to a status mismatch based on gender: the meaning of his status ("man") conflicted with the meaning of his role ("unemployed"). This mismatch threatened his identity as a man. Now that Charlie was no longer a breadwinner, he felt powerless and bad about himself. He used loaded gendered language to describe how losing his job meant losing his masculine identity: "I think for men especially, you are pretty much your job. If you have a reasonably good job, to dissociate that from who you are I think can make you feel weak and impotent and just at sea in terms of your identity. . . . I kinda feel bad. I don't wanna be a complete slug. . . . I think most people think that you oughta be doing something."

Throughout our lives we learn to consider the attitude of the generalized other; in other words, we learn to see ourselves as most other people in society-at-large likely see us (Mead 1934). For example, part of the reason Charlie worried about being a "slug" was because of what he believed "most people"— or society—thought men should do. This one societal expectation—being an employed economic provider—echoed throughout men's own definitions of what being a man meant to them. Ken, a fifty-seven-year-old white former chief executive officer (CEO) who had been unemployed for one-and-a-half months when I first spoke with him, explained what it was like to be a man without a job: "I think that's what's the hard part. There's a societal expectation that you're the head of the household. . . . It is hard for my identity standpoint as a man to be without a job, which is why I haven't told some people."

Ken even dismissed the financial consequences of losing his job. Instead, he emphasized how losing his job meant losing his identity, and that losing his identity diminished his self-worth: "[Losing my job] really has more to do with my self-worth than it does worrying about our financial situation. . . . While the economic loss exists, the self-worth loss has been far greater. I have kind of defined myself by my job."

Saul, a forty-eight-year-old African American former senior banker, echoed Charlie's and Ken's thoughts on the connections between male identity, jobs, and distress. Saul had been unemployed for about six months when I first spoke with him, and he had experienced severe depression during that time:

> I think our jobs become kind of what [men] are because . . . you're expected to be the breadwinner and do what it takes. So you just take on the job as your identity. . . . With jobs coming and going . . . it gets crushed. . . . I was really in bad shape. . . . I got to the point where [Saul clears his throat] I didn't really wanna do anything at all. I didn't wanna even be around the kids. . . . I just wanted to be alone, felt like a failure. I won't say that suicide came to my mind but I thought, boy, I'd rather not be here.

The consequences of losing a job were profound. For many men losing a job meant losing who they were as men, and it left them feeling depressed, valueless, and even close to suicidal.

So Who Says You Have to Be a Breadwinner?

Why did so many men feel less masculine after losing their jobs? Did their friends, neighbors, or wives say they were no longer manly? Did they internalize society's stereotypes about the meaning of manhood? Or did both factors play a role?

Despite stereotypes of the "nagging wife," women are less likely than men to view a man as less masculine if he loses his job (Michniewicz, Vandello, and Bosson 2014). Similarly, most of the men who shared their stories with me were adamant that their wives were steadfastly supportive and uncritical, and that neither friends nor neighbors had criticized them. Even so, men made society's expectations of manhood predominant, and judged themselves by those standards; this overrode their wives' support. For example, when Saul's wife, a lawyer, tried to tell him he did not need to be the main breadwinner, Saul challenged her: "I said, 'Sweetie, don't say that.' . . . It's [men's] job to take care of the family. . . . She could really take care of the whole family [financially] and I could be the housedad. But she knows that in my psyche, I wouldn't feel good about that."

Similarly, Charlie's wife Janette had returned to work full-time after Charlie lost his job and she now financially supported the family. Initially, when Charlie told me how Janette responded to his job loss, he pointed out that she had never complained, nor had she criticized or nagged him: "My wife is amazing. . . . I don't feel any pressure. . . . She never says, 'What did you do today?' or . . . 'You said you're gonna clean out the basement. How come you haven't done that?'"

But despite the valued support that Charlie and many other men described, they still believed they should be the kind of man that they thought society expected them to be, and they worried about what their wives "really" thought about their unemployment. For example, Charlie told me that Janette had not changed the way she treated him since he lost his job, but then once again used the term "slug" to describe how Janette "might" see him:

CHARLIE: [Janette] obviously is going through something herself. . . . This is a big adjustment to her. I'm home all the time.

ME: Do you think she does see you any differently . . . than before?

CHARLIE: Yeah. I'm sure she must.

ME: Now has she said anything to that effect?

CHARLIE: Like slug? [Charlie laughs vigorously, with intermittent gasps.] No. I don't know. No, she hasn't. No, no. That's what I'm saying. She hasn't. I think that she knows me well enough to know that would not be productive.

At first, Charlie only focused on the emotional support his wife gave him. But as our conversation continued, Charlie slowly became uncertain. He began hedging ("I don't know") and started laughing frantically and nervously. Eventually, he admitted that he was concerned that Janette actually saw him as useless and less masculine, even though she never said so: "[She] sees me in a different way—not the breadwinner. In the sense that I'm [no longer] 'Me caveman. I go out. I club deer. Bring 'em home.'"

Ken also believed that his wife saw him as less of a man, but he had little evidence to support that belief. Although right after he lost his job, his wife had made some "not so pleasant comments" and had asked "How could this happen?" she had not acted disappointed or treated him like he was less masculine since that time. But, like Charlie, Ken believed that his wife's "real," unspoken thoughts differed from what she said: "Regardless of what women say, they still want the man to be . . . the man. . . . Women give you mixed messages, that they want to be equal . . . but my wife still wants me to take out the garbage." As Ken continued, tears welled up in his eyes and he looked down. His voice got quiet and hoarse and began to break as he told me what he believed his wife thought about him since he lost his job: "She doesn't ask me very much about it. . . . It would be interesting to hear what she had to say about that 'cause you perceive what the other person's thinkin' but you're not always right. Down deep, I think she's disappointed in me. . . . It makes me tear up like I am right now. Makes me sad. . . . I guess it makes me a little disappointed in myself."

Only one man I spoke to, Theo, downplayed the connection between masculinity and employment.[2] Theo, a divorced sixty-year-old former computer programmer, may have been more comfortable with dismissing mainstream culture's expectations of men as providers because he strongly identified with hippie counterculture and was generally comfortable with being a "nonconformist": "I have zero regard for what society thinks of me. When I was a little kid I really wanted to be popular but it just didn't work. I was a fat little kid and I had a real hard time and I finally just gave up tryin' to conform . . . and now I actually take pride in myself being a nonconformist."

Theo's viewpoint notwithstanding, it is common for men to equate male identity with employment (see Cottle 2001; Newman 1999 [1988]; Nixon 2006). Yet a few authors (Demantas and Myers 2015; Lane 2009, 2011) found that some unemployed men are comfortable taking on a more domestic role and do not see employment as so central to masculinity. This may be partially due to their somewhat younger samples of men (primarily in their twenties to fifties) compared with the men in my study (primarily in their fifties or sixties), who may have held more traditional views about gender.

It may also be that the initial "surface" claims of the men in Carrie M. Lane's (2009, 2011) study do not match what lies underneath. At first, Charlie, Ken, and Saul all emphasized personal connections—support from their wives—making it appear that all was well regarding their manhood. At first glance, they thereby bypassed questions about masculinity. However, as they continued to tell their stories, they betrayed a strong concern rooted more deeply in society's messages than in their wives' feedback—that their wives "really" thought they were less masculine. The men in Lane's (2009, 2011) study might also harbor deeper, more complex thoughts about their manhood that they did not disclose.

Society's messages are central to the process of threatening the male identity, even when people close to the man are supportive, and even when others do not know he has lost his job. For example, Ken skillfully hid his unemployment from most of his friends, peers, and neighbors. Yet he still worried about what they "really" thought, but would not say to him—that he had lost his job because he was incompetent: "[My neighbors] wouldn't react negatively to me face-to-face, but behind closed doors they'd go . . . 'He must have really screwed up, must be incompetent or something. . . . What'd he do wrong that this happened to him?'"

When Ken still had his job, his employee identity was reinforced by the people he "hung with," many of whom were employed in high-level professions. Today, when he compared himself—an unemployed man—to his friends, peers, and neighbors, he felt bad about himself: "[My identity] took a pretty big hit. [Ken sighs] The people I hang out with . . . are successful attorneys. . . . The milieu you hang out with in some ways defines you. . . . In that social circle and the neighborhood I live in, people are very successful, and [being unemployed] just makes you feel not so successful . . . makes you feel like a failure." Recall that Ken's friends, peers, and neighbors had said nothing of the sort and that, in fact, most of them did not even know Ken had lost his job.

Direct feedback from others can help you feel solid in your identities. But without it, your identities can wither (Burke 1991, 1996; Burke and Stets 2009). For example, Charlie began to lose his director of training identity when his boss kept reprimanding him (see chapter 3). However, the generalized other may, at times, be incredibly powerful. It can be strong enough to override positive direct feedback and support from people you know personally, and can reverse your normally good feelings about who you are.

You can also compare your own behaviors and circumstances to what a role or status specifically means to you (Burke 1991, 1996; Burke and Stets 2009); that meaning is likely influenced by the generalized other (Mead 1934). If you come up short in your comparison, even if you have not received negative feedback from anyone directly (Norris 2011), you may become distressed (Burke 1991, 1996; Burke and Stets 2009).

In these status mismatches, feedback from wives, friends, and neighbors was not what made Charlie, Ken, or Saul feel like they were no longer men, nor was that what made them feel unsuccessful or depressed. Their thoughts and feelings came from internalizing society's views of men and unemployed people. The cultural meanings of manhood and unemployment superseded the one-on-one emotional support from these men's wives.[3] And when they got no feedback (such as when Ken's neighbors said nothing to him about losing his job), they assumed the worst as they based their ideas on society's views.

For good reason, many authors (for example, Cottle 2001; Lane 2009, 2011; Newman 1999 [1988]) emphasize how, after losing a job, the masculine identity is negotiated through one-to-one interactions. Other authors (for example, Ezzy 2001) emphasize the importance of cultural standards to men's self-views when they lose their jobs. This emphasis on large-scale factors is further supported by Ofer Sharone's (2013a, 2013b) research on how the structure of the labor market influences seemingly individual job search strategies. Charlie's, Ken's, and Saul's stories add to this body of knowledge by examining just how much men used one-to-one interactions versus cultural standards in determining who they were as men. Personal interactions remained important to them, but the cultural meanings of manhood were more powerful than personal interactions when it came time to decide what others "really" thought of them and when judging themselves as men.

On the surface, unemployed men described the general feeling of being less masculine, just as other authors have repeatedly documented. However, there is more going on behind the scenes. Lost masculinity actually involved very specific ideas and meanings that were part of men's identities, as illustrated by Charlie, Ken, and Saul. A mismatch between the male identity (based on a status) and the "unemployed person" identity (based on a role and a status) was at the heart of these men's emasculation and distress.

Status mismatches are not limited to gender; they can also be based on age and education levels. Next, you will read about Cindy and Skip, who believed their identities as "older" people conflicted with their former occupational identities. You will also read about Amber, who believed that being a thirty-year-old meant she should not be an unemployed person or a dependent. Finally, you will hear from Saul (as well as Amber again), who both experienced mismatches between their identities as college-educated people and the identities implied by the lower-level jobs they ultimately accepted.

Has-Beens and Underachievers: Age-Based Status Mismatches

No one directly criticized Charlie's, Ken's, or Saul's manhood. Similarly, no one explicitly told Cindy (the former travel account executive) that she was too old to work in her chosen field. Cindy's bosses never mentioned age, but they criticized her when she needed them to repeat instructions to her: "[My boss's boss] said, 'Cindy, part of it is that time and time again we have to repeat everything to you over and over and over again. . . . It doesn't stick with you.'"

There are many reasons you might need to hear something several times before you learn it. Perhaps the speaker is talking too quickly, too many things are being communicated at once, or the information is complex. But age often becomes part of identity (Weiss and Lang 2012; Westerhof and Barrett 2005) and can become a lens through which we view our interactions and make choices (Weiss and Lang 2012). This is what happened to Cindy.

Cindy noticed that at work she was surrounded almost exclusively by younger employees, including her new thirty-three-year-old boss. When you are the only older person among many younger people, age can stand out for you (Norris 2011). This, combined with her bosses' general criticism of her performance, triggered a focus on age stereotypes. People generally conform to society's expectations about age (Krekula 2009; Moore 2001), especially if they are reminded of age or age-based expectations (O'Brien and Hummert 2006), such as the stereotype that older people are forgetful or incompetent (Ryan 1992). Cindy began to believe that her identity as a sixty-two-year-old did not match her treasured identity as a travel executive: "I just felt like I wasn't with it. . . . I really felt that a lot of it was just age, because I quote 'didn't get it,' that it was because I didn't fit their format of their new type of employee. . . . Everyone that was being hired was very young."

Cindy thought her age was part of why she was struggling with her work. She still needed a full explanation for what was going wrong, and so she gravitated to an age-based explanation of "not getting it"—dementia. She went for medical testing to find out if this was true. You may recall Cindy's statement from chapter 3: "[My boss's boss] said, 'You just don't seem to get it.' . . . It was horrible. That's when I thought 'Maybe there's something wrong with me.' . . . I had this family history of Alzheimer's . . . and I thought, 'Maybe I am having . . . early signs of dementia.' . . . So I went through . . . a series of tests."

Although Cindy's age had not changed overnight, the criticism she heard, combined with seeing mostly young people around her in the workplace, may have led her to reinterpret the meaning of her age. She took the attitude of the generalized other—that "older" people may have dementia—and endeavored to find out if this was true for her. When Cindy got the test results, she had trouble believing them—her intellectual abilities were all normal or above average. Cindy was relieved to be able to rule out dementia as an explanation for the trouble she had at work. But, as you may recall from chapter 3, she so strongly believed that her age was to blame that the results confused her: "I had this huge document that shows all the results and everything. And the result was no, I didn't . . . [but I was] somewhat disbelieving."

She found herself still trying to make sense of why she was not "getting it," what it meant to be older in an office of younger people, and whether her identity as a sixty-two-year-old made being a travel executive impossible. If she did not have dementia, what other reason was there for her not being a "good" travel executive? And did that reason have to do with age in any way?

Before the merger and her bosses' negative feedback, Cindy was very happy at her job, believed she was very good at it, and saw no conflict between her identities as a sixty-two-year-old and a travel executive. But, as Identity Control Theory (Burke 1991, 1996; Burke and Stets 2009) might suggest, Cindy's executive identity weakened when people told her she was not good at her job. As she put this together with society's beliefs about older people, she assumed it was due to a conflict between the expectations for her job and those for her age.

The way you understand the meaning of your roles can make a difference for your mental health (Simon 1997). When you are trying to interpret several roles and/or statuses at once, things get even more complex. Her beliefs about the conflict between her age and her former occupation persisted even after she left her job. Cindy told me that because she was older she had "peaked," because to be a travel executive meant to be "young":

CINDY: Have I peaked at this level and I really do need to look at other options?

ME: What makes you think that could possibly be the case?

CINDY: Just looking around and the industry's still very young. . . . It's like somebody saying they're part of the Who's Who of the Has-Beens.

Cindy told me that the stresses and pressures of that type of job were inappropriate for someone her age, but that she would consider taking a lower-level position in the travel industry. She targeted a travel-oriented receptionist job, but when the employer tried to talk her into taking a high-level position instead, Cindy declined:

> When I actually went to them initially, I just said, "I see where you have a job for a receptionist." . . . And they said, "Oh, Cindy, you're so much more than that. Why would you even think about it? It doesn't pay anything. It's a nothing job." And so that's why they put me in touch with this other person, to interview for this really high-level job. And I listened to the interview and I talked in the interview and I just said to the woman "I'm not your person."

Cindy also turned down another potential higher-level position that a friend had begun to arrange for her. She specified that she was avoiding these jobs because she believed she was too old for them:

> I had a great interview . . . and I knew people there and it looked really promising. . . . And I just kinda let it drop because I really don't wanna— . . . the quota . . . the brow-beating, why didn't you make this sale? . . . They don't wanna pay for experience. They want someone just to go out who has lots of energy. Well, I don't have that kind of energy store. I used to. I used to work all the time, weekends. . . . And I do think that age has a lot to do [with it], 'cause I don't see anybody my age [in those jobs].

Cindy illustrates what Clary Krekula (2009, 22–23) refers to as "age-based norms and deviance" in which certain activities are "more appropriate for some age groups than for others." By attributing having "lots of energy" to younger people, she positions herself as "normal" for avoiding the high-level travel industry job (and deviant if she were to take it). However, she described herself as being very energetic before the merger and before getting negative feedback from her boss: "I felt always that I had energy, that I always could do the job. It had nothin' to do with age."

But when her new bosses told her she was not doing a good job, she used age as a "justifiable" explanation for why this was the case: it was just not normal for people her age to succeed at these tasks. She had finally, as she had put it, "peaked."

Because of her beliefs about age (which reflected society's stereotypes), Cindy started looking for "retirement jobs" in the field, even though she had not been thinking about retirement while she was still employed: "I would love to be like the concierge. . . . There are all these different organizations like RetirementJobs.com. . . . I'm also looking at quote-unquote 'administrative assistant' things."

Cindy ultimately abandoned her search for travel industry "retirement" jobs. And although she was somewhat comfortable considering retirement jobs outside of the travel industry, she had some reservations about whether she could still feel valuable if she took them (as noted in chapter 3). However, she applied for them because they were congruent with the meaning of her age identity as she saw it: "I answered one ad to be a school bus driver for Smithsville city schools. . . . I'm really observant about people in stores, things like that, their ages. . . . Trader Joe's—I noticed there are some older people [working] there."

By the time I spoke with Cindy again three months later, she did not identify as a travel executive, and had been employed for two months in a "retirement" job as an administrative assistant in a different field—the media industry. Although Cindy described her overall emotional state as "good," her new boss's habit of alternately praising her, criticizing her, and "freaking out" on her made Cindy anxious, depressed, and angry. Despite these stresses, Cindy still did not search for another executive position in the travel industry because of the status mismatch she perceived between her age and former occupation: "[The] thought of having to go back into the [travel] industry just . . . makes me crazy. . . . I don't know though that somebody at my age . . . could be valued in the [travel] industry. It's really made up of much younger people now. . . . That's old and done with and I'm finished."

Cindy did not happily transition out of a job from which she was ready to retire. She still very much loved who she had been as a travel executive, but she thought she had no choice but to abandon that identity because she also identified as a sixty-two-year-old. She was even willing to accept a job she did not especially like because at least it did not produce an identity mismatch. Her decision was not primarily due to financial problems; her husband's retirement funds and part-time job ensured that they lived very comfortably.

Skip and Amber also experienced age-based status mismatches. Skip, a fifty-three-year-old white former bank vice president, believed (like Cindy) that he was too old to apply for jobs in the field in which he had worked for more than twenty years. Unlike Cindy, Skip's status mismatch did not cause him emotional pain, but (like Cindy) it did constrain his job search. Skip said his identity had always been based on his job, and although he claimed to have been tiring of banking even before he lost his job (possibly in an effort to cope with the loss), he also said he still enjoyed working with money, and described enjoying being a volunteer on his church's finance committee. Nevertheless, he thought the banking field itself was now "a young man's game": "Historically, I've always felt that my job is me and I'm my job. . . . Modern banking . . . is very much a young man's or young person's game. . . . Long hours and . . . Blackberries and very much expected to respond to calls and email even over the weekend. . . . That's not me [Skip laughs] . . . I'm getting out of banking."

You can see the similarities to Cindy's statements about the kinds of activities appropriate for "older" people. Skip linked intense work schedules and high energy levels with being young. Conversely, he said that to be in your fifties meant you should balance work and personal life, avoid high-energy, middle management positions (such as those he believed were available in the banking industry), and look for a position that was for mentors and "sages":

> When you get into your forties or fifties . . . you've been around the block a few times. We're excellent mentors. . . . What we have to do is sell ourselves as the sage. . . . [People who are age] twenty-five to maybe high thirties . . . have a much higher energy level and they don't necessarily have a work-life balance. . . . At my age I'm a lot more sensitive to the importance of family and the importance of having time off and relaxing and recharging and just shifting gears.

He even went so far as to dismiss the possible role of age discrimination in hiring. Instead, he said that the meaning of one's age should match the meaning of the job one targets: "If you're complaining about age discrimination, it's because you're shooting . . . at a position that perhaps [is] not even appropriate for you in the first place."

His beliefs about age discrimination may have been too simplistic, however. Ageism is widespread in employer attitudes and behaviors (Berger 2009). In fact, several people I spoke to who were in their fifties and sixties described encountering illegal, discriminatory questions and comments at their previous jobs or during their job searches. For example, Uma, a sixty-two-year-old white systems engineer with two master's degrees, told me that a forty-three-year-old male interviewer asked her "How long do you think you'll stay in this job?" then snickered. Some people told me that they or other people they knew dyed their hair, tried to lose weight, or even had plastic surgery to make themselves appear younger while seeking work. Others, like Charlie, noticed that it was the older employees who constituted the bulk of the layoffs. But some older job seekers themselves also believed the negative age stereotypes. For example, after attending a networking event for older job seekers, Charlie told me that he would not hire the attendees because they were "unemployable," "naïve," "clueless," and "desperate." Others, like Skip, dismissed age discrimination as a concern.

In the end, Skip could not reconcile being fifty-three years old with a "banking industry" identity, so he did not search for work in that field. This may have made it harder overall for him to find work. He avoided banking even though he still enjoyed working with finances. And he avoided banking despite his serious financial problems: impending foreclosure on his ex-wife's home (where three of his four children still lived) and his inability to pay rent or his full alimony amount.

Not everyone subscribes to or internalizes age stereotypes. In some situations, older unemployed people avoid taking lower-level jobs because it does not match their former professional identities (Riach and Loretto 2009). (See the next section on education-based mismatches for a discussion of this.) However, most people do try to behave in an "age-appropriate" manner, and do consider age when they interpret their interactions with other people (Krekula 2009). Cindy and Skip make this phenomenon very clear: Cindy tried to rationalize what made her "not get it" (as her bosses claimed), and Skip and Cindy avoided taking jobs they believed were age-inappropriate.

On a final note, younger people also try to be age-appropriate, but it may look a little different for them than it does for older people. In contrast to Skip and Cindy, Amber, a thirty-year-old white woman, felt that her age did match her former newspaper reporter identity. But she felt depressed because her age did not match her new identities as an unemployed person and dependent (who now lived in her parents' basement). In her first interview with me, two weeks after losing her job, she told me: "I'm thirty years old. By this time, I would think I'd be able to take care of myself and that I'd be able to at least make enough to support myself. The fact that I can't is just really, really depressing. . . . I feel like I haven't really launched anything of myself. You know? Other people can say 'my apartment.' I can't. I can say 'my dad's basement.' . . . Over time it just sort of degrades your self-esteem."

Cindy, Skip, Amber and others who spoke with me told me that their age identities conflicted with who they were in their former fields or who they were as unemployed people. This status mismatch added to the stress some people already had about how they would pay their bills after losing a job, but even people who did not experience much financial stress suffered when they had a status mismatch. In particular, status mismatches lowered people's self-esteem, made them feel depressed or useless, and restricted the jobs for which they were comfortable applying. Amber, unfortunately, was coping with two status mismatches at once: one based on age identity and one based on education level. In the next section, you will read about one final status mismatch—one based on people's identities as college graduates.

I Can't Escape from the Blue Collar: Education-Based Status Mismatches

The first time Amber spoke with me, she told me that being a college graduate was an important part of who she was. Amber had struggled with mental health problems and substance abuse for years. But in her mid-twenties she had finally graduated with a bachelor's degree, which may have helped her start to leave her "junkie" identity behind: "I sort of just view [the bachelor's degree] as a personal triumph for me because at the time when I decided to go back to school, I was a junkie and I was hurting in a lot of ways. . . . I view getting my bachelor's in and of itself as just this great triumphant moment when I was actually able to complete something."

Before earning her degree, Amber had worked as a waitress. Now that she had lost her job, she feared what it would mean if she could not find work that matched who she was as a college graduate: "The scariest part of [competing for jobs] is the prospect of having to wait tables for the rest of my life. I went to college so that I could escape from that."

But after two months of unemployment, her parents threatened to kick her out of their house. Amber became desperate. She broke down and took a waitressing job at a "dirty spoon" chain restaurant so she could pay her bills. She told me the times she felt the least hopeful were when she compared being a waitress with who she was as a college graduate:

> I think "Oh God, please don't let me end up [waitressing] full-time again." . . . When I graduated college and I had all these lofty aspirations, I was like "Yay! I'm gonna get a great job with my degree and I'm gonna be doing really cool stuff. I'll be able to be proud of what I do for a living." . . . Working at the restaurant, it's a bit different atmosphere. There are a lot of high school dropouts there. . . . I think the worst part about it is . . . [Amber pauses for about five seconds] coming home and peeling off my uniform and seeing my degree. That is really crushing when you have to do that.

Others have documented this "crushing" experience of going from a higher-level "college graduate" job to a lower-level job that does not require a degree. It happens to recent college graduates (Feldman and Turnley 1995) like Amber, as well as to middle-class adults who have held their degrees and worked in their fields for many years.[4] Their descent (Newman 1999 [1988]) into becoming lower-status workers triggers identity problems (Mendenhall et al. 2008; Riach and Loretto 2009).

But it is not just downward mobility or a "lower-status worker" identity that leads to the distress that follows these "demotions." Instead, as Amber tells us, the mismatch itself—between the "college-educated" and "non-college job" identities—produces a substantial amount of the distress or discomfort that downward mobility researchers (for example, Feldman, Leana, and Bolino 2002; Newman 1999 [1988]) have documented.

Amber's discomfort did not come solely from the admittedly high pressure of a low-wage job or from downward mobility itself. It came from the job's mismatch with who she was as a college graduate. Saul also felt uncomfortable with the mismatch between his educational identity and the new exterminator job he finally took at PestFree in order to pay the bills. After six months of being unemployed, Saul believed he had done the right thing by taking a blue-collar job. However, he was also somewhat ashamed that it did not match up with his college graduate identity: "I said, what the heck? I'll do blue-collar. . . . I was really looking for something in management. . . . I figured, well, they're hiring. Maybe I can just do this temporarily until I can find something else."

One of Saul's coworkers at PestFree (who was also a former white-collar worker) told Saul that others might question why he was now an exterminator, and that Saul would probably feel embarrassed about working a blue-collar job. Saul echoed this thought when he contrasted his former white-collar, college-educated self with his new blue-collar self: "And [my friend said] 'You're probably gonna even feel embarrassed' . . . [and] I have because . . . when you graduate Who's Who in American Colleges, when you graduate most likely to succeed, when . . . a lot of people went to [Ivy League colleges] from your high school and you're voted over them to be most likely to succeed, it sort of sets an expectation."

Despite Saul's embarrassment, he may have seen himself as "too manly and responsible *not* to take the low-status job" (Lane 2011, 106, italics mine). Thus, taking the job at PestFree may have helped Saul to reclaim his masculine identity because, as Saul put it, "the ideal man is someone who's willing to do whatever it takes to make sure the family is safe and secure financially. . . . If someone is to sacrifice, the man will step to the plate, the man will sacrifice for his family."

Similarly, when Amber took the waitressing job (and eventually another part-time job as a reporter), she was able to move out of her parents' home and feel like the independent thirty-year-old she wanted to be. However, in order to resolve one status mismatch (gender-based for Saul, age-based for Amber), each of them had created another mismatch based on education. The relationship between status, jobs, and identities is complex, involves the past, present, and the future, and is not always easy to manage, especially in an economy that offers few choices.

The identity problems described by Amber, Saul, and many other people I spoke with were not just about losing (and trying to reinstate) high-prestige identities. Rather, people were distressed by the mismatch itself, whether the mismatch left them in a lower- or higher-prestige position. Darren Nixon (2006) found a similar pattern for laid-off blue-collar workers: poorly educated manual workers preferred to remain unemployed rather than take an office job where they could be seen as a "college boy" and would be unable to do the manual work with which they identified. Although prestige can be important to education-based mismatches, what seems to be more important is having a role that is consistent with the status you held before losing your job, regardless of whether that status was high or low.

Summing Up Identity Mismatches: Chapters 3 through 5

The stories of Charlie, Cindy, Amber, and others reflect a multi-level social process. During the macro-level event of the Great Recession, these men and women lost their jobs within meso-level institutions—specific workplaces. The ongoing mismatches between identity meanings acted as a chronic strain and led to micro-level experiences of depression, anxiety, and anger.

People often turn to their statuses to help them define who they are (Pearlin 1999). Existing research on work and unemployment suggests that identity (Ezzy 2001; K'Meyer and Hart 2009; Sharone 2013a) and status (Tausig 2009) are important to the amount and kinds of distress people feel after losing their jobs. The people described in this book made it clear that their distress went beyond financial losses, downward mobility, a lack of social support, or having too much time on their hands. Their discomfort and pain often centered on who they were (or were not) and how it supposedly did not match other aspects of who they were.

Specifically, the experiences of the people in this chapter highlight the importance of status during and after losing a job. The stories they shared build on the Stress Process Model (Pearlin et al. 1981) by showing that what these statuses mean to people—and not just objectively inhabiting a particular status—influences how people are exposed to and experience stress. Like Ofer Sharone (2013b, 1447), who writes that people's job search strategies result from the links of "labor market institutions to subjective selves," I show that subjective experience and status location in the social structure are critical to the kinds of jobs we seek out or avoid, as well as to our mental health.

Furthermore, the accounts in this book show that we cannot assume that having a middle-class status, which in theory provides people with a sense of control that carries over into unemployment and helps protect mental health (O'Brien 1985), actually results in feeling control over the situation. This may be because many aspects of personal control are based in the many other social statuses we hold. The accounts in this book also suggest that we cannot take for granted that a given highly ranked status, such as being male, will automatically confer a high sense of control and power after losing a job. Rather, we must think about how people see the meaning of that status in the context in which events occur. For example, consider how painful being an unemployed man was to Charlie because of how he defined manhood.

The experiences of people discussed in chapters 3, 4, and 5 demonstrate that when your identity is threatened, it can become a chronic strain. They substantiate Leonard I. Pearlin's (1999) claim about the importance of status to our identities, as well as others' (Ezzy 2001; Markus and Nurius 1986) ideas about the centrality of time to identities. Scholars (for example, Stryker and Burke 2000) recognize the value of joining structural and meaning-focused approaches to identity. Identity Control Theory (Burke 1991, 1996; Burke and Stets 2009) emphasizes role meaning and feedback. The Stress Process Model (Pearlin et al. 1981) highlights social structure, status, and processes that occur over time. If we combine the strengths of these models, we could greatly enhance our ability to explain distress. The purpose of this book is to take a step in that direction.

Who Will They Become?

Chapters 3, 4, and 5 demonstrated how distressing identity mismatches can be. You might experience a time mismatch and no longer feel like the person you were before your lost your job. You might go through a feedback mismatch when people treat you like you are bad at your job. You might experience a status mismatch if you no longer feel like a "real" man after losing your job, or you do not feel like you are the "right" age or have the "right" education level for a specific job. Identity mismatches created emotional pain, and sometimes diminished employment prospects.

The people in chapters 3 through 5 had lost parts of their identities in many ways. They now had ahead of them the task of reassembling their identities. Who were they now? Would they be similar to the people they used to be? If they adopted new identities, would other people validate them? And how would any of their new identities fit in with their genders, ages, or education levels? As Charlie put it during my first interview with him, finding a new identity takes work: "So I think I'm working on my story. . . . I think I'm coming to a new identity. . . . So [Charlie taps repeatedly on the table] what do I want that story to be?"

In the next few chapters, you will explore the answers to that question by reading about the complex "identity work" (Snow and Anderson 1987) people did to try to manage their damaged identities, as well as the structural factors that helped or harmed their efforts toward identity work.

6

"On the Mommy Track"

Shifting

In chapters 3 through 5, you read about three ways (time mismatch, feedback mismatch, and status mismatch) that your identity can be threatened and cause distress after you lose your job. But if identity threats cause the suffering, can you also use identity to repair the damage? If so, are there limits to who can successfully use identity in this way? Chapters 6 through 8 explore these questions.

When your identity is threatened, you may seek to protect it by using "identity work" (Snow and Anderson 1987). This book highlights two types of identity work—shifting and sustaining. You may try to shift toward a newly emphasized identity—an "identity magnet." An identity magnet draws you to it because it is easily available, matches what society expects for you as a woman, or a man, or a twenty-year-old, etc., and is thus supported by other people. Alternately, you may attempt to sustain the identity connected to the role you lost (see chapter 7). Moving toward a new identity is common for people who voluntarily leave a role they did not like (Ebaugh 1988). But what about people who did not want to lose their role? Can they shift to a new identity?

Shifting operates through "buffer roles" (Sieber 1974, 573) that may help you feel better. When you lose your job, identifying as "unemployed" is an undesirable option because it lowers self-esteem (McFadyen 1995) and increases depression and anxiety (Cassidy 2001). So instead you may downplay the threatened role while emphasizing a different one (Gecas and Seff 1990; Sieber 1974). For example, people who have few promotion opportunities at work may downplay their "worker" identities and look for happiness outside of work. This may help them maintain a sense of control and self-worth (Kanter 1977). Research evidence supports, but does not directly test, the idea of using shifting as a coping strategy when your identity is threatened (Gecas and Seff 1990; Schöb 2013).

This chapter shows that some people do shift when their identities are threatened, and that this reduces their distress.

However, not everyone has equal access to opportunities to successfully shift. Structural factors, like involvement in social institutions (Stryker 1980), and social statuses (such as gender or education level) (Pearlin 1999, 398; Simon 1997; Thoits 1985, 1986) are important to your identities, so they may expand or restrict your identity work options. For example, when you shift, it may be easier to select an identity from an existing role in a social institution you are already involved in, such as family or a volunteer organization. Social statuses are also important. It will probably be easier to adopt an identity that seems to "fit" your beliefs (or society's beliefs) about being a man or a woman, or what having a college degree means to you. Ensuring this "fit" will also make it more likely that others will give you confirming feedback that you are the person you claim to be. For example, people are more likely to praise a woman than a man for being a stay-at-home parent because manhood is often more commonly associated with breadwinning (Townsend 2002). This societal approval and confirming feedback will likely make it easier for a woman to shift her identity from employee to parent.

This chapter begins with the stories of Charlotte and Lorna, whose identities were threatened when they lost their jobs. They describe how shifting to "wife and mother" identities helped reduce their distress. They also describe how two statuses—being a woman and being middle-class—made this shift easier. The second section of this chapter describes Marcus and Amber, who successfully used past and hoped-for future identities to reduce their distress. As with Charlotte and Lorna, their social statuses (man and college-educated thirty-year-old, respectively) helped determine which roles became identity magnets. All these stories show how social structure, status, and time are important for successful identity work.

"I Can Be Supermom": Shifting to Wife and Mother as "Identity Magnets"

Identity Uncertainty and Distress: Charlotte and Lorna

Charlotte, the former chief financial officer (CFO) briefly introduced in chapters 3 and 4, had worked at the nonprofit Patenko Institute for eighteen years, nine of them as CFO. She usually worked weekdays from 8:30 am to 6 pm, and a typical day consisted of reviewing financial statements, meeting with other executives, preparing for audits and board meetings, and managing employees. She enjoyed the autonomy of her position, a great working relationship with her original boss, Rod, and a friendly and comfortable relationship with her employees.

But when Charlotte's new boss, Shannon, repeatedly told her she was not cut out to be a CFO, Charlotte's long-standing CFO identity was threatened. This feedback mismatch made her anxious, "tearful," and depressed. She described her relationship with Shannon as "abusive," and often desperately hoped that Shannon would tell her that, at least this time, she had performed her job right. This rarely occurred.

When Shannon finally told Charlotte that she would be reassigned to a "special projects" job, Charlotte felt like she was losing the identity she had held for so many years. This time mismatch was highly distressing. In a futile attempt to psychologically hold onto her CFO identity ("I'm a CFO between jobs"), Charlotte left her job before officially starting the "special projects" position. But Shannon's feedback had created long-term effects. Even after losing her job, Charlotte questioned whether she was a CFO, or could ever be one again. She was losing her CFO identity.

The first time I interviewed Charlotte, four-and-a-half months after she lost her job, we sat together under the shade of a large tree behind a public library. She placed a bright pink towel on the grass for us to sit on, and we snacked on chips and Starbucks iced coffee on a pleasantly warm and sunny summer day. She dressed casually in a short-sleeved sky-blue Oxford shirt, a flared denim knee-length skirt, and brown leather thong sandals. Her shoulder-length hair was clipped at her crown with a barrette, and she sported several brightly colored plastic children's Silly Bandz bracelets on her left wrist. Despite losing her job, she seemed happy and friendly as she told me her story.

For most of her adult life, Charlotte had defined herself in terms of her work. Even after having children, she questioned whether she was a good mother, and she and her husband agreed that he would be a stay-at-home father while she earned money for the family:

> [Before I lost my job] I had this picture of myself that I was the worker and my husband was the caregiver and that that was just the way it was and thank God that that was the way it was because apparently I was very good at work and just really stinky at this parenting thing. . . . I'm yelling at the children. I don't have any patience. I guess I wasn't cut out for this. I'm really glad that I have crafted my life in such a way that it is my husband who's the primary caregiver of these children because if it were me, boy, this would be really messed up.

Charlotte mentioned that, for the first two months after losing her job, she felt "weird" because she had been with her former employer for so long: "The first two months were kinda weird. . . . Eighteen years is a long time, and to just all of a sudden get up one morning and not go to that place where you've been for eighteen years? . . . Those first two months there was a lot of . . . 'What am I doing? Why don't I have a job?'"

At first, being unemployed was confusing and stressful for Charlotte. But after about two months, she began to shift toward a mother identity, which helped relieve the distress surrounding her identity. When I asked Charlotte what her moods had been like since she had lost her job, she replied: "About two months in it was like, this is great. I don't know what I'm meant to do for the next twenty years, but for the next couple months, I am meant to just enjoy these children." This shift strengthened and her identity-related distress continued to decrease the longer she was unemployed.

Lorna (briefly introduced in chapter 4) also suffered from identity threats after losing her job. Lorna was a fifty-one-year-old African American woman who had worked in the broadcast entertainment industry at a company called JCC. After she lost the job she had held for twenty-eight years, she felt that she was no longer the same person. Lorna's job had been a big part of who she was for a very long time. She had said that she was "used to bein' in broadcasting" but that now she had "lost her whole music identity" and that "it hurt." Working at JCC had provided her with a salient and valuable identity that had benefited her well-being by giving her a consistent sense of who she was. But it also provided her with self-esteem and respect from others. For Lorna, losing her job meant that other people would no longer respect her, and she told me that her JCC identity:

> . . . made me somebody. . . . When my kids were little, they'd really be in awe of the different people who I would come in contact with. Like my kids used to say "Mom, you were in the elevator with D Grim Crush? . . . Mom, that was D Grim Crush and his boys! Aren't you excited?" . . . There was a time I could walk in a room . . . everybody'd be quiet and listen to what I had to say. . . . [Now] I'm just like the average person. . . . It makes me not as important as I used to be.

She had also felt respected and important because of the way her former subordinates acted toward her and the way the general public treated her when they found out where she worked: "All my immediate crew looked up to me. . . . They were always respectful. . . . JCC was my life. . . . I could go anywhere in the world and people wouldn't give a rat's you-know-what about me. But if for some reason I had to tell 'em where I work, [as] soon as I said that, 'Oh, you work for JCC?' and then their whole attitude would change."

The first time I interviewed Lorna, she emphasized the importance of honesty and kindness in her personal and work relationships. She was friendly and spoke slowly and quietly, with an air of innocence. It was a hot and humid day, and Lorna dressed for the weather in a T-shirt, jeans, and sneakers for our meeting in the children's section of a public library. She told me her usual work schedule had been on weekdays from 9 am to 5:30 pm, but if problems arose she occasionally worked as late as 9 pm, and even occasionally worked on weekends if problems arose. She told me what an average day was like at her old job supervising eight employees in the broadcast industry:

> I'm in charge of a team of people . . . two shifts . . . a day shift and a night shift . . . who are looking at the shows and recording them into digital servers . . . to make sure that that show is of broadcast standard. No audio or visual errors. . . . For example, [there] may be a curse word in the show. . . . I would [create] the schedule for both shifts. . . . I normally worked along with the day shift. . . . We look at the show in real time, from start to finish.

Lorna's eventual dismissal started with a series of disagreements between the way her boss, Sandra, wanted things done and the way Lorna did them. When I asked Lorna to tell me more about her relationship with Sandra, she was hesitant:

LORNA: Permission to speak freely?

ME: Please do.

LORNA: [Lorna mumbles almost inaudibly] . . . What I really wanna say . . . [Lorna stops]

ME: Oh, please do. It's important to the study.

LORNA: [Lorna pauses for five seconds] She was a two-faced bitch. . . . She will sell you down the river to save herself. . . . She would not look me in the eye and tell me the truth. . . . I mean, one day I was sittin' in her office, and she had like a doorway and then like a little glass area . . . and one day I was so mad, I saw myself pickin' up a chair and throwin' it through that glass window. That's how angry I was.

Despite her angry feelings, Lorna described her actual behavior toward Sandra as always respectful: "I would go out of my way—because she was my boss; I do owe her that respect—to still be respectful of her. . . . On days that she was pissed off, or in a bad mood, or just didn't wanna say anything to me . . . I just went about my business."

This tension continued for years, but it escalated when Sandra emailed Lorna's performance evaluation to the company's vice president with comments meant for his eyes only. However, she accidentally sent it to Lorna, and Lorna's trust in Sandra dwindled. This mistrust, the arguments about how to accomplish specific tasks, and disagreements about how Lorna managed her employees ultimately led to her being fired. The year that she got fired, Lorna did not get evaluated when evaluations were due. She questioned Sandra about it, but was given the run-around:

> A week before I lost my job, it was around the Thanksgiving time . . . [and] bonuses were based on the evaluations. . . . Payroll lady gets off the

elevator and she puts her arm around me and hugs me . . . and said, "Lorna, I got your paycheck, but I didn't get a bonus check. . . . You need to check with your immediate boss . . . and find out why you didn't get a bonus." Sandra still hadn't evaluated me. She had me evaluate everybody in my department . . . but she hasn't done my evaluation yet. . . . I had said to her, "You gonna do my evaluation?" [She said] "Yeah, I'm gonna do it. . . . I'll call Hugh [the vice president] and find out what happened [to your bonus]." . . . Around four o'clock I go back to her office and I said, "Sandra, did you check with Hugh? Did he say anything about where my bonus is?" She said, "He said he's workin' on it." So I made a joke . . . I said, "Sandra, you and Hugh are not tryin' to tell me anything?" And she was sittin' there at her desk . . . looking down and writing something and she wouldn't look up at me. That was my first clue. . . . I started to worry. . . . Went home Thursday and all night long I couldn't sleep 'cause I knew next day I was gonna get laid off.

The next day, Lorna's worst fears came true. Sandra told Lorna:

"Come on back from lunch. Hugh wants to talk with you." . . . Comin' down the hall is our senior vice president of Human Resources with a file in his hand. And I went "Oh, here it comes." So then he comes out. They sit and talk to me. And they're like, [Lorna speaks very quietly] "We're lettin' you know that your position is bein' abolished. We are restructuring the department and we no longer need your services." So I said, [Lorna speaks slightly louder] "Ohhh, so now you wanna talk to me? Friday at two o'clock?" . . . I said, "Now you wanna come talk to me," and I went "I don't really wanna hear it, anything you twos have got to say." . . . I was angry. I was real angry. . . . I didn't call 'em rat-bastards, but I said, "I hope you two 'rat-Bs' can sleep tonight and I hope when you get up tomorrow you can look yourselves in the mirror. Because you didn't have to do this to me."

Losing her job created a time mismatch for Lorna, and she also felt like she was no longer important without her work-related identity. Although she had the roles of wife and mother available to her, she did not initially identify strongly with them when she lost her job. After six months of unemployment, she did not find herself "immersed in motherhood" like Charlotte had been. Instead, Lorna said motherhood: "keeps me busy but it doesn't make me happy. It's not what I really wanna do. . . . It's not me."

She was between identities: although she was in the mother role, she had not psychologically shifted to a stronger mother identity at that point, and was still going through a lot of identity-related distress. However, she told me she needed to fill her time, and that she tried to do so by investing her energy in her responsibilities as a wife and mother. At that time (six months of unemployment), those roles had not become her primary identities, but she did notice a slight reduction in some of her distress because they helped fill her time and distract her from being unemployed: "The every day bein' a mom and a housewife type thing . . . I don't mind it and I don't put it down for anybody who wants to do that. . . . But it's not what I wanna do. It's not me. But I'm doin' it. . . . If I didn't I'd probably go crazy. I wouldn't have anything to do. . . . It takes my mind off of not having a job and being depressed. So it helps keep me goin'."

Making dinner and cleaning the house helped Lorna feel a little better because she felt more productive and was distracted from thinking about losing her job. However, her time mismatch was still very hard for her. Tasks, distraction, and filling her time did not address the emotional pain that came from a damaged identity; she needed solid identity work for that. Although it took Lorna a little longer than it did Charlotte, they both ultimately invested their identities more strongly in the wife and mother roles.

Making the Shift: Charlotte and Lorna

During Lorna's first interview with me, she had told me how upset she was about no longer having the work-related identity she had had for twenty-eight years. This time mismatch made her feel depressed: "Sometimes [I'm] depressed because I'm used to bein' in broadcasting and that's what I would like to do and I'd like to go back to it and get paid for it."

By Lorna's second interview with me, after eight-and-a-half months of unemployment, she was struggling with a tight budget. Her severance pay had run out, and she was receiving an unemployment check of less than $1,200 per month. She was worried about money. But in many ways her distress had actually decreased. Although Lorna attributed some of this to maintaining a schedule and keeping busy, she said she mostly felt better because she had shifted more strongly into her wife and mother identities:

> My identity now is a unemployed mom who's lookin' for a job, but just tryin' to keep the unemployed mom-slash-housewife [identity]. . . . It's real important to me. . . . I've got more time to sit back and really look at what my kids are doin', which has been a lotta fun watchin' them get themselves together and hopefully become the people that they need to be. . . . I've got a lot more time to focus on that. . . . I'm not an employee anymore, so I don't have that.

This was such a strong contrast to what Lorna had said in her first interview that I read her old quote (" . . . keeps me busy but it doesn't make me happy. It's not what I really wanna do. . . . It's not me") to her to find out more about why and how this had changed. She reacted with disbelief: "I said that? . . . Oh my God . . . I'm shocked at myself. . . . You got that on tape? . . . Because it is me. It is me. . . . Bein' a mom is a real big deal to me, and until those kids grow up and go off and get married and have their own lives, right now, that job is just as important as bein' an employee somewhere."

After eight-and-a-half months of unemployment, shifting to a wife and mother identity had helped Lorna feel better. She noted that (to some degree) she shifted on purpose to help her move away from the "funk" she was in after being fired: "I really feel [being a mother] has been a positive aspect that has helped me kinda get outta that funk I was walkin' around in, that hatred that I had for people. . . . It grew out of . . . tryin' to get past some of the negative thoughts that I had about people that I work with . . . and getting laid off."

Focusing on her mother identity did not take away all of Lorna's stress about losing her job. But because it did help, Lorna tried to "intensely" use her mother identity to help repair her personhood:

ME: What does it mean to you right now to not have a job?

LORNA: [Sighing] It's disheartening. It sometimes makes me feel like I'm a less of a person, which is why I stay on the mommy track so intensely.

When I asked Lorna if she felt like she was the same person as she had been when we had spoken two-and-a-half months ago, she pointed out that she had actually become much more positive over time: "I'm way more positive. . . . I'm more happy about life, even though I still . . . got financial obstacles to look at. . . . That's about the biggest thing."

Lorna's financial situation was indeed getting bad. At one point, she and her husband had been four months behind on their mortgage. They withdrew some of her husband's retirement funds to pay some of these bills. Nevertheless, at the time of Lorna's second interview with me, they were still one month behind. They had even had to use some of their daughter's college funds toward their household bills, leaving their daughter unable to attend the prestigious college to which she had been admitted. Despite these serious financial problems, Lorna's overall mental health had improved, and she attributed this to shifting to new identities.

Charlotte's identity shift had helped her mental health improve as well, even while she, too, faced diminishing finances. As Charlotte's unemployment passed the eight-month point, she was actively searching for work, but she strongly clung to identifying as a mother although she was becoming increasingly worried about money: "There were days when I was just convinced that we were gonna live in my mother-in-law's basement . . . [and I thought] I have jeopardized my family's financial security. What have I done?"

Charlotte had had a really tough time when her identity was threatened (see chapters 3 and 4). But the second time I interviewed Charlotte, she told me that despite her previous strong worker and CFO identities, despite her former belief that she was a bad mother, and despite her financial concerns, she now saw herself as "Charlotte 2.0"—a Charlotte with a new identity as a mother: "Charlotte 2.0 is all about strengths of my relationships with my family and friends. . . . Now my entire identity is wrapped up in being a mother . . . partly because I have so much time for self-exploration [Charlotte laughs] . . . not because I'm a brilliant parent—[Charlotte speaks in a "sidebar" voice] [but] I think I might be."

Charlotte was looking for a job, but was aware she was strategically using the mother identity to help her deal with threats to her worker identity. She found her mother identity especially useful when searching for work:

> I think I found comfort in that [mother] identity on those days when I wasn't succeeding on my job search. It was okay, well, let's make caterpil- lars out of egg cartons. I can be supermom. So I think I turned to it as a way to make me feel better and I found a lot of solace in being the kind of parent that I always wanted to be. . . . When [the job search] wasn't going well, I could ditch my job search and immerse myself in motherhood.

She continued by telling me that once she got past the "weirdness" of not having a job: "I really did not think of myself as a worker at all. . . . Probably 10 [percent worker] and 90 [percent mother]. . . . I have been to the promised land. . . . I will never go back to [identifying as] a 100 percent worker."

Identity shifts did not necessarily involve a straightforward acceptance of a new identity and rejection of an old one. People were sometimes conflicted about their shifts. For example, Charlotte second-guessed her shift to the mother identity, which she had been referring to in somewhat tongue-in-cheek biblical terms as "the promised land." Although her identity shift did reduce her distress and help her cope with identity threats, she realized that she might not be comfortable prioritizing her mother identity for the rest of her life: "Would I feel differently about that if my plan wasn't to go back to work? If our roles were reversed and [my husband] were working and I thought, 'Well, this is my future,' I think I might throw myself off a bridge."

Lorna also had mixed feelings about not having a work-related identity. She wanted to return to her field and was actively searching for jobs, but was wor- ried that as time went on, she was losing more and more of her broadcasting employee identity. She was focused on being a mother, which helped her, and she wanted to keep that focus even if she got a job. But she was still upset about being unemployed and the loss of identity that accompanied her situation: "I still wanna do [broadcasting] because I do it and I do it well. . . . If somebody came in here today and said 'I got a [broadcasting] job for you,' I'd be like 'Okay, Dawn. We need to finish this up 'cause I need to go.' [Lorna laughs] . . . [But] even if I do wind up gettin' a job and getting back into my career, the mom job part is really important to me."

Although identity shifts may help people manage the troubling experience of not being the same person anymore, they are not always easily achieved. Even if you voluntarily leave a role, part of your old role often lingers as a persistent "hangover identity" (Ebaugh 1988, xiii, 149, 173). As chapter 4 explored in depth, it is hard when you feel like your identity has become inconsistent (Stets and Burke 2014; Swann 1983), and although a shift may help you find a replacement identity and a sense of who you are, it may not provide the identity consistency that is important for mental health.

However, the ability of unemployed people to shift to emphasize a non-work identity calls into question the centrality of work to our identities, as proposed by Marie Jahoda (1981, 1982) and Peter Warr (1987), and as shown by other scholars (for example, Ezzy 2001 and Sharone 2013a). The relative ease with which some people shifted suggests that as a society we may be at a mid-point between two extremes: work being central to who we are and work becoming less relevant to who we are. Perhaps we are adapting somewhat to the current unstable economic conditions by developing the flexibility (at least in the short term) to move into and out of work-related identities when it is necessary to protect our mental health.

"Shaped by My Circumstances": Social Institutions, Status, and Feedback

Charlotte and others may have hedged their "identity bets" by shifting to new identities even though they did not want to completely give up their work-related identities. But who you are is strongly shaped by your relationship to your external circumstances, such as structural forces and social institutions (Stryker 1980) like the workplace. Charlotte recognized this: "I think until I get the job [my identity] will still very much be weighted toward parent because I'm not working, so I don't think of myself as a worker. . . . I think I allow . . . my identity to be shaped by my circumstances. So even though I'm focused on getting a job . . . it's probably 75-25: 75 [percent] mom [right now]."

Being in a role and interacting with other people who have something to do with that role—such as mother and child or boss and employee—greatly influenced the identities of the people who told me their stories. Social institutions were therefore critical to identity work.

Social status is also important to how people cope with financial insecurity (Cooper 2014) and unemployment (Schöb 2013), as well as the options they have for identity work (Khanna and Johnson 2010). This is partially because "one's emotional life is influenced by one's place in the power structure" (Cooper 2014, 214). Women's gender, in particular, may constrain their identity work during times of career uncertainty, so they may use other aspects of their identities (such as religion or hobbies) to help in "making their careers meaningful" (LaPointe 2013, 142).

Studies that examine differences in unemployed people's mental health by their gender and relationship status support the idea that people may shift when they need to cope with identity threats. Women in relationships are the least distressed (compared to all other categories) when they are unemployed. In contrast, men in relationships suffer the most. Single men and women are somewhere in the middle (Schöb 2013). This may be because American culture deemphasizes the employee role for women (McFadyen 1995; Thoits 1986) and heightens its importance for men (Townsend 2002), allowing women to more easily recategorize themselves as wives and mothers to reduce their distress (Schöb 2013). Men, on the other hand, may be unable to shift in this way (Schöb 2013), and so may be more likely to try to somehow sustain their "worker" identities even though they are unemployed (see chapter 7). The accounts in this book show that statuses do not necessarily play out in the expected ways, such as higher statuses automatically leading to more power or options.

Charlotte was able to shift to motherhood, which served as an identity magnet. The mother identity was easily available in a social institution that she had already been involved with before losing her job—family. Furthermore, it was socially acceptable for her as a woman to be a non-employed parent. This made it easier to earn social approval that would reinforce the identity. To illustrate this, Charlotte contrasted how people treated her with how people treated her husband when each of them played with their daughter in the park:

> I think it's much easier [for me]. . . . When I'm in that park with the kids during the day, they don't see me as an unemployed person. But when [my husband] is in that park, I'm sure they think "Oh, did he take the day off to spend the day with his children?" And I just think that's so much harder for him. . . . People talk to me all of the time. And [my husband] says they never talk to him in the park. . . . [They] seem annoyed mostly.

When people accept you in your role and act as though you belong in it, it helps you maintain that identity (Burke 1991, 1996). These reactions aided Charlotte's transition from being a "stinky" parent to "supermom." When one of our social statuses (for example, woman) lines up with what society expects of a role (such as full-time parent), we may be more likely to get feedback that tells us we are who we claim to be (Burke 1996; Thoits 1985, 1991). Not only did Charlotte perform an activity that mothers may be expected to do with their daughters—playing in the park—but because she was a woman, others interacted with her as though this was natural and normal. This most likely made performing the mother identity more comfortable and more rewarding.

Feedback also helped Lorna solidify her shift to the wife and mother identities. She overheard her husband talking to other people and praising her cooking skills, even going so far as to say that that was why he was happy she was home more often. Lorna behaved in a way consistent with those expectations: "My husband, I overheard him tellin' some people, 'I enjoy having her there 'cause she cooks more.' And I grab the cookbooks . . . and cook gourmet meals."

Women were praised by others, or at the very least assumed to be normal by others, when they were not working and when they performed the roles of wives and mothers. In contrast, not one man in my study told me that his wife had praised or tried to encourage his domestic contributions. Social status was critical to the reinforcing feedback that helped women shift to wife and mother identities. Perhaps getting this feedback is one reason why Charlotte tried to quickly let others know she was a mother, and why she wore specific things to show this to others: "When I do meet somebody, [I] quickly bring up the children to make sure they know that I have them. . . . I'm pretty sure that's why I'm wearing the Silly Bandz [children's bracelets] all the time, so people will see me as a mother."

According to Erving Goffman (1959), a great deal of maintaining your identity has to do with convincing others that that is who you are. Charlotte used the Silly Bandz as a prop—or what Goffman refers to as a "sign vehicle"—to show other people she was, indeed, a mother. Doing so also likely helped her get the feedback that would continue to strengthen the mother identity that was helping her emotionally.

Other statuses, such as social class, can also shape our responses to financial insecurity (Cooper 2014). Charlotte's relatively high class afforded her the option of using shifting as identity work. Charlotte was aware of this, telling me that the "severance package that bought her some freedom" had given her the time to really engage in being a mother: "If I had to go out and get a job the next day 'cause we wouldn't eat otherwise, then I don't think I would have been able to have as adeptly made this transition."

Lorna did not have as much money as Charlotte. But interestingly, Lorna's financial troubles actually pushed her to perform "wife and mother" behaviors more often than she thinks she would have if she was more affluent. Because her family had less money, they could not eat out as often as they used to. This meant Lorna had to cook more: "We did kinda have to curb that a little bit and stop eatin' out so much. We still eat out a lot, but it's a lot less. And that's the part where cooking more came into play. . . . I am a good mom. . . . I try to work hard and perfect the craft of whatever I'm doin'. . . . I like to have dinner ready for everybody when they come home."

Losing your job can strain your identity and your finances. Identity work can help you solve problems related to a threatened identity, and money or other material resources might help you reduce the stress of a shrinking bank account. But identity work will not help with money stress, and money will not necessarily help you repair your identity. Charlotte and Lorna were worried about their financial situations, but they still benefited emotionally by shifting because doing so addressed the identity component of their stress. There may have been little Charlotte and Lorna could do at the time to keep from being stressed out about money, but they could at least feel better about who they were. Performing the identity work of shifting did not get rid of all of their distress, but it was likely much lower overall than it would have been if they had not addressed their identity concerns. Some distress reduction is better than none and is welcome in the midst of such painful circumstances.

Sometimes people do not perceive their very real problematic situations (such as financial troubles) as disturbing. Although you might say these people are just deceiving themselves, such beliefs can have a protective effect on mental health. Financial problems do have real consequences, but distress is not solely determined by these tangible financial problems; sometimes how you feel about and cope with the problem (Cooper 2014) are just as important for your mental health. How you see the meaning of your identity, your perception of whether your identity has been threatened, and how you might be able to redefine yourself are some of the subjective areas that are critical to understanding distress and coping after losing a job.

Repairing Old Identities

Shifting to new identities after losing a job helped reduce the pain of identity mismatches. But sometimes shifting carried with it an additional benefit: it helped repair old identities that people thought they had performed poorly in the past. This may have been an unexpected benefit. Alternately, the identity may have been chosen precisely because it needed to be repaired (according to the person shifting). Women who are trying to balance the wife and mother roles with the employee role often feel that they cannot give enough energy to both roles (Simon 1997). If the wife and mother roles were close at hand, and these women felt that they had not been the best wives and mothers in the past, it makes sense that they would gravitate to, and ultimately shift to, wife and mother identities. By doing so, they could both downplay their threatened worker identities and reduce a (perceived) past mismatch between their actual and ideal behaviors as mothers. As theorists would predict (Higgins 1987; Large and Marcussen 2000; Marcussen 2006), shifting to an identity that could "repair" these supposed failures improved their mental health.

For example, Charlotte criticized herself for acting like what she thought was a "bad mother" in the past: "Someone spills a glass of milk. I lose it. I'm like [Charlotte speaks very rapidly] 'Oh my God. That's so stupid. I can't believe he did that.' [Charlotte speaks at a normal pace.] Then I would [think], 'Oh, I can't believe you. You yelled at Jacob. He's three. He doesn't know how not to spill milk.' And then it became like, 'Oh, I'm such a bad mother.'"

Although Charlotte was actively looking for a new job, she was thrilled that, while unemployed, she had transformed into what she called a "brilliant" parent (see earlier in this chapter).

Lorna also chose the wife and mother identities because of what she perceived as less than successful wife and mother behaviors in the past. Even the first time I interviewed her—before she had fully shifted to these identities and reaped the full emotional benefits of them—she was aware of her reasons for selecting these particular identities. When I asked her why she had gravitated toward being a wife and mother, she replied:

> I felt like I wanted to give back to my kids and my husband for all those times that I've worked when they were little and [I] couldn't necessarily go to the plays . . . and recitals and the concerts and takin' 'em to band practice. . . . A lotta times I had to work nights . . . and I wouldn't be there to put my children to bed . . . I wouldn't be there to give 'em a bath or read 'em a story. . . . Some nights if I was there, I'd be so tired I'd tell them to read me the story. . . . Sometimes I would go to sleep and they would get up and cut the light out. . . . I'd fallen asleep . . . I felt bad . . . I'd go "I can't even stay awake to read the story."

Lorna was a dedicated mother. Despite working long hours to support her family, she had always tried her best to be there for them. And despite Lorna's appraisal of the situation, her children may have greatly treasured the times that "mom fell asleep" with them in bed. Lorna said she needed to do a better job this time around, and that this would help her identity because she would "complete another phase of me": "I gotta do it . . . I wanna try to do it right. That I didn't used to do it the way I really wanted to do it 'cause I had to work. So now I feel I'm completing another phase of me because I've been given the opportunity."

By her second interview, once she was more strongly entrenched in her wife and mother identities, she proudly told me that she had succeeded at "doing it right": "I try to be good at what I do. And I have to say today . . . I'm a good mom. I perfected the craft of bein' a mom."

People who lost their jobs went from feeling like they were no longer the same person they were in the past, to trying to shift to other identities that they thought they had done poorly in the past. Sometimes a complete turnaround occurred. They felt they had "perfected" these identities, or that they were now "brilliant" at doing them. Shifting thus had a double benefit: reinstating a sense of self that had been lost after losing a job, and repairing another identity at which they thought they had done a bad job before. This pattern of repairing old, "poorly performed" identities also occasionally occurred with the identity work I refer to as "sustaining" (see chapter 7).

Using the Past and Future to Support "Identity Magnet" Shifts

Having roles readily available in social institutions supported shifts to other identities, especially when these roles matched society's expectations for the person's gender or other statuses. But identities may also be based on the past or future (Markus and Nurius 1986; Sieber 1974). Some of the people I spoke to used their past or their possible futures to help support their identity shifts.

For example, Amber, the thirty-year-old former newspaper reporter briefly described in chapter 5, struggled with two status mismatches. The first was based on her age status. She saw being a thirty-year-old as mismatched with living with her parents, and she described this status mismatch as "really depressing" and "degrading her self-esteem" (see chapter 5). Then Amber took a waitressing position to earn money, which allowed her to move into her own apartment. Now that she was a thirty-year-old living on her own, that status mismatch disappeared. However, a second status mismatch emerged. This one involved her education status. Taking the waitressing job spurred thoughts about her movement from a higher-level occupation (reporter) to a lower-level one (waitress). This downward movement generally harms mental health because it threatens identity (Mendenhall et al. 2008), and Amber confirmed this. Her waitressing job did not match expectations for having a bachelor's degree, which she described as "crushing" (see chapter 5).

Amber had been fired for her poor performance, so she was hesitant about whether she wanted to be a reporter again. It could be risky to make herself vulnerable to being rejected again from potential reporter jobs, because that would be additional feedback that she was not really a reporter, which would further threaten her identity. During her first interview with me, she did not mention looking for reporter positions or any desire to go back into reporting, editing, or any publishing-related fields. Instead, she looked back to her past—she had once wanted to be a teacher. She pulled a potential future identity—teacher working abroad—from it, and mentally began shifting to this new identity: "One of the things that I'm looking into is teaching abroad. . . . I went to school originally to study education. I wanted to be a teacher. . . . So that's my biggest thing and that was my original intent going to college."

But by the time I interviewed her again, six months later, she had found a part-time newspaper reporter/copyeditor position to supplement her thirty-hour-per-week waitressing position that paid the bulk of her bills. She had not sought out the reporter position; rather, she "fell into it" after being recruited by a friend's relative who worked at a newspaper and knew she needed a job. She described the copyeditor position as matching her identity: "It's sort of like fulfilling a natural proclivity, I guess [Amber laughs]. It fits."

She noted that she had really just been using the potential teacher identity to buffer her from possible rejection as a reporter, and that a reporting/publishing career would now make her happy:

> I think I was grasping at straws when I said that [about being a teacher]. . . . When I lost my job at *Johnson County Weekly* I don't think that I really thought I'd find another newspaper job. . . . Now that I'm in a different position that seems to have some possibilities, I'd rather explore those. . . . It still seems like a great, wonderful profession and I would love to be able to call myself a teacher. . . . It's just probably not a good fit for me.

When I asked Amber why her interest in teaching had changed, she pointed to "circumstances"—her involvement in specific social institutions—as being critical to her identity: "It changes with my circumstances. . . . The fact that I have found another newspaper job I think is just the biggest point for me. Because I could see myself being very happy with a career in publishing and editing and writing 'cause it's what I enjoy doing most."

Now that Amber had her foot in the door of the newspaper industry again, she could once again envision her identity—both in the present and the future—as a reporter. Despite a brief mental shift to a future teacher identity, Amber ultimately preferred consistency in her occupational identity once it was safe enough to say so. This supports research showing that our need for identity consistency often overrides our need to hear good things about ourselves (Stets and Burke 2014).

At the time of the second interview, Amber seemed much more relaxed and happy compared to the first time I had spoken with her. She smiled more and this time her smile seemed genuine rather than forced. She contrasted her emotions with the last time she had spoken with me: "I'm a lot better today. I'm smiling . . . I have a direction . . . a foundation . . . [I'm] hopeful. . . . [In the past] I've always been a pessimist. . . . I know there's a lot of things that I probably shouldn't be hopeful about, but . . . [my new reporter job] puts me in a good mood. It makes me feel relaxed."

Getting the new publishing job, even on a part-time basis, helped Amber re-identify as a reporter, and her emotional well-being had improved, probably due in part to continuing an identity that was consistent with her education status. Making money also helped reduce her overall distress level, and also provided a second benefit: it allowed her to support herself at age thirty, and so eliminated the age-based status mismatch. The combined income for herself and her fiancé was only about $35,000 a year, and most of her money came from waitressing. They certainly were not living a life of financial ease in this expensive region of the country. So although making money helped her mental health, it is unlikely, given her relatively small salary, that the money alone accounted for her mental health improvements.

In fact, despite Amber earning most of her money from waitressing, she said she felt her least hopeful when she thought about getting stuck in waitressing for the rest of her life (see chapter 5). This suggests once again that money alone could not have alleviated her distress. Further supporting the importance of identity for mental health, she said that being a reporter again helped to reestablish a consistent sense of who she was, and that that felt very satisfying: "The best thing about the job at the paper is, number one, I get to say I work at a newspaper again. . . . I get that satisfaction . . . being able to geek out over what I normally do." Having the reporter job also took the edge off of her education-related status mismatch because she could envision a "future self" as a full-time copyeditor, and even thought about moving up into higher-level positions at the newspaper: "I'd like to get a full-time job at the *Daily Banner*. . . . Eventually I think I'm gonna be moving over into page design and probably learning everything I need to do to do [the senior editor] job, because that's the job that I want."

In other words, it was not the small amount of extra money she was earning from her new newspaper job, but how the job affected her identity that helped her distress decrease. Until Amber found a new reporter position, she identified with (and hoped to become) someone she had wanted to be in the past—an (aspiring) teacher. She was involved with few other social institutions that could have provided an identity that would have addressed her emotional needs. Therefore, she delved into her past to find one, and used it until she no longer needed it.

Marcus, a divorced forty-seven-year-old African American man, also used his past to help him shift to a new identity after he lost his job. The father of a teenage son who visited him on weekends, Marcus had worked as an operations director at an environmental technology company until the company folded seven months before I first spoke with him. When I first interviewed Marcus, he dressed conservatively yet casually, in a white button-down shirt, jeans, and a baseball cap. He was slender, with dark brown eyes and a closely cropped black mustache; he seemed calm and laid-back but hesitant to discuss his emotions.

Marcus had lost his job under unusual circumstances. At first, his boss stopped paying everyone. A government investigation ensued, and the boss abandoned the company and could not be found. Marcus continued to come to work for several weeks after the paychecks stopped, trying to stabilize his employees' morale, and even paid some of the people he supervised with his own money to help them hang on. But eventually it became clear that the company had completely collapsed. Fortunately, despite receiving no severance pay, Marcus's financial situation was relatively stable even after he lost his job. He attributed this to a history of smart investing and saving habits, but he also had cashed in one of his CDs and was relying on unemployment checks to help him pay his bills.

He had strongly identified with his job, primarily because it allowed him to be an economic provider, which was central to his definition of being a man. To him, that meant "the whole provider thing. . . . If I compare myself to somebody, it would probably be my dad in terms of just trying to make sure that I'm always providing for my son."

After losing his job, Marcus feared that at some point he would no longer be able to provide, and he was anxious because of this anticipated status mismatch: "Not being able to provide would make me feel like I wasn't being successful in terms of that role. . . . I'm not saying I'm comfortable. I'm taking care of my obligations, but I don't want that stack [Marcus laughs] to get too small."

But even though Marcus worried about the possibility of not being able to provide, when I first interviewed him he was able to do so with the resources he had at hand, and was generally in a positive emotional place. In fact, he was surprised at how relaxed he felt: "I've been so laid-back, it frightens me [Marcus laughs]. . . . I'm pretty even-keeled. . . . I'm not keyed up."

He then told me that his relaxed attitude was due to putting more energy into another identity, one that was based on a role within a social institution (volunteer organization/sports team) that he had been involved with even while employed. But since he lost his job he had begun to spend more time in the role—children's basketball coach—and it became a stronger identity that helped his mental health. Furthermore, the identity was sports-related and therefore tied to traditional masculinity: "I think I'm channeling my energy in a different—spending time with the [team] kids more. . . . I've kind of thrown myself into that. . . . I kind of spend time tryin' to mentor some of those kids. . . . That kinda makes me feel better."

The coach identity may have reinforced his masculinity. When I asked Marcus what it meant to him to be a man, he replied not only in terms of being a provider, but also by referring to his mentorship as a basketball coach: "I think it's being a role model . . . to help people and make the world a better place. . . . I'm like Charles Barkley . . . reaching out and helping people."

His coach role also connected to an identity he had longed for decades ago but had not pursued because it would not have allowed him to be a provider: "I was an athlete in high school and in college. What I really wanted to do was to coach. . . . But I kinda got away from that because [they] don't make a lot of money. . . . What was driving me was income. . . . But what was rewarding [was] when I coach. That's probably when I'm my most relaxed."

By the second time I interviewed him, after he had been unemployed for a full year, Marcus's coach identity had strengthened even more. Although he had also had a small amount of paid consulting work, he was largely uninterested in returning to his former line of work, or even in making large amounts of money. Instead, he was strongly considering (and pursuing) paid coaching jobs that paid much less than what he used to make. Marcus found he could maintain a sufficient provider status without having to make large amounts of money. And he had secured an identity that connected to both traditional masculinity and his past desired identity of coach, which he now referred to as a calling. He reported feeling great joy from this "calling," and even pondered whether he might really have been meant to be a coach all along, that that was who he "really" was: "I coach basketball. . . . I really enjoy that. That's my passion anyway. . . . I'm thinking maybe [coaching is] my calling. . . . And I don't know why that's all of a sudden important to me. Before it was like, yeah, okay. But now it really just makes me feel good. . . . It made me start to wonder, has my calling changed? Or maybe I was supposed to be doing this all along and I ignored it."

It may have been that coaching was "all of a sudden important" because he needed it for his identity and his mental health after losing his job. After one year of unemployment, Marcus also described his mood positively, and he had become much less concerned about his employment status and his identity as a manager and provider, even though he was only earning about half of what he had earned the previous year (mostly from unemployment checks): "I've been great. I've been pretty lighthearted . . . and I'm almost surprised at the fact that I'm not concerned. It is my goal to find employment, but I'm not overly concerned about not working. . . . We are measured by what we kinda have, the house where you live, what you drive, what you wear. And I got caught up in that for a little while. But now . . . I don't care."

He ascribed this new attitude to feedback he got from his son:

My son and I had a long talk one evening. . . . He gave me some compliments. . . . I was sayin' "Well, do you wanna do this and go here?" . . . And he was like "No, Dad. I just wanna spend time with you. That's the most important thing to me." And a light went off. . . . It seemed like such a profound statement. . . . It's about the time and not about the money. . . . They value that time that an adult, especially a male, is spending with them. . . . That's really what's the most important, is time. That just kinda was my—for lack of a better word—epiphany.

In Marcus's mind, his son had given him "permission" to prioritize time instead of money, offering him feedback that encouraged a masculine identity distinct from that of provider, and giving him permission to be a different kind of father and a different kind of man than the way he had defined it for himself in the past. He no longer had to provide at a high level, but just spend time with his son. This helped him further distance himself from the managerial identity and move further toward the coach identity.

Having a social institution readily available—especially one that offered him a masculine role—facilitated Marcus's shift into the coach identity. This shift was given additional support by his past desired identity as a coach (or at least, while he did not have a job, he claimed that was who he had always wanted to be). Shifting his focus more strongly to a different identity made him happier and more relaxed, just as it had for Charlotte, Lorna, and Amber.

Recap: When Do We Shift? Why Is It Important?

When your identity is threatened by a mismatch, you need an identity-based solution. Shifting your focus to a different identity is one potential solution. Some people who lose their jobs use a "romantic narrative" to frame their experience. They claim that losing their jobs is a relief and that they are better off for it, and then seek or even move into a new career (Ezzy 2001). The stories of the people in this chapter show that shifting may occur even in cases where job loss is not seen as a relief. These stories also show that shifting is used strategically to cope with identity threats. Unfortunately, shifting may not be available to everyone at all times. In order to successfully shift, you need to have some level of involvement in a social institution that can provide an "acceptable" identity—one compatible with expectations for your social statuses. (This will be discussed further in chapters 7 and 8.)

Leonard Pearlin's Stress Process Model (Pearlin 1989, 1999) posits that status encompasses most aspects of the stress process, including the kinds of things that stress us out and the alternatives we have to cope with them. However, the model does not fully address the subjective aspects of status (for example, what our statuses and identities mean to us) that are likely to be important to our mental health after losing a job (Schöb 2013). Status is also important for our identities (Pearlin 1999, 398; Simon 1997; Thoits 1985, 1986), and so these more subjective aspects of status also strongly affect what harms us emotionally and how we can (or cannot) repair the problem. In this chapter, Charlotte and others showed that perceptions about what various statuses mean can shape whether shifting is a viable identity work option. For example, Charlotte and Lorna were able to shift to wife and mother identities relatively easily because social expectations of women may still emphasize them as nurturing mothers, whereas expectations regarding paid labor are more flexible.

In line with predictions from Identity Theory (Burke 1991, 1996), feedback helped fortify these newly strengthening identities. When Lorna's husband said he liked having Lorna at home because "she cooks more," this encouraged her to continue to cook, which helped her further identify as a wife. And when Marcus's son told him that he did not need Marcus to buy him things or take him to do things that involved money, Marcus felt more comfortable moving closer to the coach identity that he had been edging up to.

The concept of time is also pertinent to shifting. When Charlotte and Lorna shifted, they selected identities that were not only available and acceptable, but represented roles they regretted having done "poorly" in the past. This may have allowed for an even greater boost to self-esteem or emotional well-being because they not only could say they had a new, acceptable identity, but that they were "making things right" with the past.

People also thought about their pasts and futures when they shifted. Perhaps to maintain the identity consistency that is crucial for mental health (Stets and Burke 2014; Swann 1983), they tried to connect past, present, and future identities in some way. For example, after Amber lost her reporter job, looking for reporter positions might have further threatened her identity and harmed her self-concept. So instead she started to shift her identity to "future teacher," which she said had been her original goal in college. Thus, she used both past and future in a way that helped her manage her present identity and buffer her mental health. When Amber found a part-time reporter position, she no longer needed these past and future identities for her emotional well-being, and discarded them.

So what happens if you are not involved with a social institution that offers you a role compatible with your status? If you cannot shift, is another form of identity work available to you? Chapter 7 addresses this by focusing on another identity work strategy—sustaining the employee identity.

7

"It Was Like I Was Still Working"

Sustaining

In chapter 6, Charlotte illustrated why social institutions and statuses are important for successful shifting. At the time Charlotte lost her job, she was also a mother. With that role so readily available, she was able to easily shift from identifying mostly as a worker to mostly as a mother. This role was also socially acceptable for a woman, and meant she was likely to receive positive, identity-affirming feedback for being a stay-at-home mom. The mom role thus acted as an identity magnet, drawing Charlotte toward it.

But what happens if the structural conditions for shifting do not exist? Is there something else you can do to salvage your identity and, if so, what factors might make this easier? One possibility is that your identity work (Snow and Anderson 1987) may instead consist of sustaining your employee identity, even though you know that you are actually unemployed. In order to feel like you are still the same person you were before, you may establish a more flexible way of interacting, talking about, and thinking about what it means to be an employee. This strategy may be very helpful because we prefer having identities that are consistent across time (Burke 1991; Swann 1983), perhaps because that lessens distress (Burke 1996). Although sustaining may not be a long-term solution to unemployment-related suffering, all the people I spoke with who successfully sustained their work-related identities felt better emotionally by doing so.

However, as with shifting, sustaining is not equally available to everyone. As Erving Goffman's (1959) dramaturgical perspective suggests, involvement in social institutions that can help you successfully "play the part" of an employee will increase your likelihood of seeing yourself as one. Much like acting in a play, to be convincing in your role you need an appropriate setting (such as an office), "props" to use (such as business clothing), and other "actors" who will react to you as though you are an employee. If you have these things, you will be more likely to get the invaluable feedback that you are who you say you are; this, in turn, should improve your mental health (Burke 1991, 1996).

If you do not have another role (like Charlotte's mother role) readily available that matches society's expectations for your gender, age, or other statuses, you may be more likely to sustain your work-related identity than to shift your emphasis to a different identity. You may find ways to still feel like a worker ("I'm still producing a product/service"), a member of your former workplace ("I'm still a Google person"), a member of your former occupation ("I'm still a scientist"), or even a "good" member of your status group ("I'm still a man").

I'm Still a Worker

For the people who spoke with me, sustaining often involved finding ways to continue to feel like a worker or a member of one's former workplace; for men this frequently also helped them feel like they were still "real men." Paul's, Ruth's, and Ken's stories illustrate how people sustained in this way, and also demonstrate the mental health improvements that followed.

Paul: "I'm Not Unemployed"

I interviewed Paul for the first time under fluorescent lights in a public library's dull gray conference room, where we sat at a long rectangular conference table. Paul, a physically fit six-foot tall white man, was fifty-six years old, but appeared almost ten years younger. His light-brown thinning hair spiked up in various directions near his forehead. He was dressed casually in black slacks, a long-sleeved black button-down shirt peppered with small faded orange shapes, and a black cotton T-shirt that peeked out from underneath it.

Paul was married and had three adult children. Unfortunately, he had been experiencing serious family problems for several years even before losing his job. These included having a chronically ill family member and marital issues severe enough that Paul and his wife had been technically separated for two years. They could not afford to live in separate households, so Paul lived in the basement of the house while his wife lived upstairs. These family problems amplified the stress Paul experienced after losing his job.

Three months before I interviewed him, Paul had been laid off from his job as a manager in a publishing company. He had directly supervised six people and had usually worked between fifty to eighty hours per week. He told me that he had been in charge of marketing, and that early in his career a typical day consisted mostly of administrative planning duties: "I was in charge of the brand. . . . I'd be talking to [the vice president] about that progress report [for] . . . whatever initiatives that we were responsible for. . . . When we got a field staff . . . then I would be involved in their performance [reviews]. . . . Almost every week, I'd be on a committee to order the product, which book will work and which genre, which title, what not to put in a network."

Later, his responsibilities evolved into those more typical of a traveling merchandising representative and brand marketer. At that point, he had to travel much more frequently to interact more directly with the companies they served: "The last two or three years . . . I'd be visiting six hundred [store branches] a year. . . . Usually I'd do two two-day trips a week."

Most of Paul's previous jobs had also been manager positions. He had even liked some of them (such as convenience store district manager) more than his job as a publishing manager. But in all these jobs, Paul gained his masculine identity from his work. Paul said that to be a man was to be an economic provider: "In my family and to myself I am known as a provider . . . the one that gets the job and gets the money in to pay the bills. . . . That's probably the number one thing . . . I'm defined by how I provide."

If to be a man was to be a provider, losing a job could mean losing his masculinity. And losing his job was on the horizon. After the company's unprofitable purchases, two bankruptcies, loss of a major client, and finally a merger, Paul's boss warned him that he and one other colleague would be laid off in about five months: "[My boss] called my counterpart. . . . My coworker and I thought . . . that we were being told that the program ended; we don't need you guys anymore. . . . It turned out at that meeting . . . he just confidentially told us that positions are probably gonna end sometime in 2010, maybe May or maybe March."

Many unemployed Americans blame their lack of work on a "flawed self" (Sharone 2013a, 2013b). Paul's self-blame, however, began even earlier—while he still had his job. Right after his meeting with his boss, Paul began to doubt his identity and his worth as an employee:

So that's when it hit . . . I was numb from the time of the meeting. . . . The world starts spinnin'. . . . I must not have been valuable to them. . . . So all of a sudden all of that hit in November as to "Who is Paul Amberson?" "Well, Paul Amberson is a guy who hasn't been doing his job well enough and the company doesn't like him enough. He's too old and the company doesn't like him enough to find a place for him."

The news of Paul's impending layoff created a feedback mismatch. Before this news, he identified as a publishing manager; now, even though company financial problems were to blame, he saw himself as such a poor-quality employee that he must be terminated.

Being told he would lose his job also created a status mismatch based on age. He thought that who he was in terms of age did not match who a prospective employee "should" be (younger), and this lowered his self-esteem. He said that just after he was told he would be laid off, he thought: "Well, I'm fifty-six years old. What am I gonna do? Who's gonna want me?"

Paul's job loss also led to a gender-based status mismatch. Because Paul so closely identified his manhood with employment and breadwinning, he also believed that if he was unemployed, then he was not a "real man." Fortunately, even after his job ended, he did not have immediate financial problems because he had received a substantial four-month severance package.[1] Paul did have some fears about what would happen financially if he did not find a job soon, but his primary concern seemed to be his threatened manhood. Although at the start of the interview, Paul had seemed fairly positive and had made lots of eye contact, he began to fidget, look down at his hands, and stutter when I asked him what it was like to be a man without a job: "[Since I've been laid off] I'm not doing my job. Um, I'm not, uh, yeah. The—I'm, I'm, uh, deficient. I'm, uh, incomplete. I'm in trouble. Um, I have to be wary. Um, worried, anxiety. . . ." His fidgeting and stuttering continued throughout much of the rest of the interview. To Paul, not having a job meant he had lost his identity as a man, which created anxiety and feelings of inadequacy.

Experiencing mismatches between who we are and who we would ideally like to be is more common for unemployed people than for those who are employed (Sheeran and McCarthy 1990, 1992), and these mismatches often lead to distress (ibid. 1992). Therefore, as you might expect, Paul was not in a good emotional state three months after losing his job. It is no wonder that Paul told me: "Throughout this process of finding out that you're going to be laid off . . . there have been times when I break down and cry."

Paul had a dilemma: he believed no one would want him as a manager because he was "too old." But he could not remain unemployed because he would no longer feel like a man. When I contacted Paul by phone three-and-a-half months later to arrange a follow-up interview, he told me he had not found work. He had now been unemployed for a total of six-and-a-half months, and I worried about his emotional state. But I was taken aback when I met Paul face-to-face for the second time.

As Paul entered the public library, I almost did not recognize him. The man who had looked downward, fidgeted, and stuttered through much of the first interview now stood tall and confident in professional clothing—a dark pin-striped button-down shirt, black business slacks, black necktie, leather dress shoes, and a black leather briefcase. He carried himself with pride and reported feeling confident. There seemed to have been a dramatic change in his well-being even though his objective financial situation had actually worsened and his employment prospects were dim.

Paul had only had two informational interviews since I had last spoken with him, and after six and a half months of unemployment, he no longer even spent much time applying for jobs. But he had become actively involved in two job seekers' groups where he received feedback that he was still the professional and "marketing man" he had once been. One of these groups was a religiously affiliated job networking group called FaithWorks!; the other was a (secular) seminar for unemployed people.

Paul planned to attend FaithWorks! after our meeting, and so he had dressed the part. At FaithWorks!, Paul would (ironically) not act like a job seeker, but instead like a marketing professional and leader. Initially, when Paul attended FaithWorks!, he had self-identified as an unemployed man, to the detriment of his mental health. But during one of his early visits to the group, a chance interaction with a staff member made him rethink his "unemployed" identity:

> Someone at that ministry saw me in a [leadership] role before I saw myself in that role. So I'm literally at the table waiting to have someone look at my resumé and . . . [the resumé reviewer] was swamped. . . . She [Paul laughs] just said, "You know what, Paul, can you do me a favor? Would you help [another job seeker] . . . with her resumé?" . . . And then she left! [Paul laughs] . . . She's obviously seeing me in a leadership role. And that's the role that I need to be . . . and I'm [now] portraying myself with some sort of image as a leader.

Similar to other unemployed professionals who were able to "preserve a sense of themselves as valued leaders" (Lane 2011, 91) through job seekers' groups, these identity-affirming interactions helped Paul move away from seeing himself as an unemployed man and toward the identity of a successful leader—a role Paul believed society expected of men and one that he had previously held as a manager. In addition to the professional interactions that are common in these groups (Lane 2011; Sharone 2013a), Paul received direct feedback from others who specifically told him he was a professional. These kinds of interactions at FaithWorks! began before my first interview with Paul, but their frequency, breadth, and impact increased between the first and second time I met with him, and they strengthened and stabilized his identities as a leader, marketing professional, and entrepreneur:

> I volunteer mostly with resumés but I [also] . . . hosted a breakout session on how to learn how to sell on [online marketing sites]. . . . And I did get a good positive feedback from one of the recruiters at the other table, that he's listened to what I've done and I am effective. So that was important. . . . Now that I'm being seen as maybe a leader, I'm not just a volunteer. . . . The more I go to FaithWorks!, the more . . . uplifted, the more confident, the more durable my emotions are.

FaithWorks! also helped Paul's emotional state by providing social support, normalizing his unemployment, and promoting a sense of "divine control" (the belief that God is in charge) (Schieman et al. 2006). But according to Paul, the biggest boost to his mental health was identity-related: the people at FaithWorks! agreed with him about who he was as a leader and marketer. With additional opportunities to enact these identities and to get feedback that affirmed them, Paul was able to once again find the interpersonal fit or "chemistry" (Sharone 2013a, 2013b) between his sense of self and an institutional role that he could treat as a job. This interpersonal fit is often critical for getting others to agree that you are the right person for the job (Sharone 2013a, 2013b), or in Paul's case, that he was the leader and marketer he claimed to be.

Around the same time that Paul attended FaithWorks!, he also attended a seminar for job seekers that was given by a CEO of a career management organization. When this CEO gave Paul an occupational nickname during the event, it stuck. This further solidified his identity as a marketer and increased his confidence: "He started calling me 'Marketing Man' during this seminar, which was really cool, very confidence building. . . . [He said] 'Hey, Marketing Man, do you think this . . . ?' 'Do you think that, Marketing Man?' . . . So two, three days after that I went to GoDaddy.com and . . . I'm embarking now on toying with the idea of being Your Marketing Man."

Paul reached into his briefcase and pulled out a brand-new business card imprinted with "YourMarketingMan.com."[2] He told me he wanted to start his own marketing and branding consulting company. In essence, his "unemployed" identity had largely vanished, and he had instead connected his past identity (marketing manager) and future identity (marketing entrepreneur) to his present "marketing man" label given to him by the CEO. Paul also connected his current volunteer role at FaithWorks! to his desired future "marketing entrepreneur" identity: "I've been passionate about volunteering at FaithWorks!, helping people with resumes. Well, that comes under what? [Paul reads from his business card] 'Personal brand counseling.' . . . I'm already doing that . . . I'm not asking for money for it, but I do that."

When I asked Paul to comment on the identity work that he mentioned the first time I interviewed him—that he was "working on who he was as a prospective employee"—he replied in Ofer Sharone's (2013a, 2013b) "chemistry" terms—by emphasizing the importance of matching his identity to a specific occupation: "I [now] know much more who I am, as you can see from the business card. [Paul laughs] . . . That's the exciting thing is I've found a business card that's me. . . . The work I did on the card and matching it up to who I believe I am may be very, very fruitful."

Paul's experiences at these two groups had now culminated in what he told me during my second interview with him: that despite his receipt of unemployment checks, his lack of paid work, and the end of his severance package, he was now a provider and he was "not unemployed." He also quickly reminded me that he equated breadwinning with manhood, and said he was now meeting this standard: "That's the biggest worry someone can have. A guy has to provide. That's what guys do . . . I'm providing. I'm getting fulfillment because it's successful."

His statement about being a successful, breadwinning man was at odds with what he had said in his first interview about feeling less manly because he was unemployed. I presented him with his quote from the previous interview:

ME: Last time we spoke, you said that at that time being a man without a job made you feel deficient and incomplete. Is that still the case?

PAUL: No, and it wasn't the case when I spoke that. That wasn't truth. Because I am not and I wasn't unemployed then. . . . The mental fact of the matter is I had a source of income when I made that statement and that source may be a career. I can make that work. . . . And so instead of saying I'm unemployed, I should have said I'm a successful small business owner or I'm a successful entrepreneur on [online marketing site]. . . . I'm not necessarily spinning because those are all true.

This flexible thinking of oneself as an "entrepreneur" is illustrated in Carrie Lane's (2011) work on laid-off (mostly male) technology professionals. In an era in which job security is increasingly rare (Kalleberg 2009), the idea of self-reliance, being your own boss, and having the power to find and retain clients may feel comforting and appear realistic. Consequently, establishing a seemingly workable form of employment led the men in Lane's (2011) study to feel positive about their futures. But is there more to their entrepreneurship than meets the eye? Perhaps they used entrepreneurship as a way to sustain their identities as workers (and possibly as men), regardless of how established their businesses or consulting firms actually were. Addressing identity threats in this way may have helped them feel better about themselves. We could expect, then, that Paul's online sales might also reduce distress, and that is what occurred.

Paul's online business only brought in about $1,000 per month—far less than he needed for his basic expenses. But Paul did not need his business to be highly profitable in order to reduce his identity-related distress. When I asked Paul what his mood had been like since the last time we met, he told me: "Just incredible positive confidence. It's awareness of yes, I'm doing the right things. I'm thinking the right things. I'm accomplishing the right things."

Paul had made an unusual claim: that he was not currently unemployed and had also not been unemployed three months earlier. Clearly, Paul was unemployed then and was still unemployed at the follow-up interview. But because he was sustaining his worker identity, he managed to hold onto the idea that he was still employed, and therefore was also still a provider and a "real man."

During his first interview, Paul had mentioned the online sales venture that he now called a "source of income that may be a career." But at the first interview, he had only referred to it as a hobby: "I kinda have a hobby . . . that my son and I are involved in, and in the last five or six years, I've developed an [online marketing site] store. . . . I buy things thinking they'll sell and they may not. . . . The basement is kinda like a warehouse of things that need to be sold but haven't been sold."

Now, three-and-a-half months later, he framed that hobby differently. He claimed it made him a "successful small business owner or a successful entrepreneur," and made him "not unemployed." Yet nothing about this online venture had objectively changed. Paul had participated in this hobby for years, and had always made about the same amount of money per month from selling these collectibles. But by framing his hobby in a new way, Paul was able to successfully sustain the idea that he was still employed, and thus still a provider and a man. His identity was no longer threatened, his confidence was boosted, and his anxiety decreased.

Ken: "Feels Like I Work Here, Except I Just Don't Get a Paycheck"

Very wealthy people, such as Ken, the former CEO, also sustained their worker identities. Ken, like most other sustainers, had access to a social institution that offered him a way to "play the part" of a worker. Even months after being fired, Ken's boss generously allowed him to continue to have an office in his former workplace's office suite to conduct his job search: "One of the biggest benefits is having this office. I was home one day last week and . . . it was kind of depressing . . . . It feels like . . . kinda lost, no direction. . . . So having this office has made a big difference to me. . . . It kind of feels like I work here, except I just don't get a paycheck." By using the office as a "setting" (Goffman 1959) in which to perform his role, Ken was able to continue acting like the successful white-collar employee he had once been, even though he had been out of work for months.

Feedback from others also helped him sustain his employee identity. After five months of unemployment, Ken's old employer gave him contract work— two simple presentations for groups of eight to ten people each. It did not pay much, nor was he guaranteed any additional work, but it helped him feel more like an employee again. Performing that role through the structure of a formal work contract with an established organization, along with feedback from the presentation attendees, helped him sustain his worker identity: "It was very self-reaffirming to go out there and feel like I did a great job. . . . The ultimate, final sense of accomplishment is when you look at the [eight participant] evaluations and they're high. . . . So not a gigantic group, but it was enough for me to affirm that I had connected with them."

This small amount of feedback from individuals at seminars allowed him to feel as though he was still a part of his occupation's group and was (to some degree) fulfilling his role as a man. The power of this feedback may have been due to it coming from a structured, workplace-like setting.

Ken had also been trying to arrange short-term contracts for piecemeal work with two other companies. No contracts had been signed yet, but he believed they would come to fruition, and this helped him feel hopeful, valued, and as if he was still a worker: "I do some consulting work for a guy I used to work for. . . . It actually feels like the place that I used to work at, and now I get kind of a smaller paycheck."

Now that Ken had this small amount of work, he abandoned his former assumption that his friends, occupational peers, and neighbors would see him negatively:

ME: Last time we spoke, you mentioned it was hard to feel positive around friends of yours who are also lawyers, because at that time you didn't have a job. Where do you stand on that now?

KEN: I think it's a little different now. . . . I think 'cause I've found some work.

ME: Last time we spoke, you also mentioned that you tended not to tell your neighbors about your contract not being renewed. Is that still the case?

KEN: I've kind of gradually told a few people. . . . They're nice people and they're not gonna judge me and think less of me.

Just like unemployed people who found it easier to "publicly revise and assert their professional identities" (Lane 2011, 97) when they were involved in "work-like" formal organizations, Ken's access to organizational structures (the office; a small amount of paid work) and a little feedback from within those structures enabled him to sustain his professional identity.

Ruth: "That's What I Would Do at Work"

Ruth, a forty-three-year-old African American woman, carefully chose behaviors that helped her sustain her worker identity. A former information analyst for a government contractor, Ruth had spent her days researching wage and job description information, as well as supervising similar work done by other people. Work had always been a large part of Ruth's identity: "I love work. When I had permanent jobs . . . I always worked more than eight hours a day. I was really a workaholic. I mean, I love to work."

Ruth had been laid off from her job six months before I first spoke with her. She told me that it was upsetting and confusing to be a workaholic without a job. In essence, she was once a workaholic and now was unemployed—who she was had changed over time—and she therefore experienced a time mismatch that made her miserable. Fortunately, Ruth had found a way to combat this; she selected specific behaviors that made her feel like she was still working and constructed a "work world" for herself, which reduced her identity-related distress: "As somebody [who] loves to work I'm miserable not working. . . . It's confusing. . . . [So] I get up every day and get dressed and go to the library, and I look for jobs in the library because to me that feels like going to work. . . . I am happier when I'm doing things that are similar to the things I did at work. Absolutely. . . . It makes me more positive."

Ruth went beyond just keeping a schedule similar to her old job. She did specific things to make the library feel even more like work, and to make herself feel more like a worker: "A lotta times I have on business attire going to the library to sit all day in front of a computer to apply for jobs. . . . So it feels like going to a workplace. . . . I have a hard chair that feels like work. . . . I take my lunch. I have my lunch, thirty minutes or lunch hour. . . . [When] I feel like I need a snack, I'll go to the vending machine . . . but then I get back to work. . . . That's what I would do at work."

Ruth also constructed interactions that were similar to those at her former workplace: "Makin' friends at the library, so I can say hi and bye to people, just like on a job. . . . I have a buddy at the library. . . . He and I go to lunch together. We can talk about non-library stuff at lunch, and then we can go back to the library and go back to our work like it's a job."

Ruth even tried to reproduce her former tendency to work overtime: "Keeping a regular schedule in the library, and usually more than eight hours [per day]. So that kinda keeps my life normal if I stay for longer than eight hours, 'cause that's what I did on the job."

Job seekers' support groups often advocate treating the job search like a job. These groups may advise their members to schedule their time and treat their job searches "as they would a real job" (Sharone 2013a, 54), with some job seekers even restricting relaxation and leisure to evenings or weekends (55). Some of these groups even explicitly suggest using some of the techniques Ruth "fell into" (and continued to use because they worked). For example, some promote dressing and presenting yourself as if you still have a job, which serves the purpose of "drawing on and reinforcing previous notions of what it meant to be a hardworking professional" (Garrett-Peters 2009, 555–556). On the surface, these strategies are meant to help people find jobs more quickly, but they may provide a secondary benefit—an "initial boost" (Sharone 2013a, 54) to their emotional states. This may be because these strategies help job seekers "proactively counter the temporal disorientation that . . . can accompany the loss of a job" (55). This suggests that the very fact of sustaining a worker identity over time may benefit mental health.

Ruth's and Paul's active efforts at identity work allowed them to create positive narratives about unemployment, similar to the identity work done by people in other stigmatized groups (Ezzy 2001; Ibarra and Barbulescu 2010; Snow and Anderson 1987). However, rather than defining their new stigmatized identities positively as illustrated in some unemployed people's "romantic narratives" (Ezzy 2001) or some homeless people's embracement of the homeless identity (Snow and Anderson 1987), they instead found ways to continue to identify with the worker roles they had lost. By doing things they would have done as workers and telling consistent stories about their identities, Ruth and Paul were able to (knowingly) achieve a moderate level of self-deception (Robinson, Moeller, and Goetz 2009; Taylor and Brown 1988) and identity consistency (Burke 1996; Ibarra and Barbulescu 2010; Swann 1983) that could benefit mental health. As suggested by self-discrepancy theorists (Higgins 1987; Large and Marcussen 2000; Marcussen 2006), reducing identity mismatches indeed helped Paul and Ruth attain more positive mental states.

I'm Still Performing My Occupation

Behaving like workers and telling identity stories were not the only ways to sustain work-related identities. As illustrated by Paul's experiences, social institutions, including volunteer organizations and job seekers' groups, often provided avenues for these efforts. Job seekers' networking and support groups may help people sustain their professional identities by providing places to do the kinds of things they once did at the workplace (Garrett-Peters 2009; Lane 2011; Sharone 2013a), or by running meetings and events in ways that simulate corporate structure (Lane 2011, 98–99; Sharone 2013a, 27). This offers job seekers opportunities to rehearse their professional identities by practicing job-related "elevator speeches" (Sharone 2013a, 35–36) or enacting professional identity "commercials" (Lane 2011, 98). The more they continue to act like professionals, the more likely they are to sustain those professional identities (Burke 1991, 1996).

Additionally, interacting with other former professionals at these groups may simulate the kinds of interactions they were used to at their former workplaces (Lane 2011, 22–23, 27). The networking groups may thereby provide places where job seekers work together in "teams" (Goffman 1959) to give one another feedback that they are still professionals and members of their occupational fields (Lane 2011). In fact, the benefits of sustaining identity may be one reason some unemployed people "gravitated toward roles [in job seekers' groups] that resembled those they held in the workplace" (Lane 2011, 90).

The importance of social institutions for sustaining worker identities was evident in the stories of people who found ways to uphold their former occupational identities, such as marketer or CEO. For example, Paul used FaithWorks! to participate in leadership positions that were somewhat similar to the marketing position he had once held. He also received feedback from others that he was a leader and "Marketing Man." FaithWorks! helped reduce Paul's identity-related distress by sustaining these identities which, in turn, also strengthened his masculine identity.

Contrasting Paul's and Ruth's Experiences

FaithWorks! did not work the same way for everyone. Ruth's emotional improvement after attending FaithWorks! involved a different process than did Paul's improvement. This may have been due in part to Ruth's lower social status as an African American woman. Generally, having a higher social status increases the likelihood that others will affirm a person's identity (Stets and Harrod 2004). To my knowledge, Ruth was not given a chance to perform a leadership role at FaithWorks!, perhaps because of the perceived mismatch between her status as an African American woman and the cultural conception of a "leader" as a white man (especially within this relatively conservative organization). FaithWorks! also did not readily provide Ruth with a chance to perform behaviors similar to those in her former job, so it did not address the threats to her identity. However, this network of mutually supportive unemployed people did provide her with social support, which is highly valuable during stressful circumstances (Pearlin et al. 1981): "It's so wonderful to be around other people that are in the same position. We're all looking for jobs. We're all trying to stay encouraged. . . . It's good to be around other people who articulate the same things that you articulate."

FaithWorks! helped Ruth stay positive, but it did not offer her a new role to which she could shift, nor did it provide feedback or a work-like role that could help her sustain her worker identity (Burke 1991, 1996).

The contrast between Paul's and Ruth's experiences at FaithWorks! illustrates the importance of examining what actually occurs during interactions, and the specific path through which they may improve mental health. For example, Paul partially attributed his reduced distress to FaithWorks! feedback that helped him sustain his occupational identity, as well as his worker and masculine identities. On its own, "generic" social support available at Faith-Works! may not have been sufficient for Paul because it would not have addressed the threats to his identity. In contrast, Ruth said FaithWorks! provided her with much needed social support. Nevertheless, it did not address the identity aspect of her distress, so she took additional measures (her library routine) to sustain her worker identity.

The variety of institutions in which Paul was involved enabled him to enact leadership and marketing roles and hear from others that this was truly who he was. These institutions also provided the structure and feedback he needed to successfully sustain his identity as a provider and a man, which ultimately increased his self-esteem and reduced his anxiety. Additionally, because connecting identities across time bolsters mental health (Markus and Nurius 1986), Paul's links between past, present, and future identities most likely also helped to reduce his distress.

As Leonard I. Pearlin's (1999) model suggests, objective social status was important to Paul's experience of stress and coping. Because Paul was a white man, people were probably more likely to give him feedback that confirmed his leader and marketer identities. But subjective meaning is also important to our identities, and so it also may affect our stress and coping experiences (Simon 1997). Paul's gains in mental health, which partially depended on successfully sustaining the idea of being a man, occurred during a time period when his actual financial situation was worsening. This meant that subjectively sustaining his provider identity—despite his financial reality—might have had a more powerful effect on Paul's distress than did his objective economic situation.

Marsha: Getting Me Back to Me

People who struggled financially also used sustaining to cope with the identity threats posed by losing their jobs. For example, one of the least affluent study participants, Marsha (the former public safety manager) initially experienced a time mismatch, but sustained to help cope with it. As with Paul, Ken, and others, the role that social institutions played was key to Marsha's successful sustaining.

Marsha had described herself as "a very service-oriented person . . . who is into safety and security." After losing her job, she no longer felt like the same person anymore, which left her depressed and anxious. But her distress varied: when she was able to sustain the idea that she was still working, she felt better; when she could not sustain this, she felt worse. Specific social institutions, such as an EMT class, helped her sustain her public safety worker identity: "At the time of the . . . forced resignation I was in the middle of an EMT class. . . . That was good because it gave me a transition. It was like I was still working." It was only after the course ended that she felt the full force of the identity threat; without a place where she could enact a public safety employee identity, she felt depressed: "Once I was out of [the EMT class] the first week I really didn't know what I was gonna do. . . . I would say that I've probably been depressed. . . . [Recently] I spent probably three days in bed probably just not motivated to go do anything."

Marsha did not become depressed right after being fired (although she was upset and in shock), but rather after the end of the EMT class that had helped her sustain her occupational identity. Without the EMT role to help her sustain that identity, she experienced a time mismatch.[3] Her distress fluctuated within fairly short time periods depending on her level of involvement in roles similar to her old job. After the EMT class was over, she became depressed, but then joined an EMT volunteer group. By doing so, she once again sustained her occupational identity and felt more like herself again: "Now I'm what they call an intern . . . where you have to get field training hours with another EMT. . . . I've already done four this week. This is my first week back after the training and I'll probably go spend an overnight. . . . I think that's getting me back to me."

Sustaining the idea that she was still working helped Marsha rebuild the public safety worker identity that had been threatened by a time mismatch when she lost her job. Marsha had been fortunate enough to be involved with a social institution—an EMT education facility—that provided her with the means to sustain her identity after losing her job. Unfortunately, when that ended, so did the stability of her public safety employee identity.

By the time I met with Marsha again four-and-a-half months later, she was still unemployed, and had completed her EMT field training. Thanks to student financial aid and a severance package that included tuition assistance, Marsha had returned to college full-time to complete the five remaining courses for her associate's degree in criminal justice. There are many possible reasons she may have chosen to do this (such as improving employability and keeping busy), but she was also well aware of how these courses could help her sustain her employee identity and reduce her distress. In fact, she dreaded the anticipated depression she thought she would feel when her college courses ended: "What I was experiencing after the EMT class [ended] is pretty similar to what I'm comin' up on here toward Christmas. . . . [It's] ominous. . . . It's really quite awful actually."

Although social institutions made it easier to perform and sustain occupational identities, Marsha (like Ruth) also found other ways to accomplish this. During my second interview with her, I asked her when she felt most like the public safety worker she used to be. She answered by telling me about the short-term classes she was now taking to gain the necessary skills to drive an ambulance for a paramedic company, and then launched into a story about a traffic incident that illustrated how she found ways in day-to-day life to behave like a public safety worker:

> I was on my way to do my [paramedic driver] duty at five in the morning. . . .
> There was something in the road. . . . As I went around it, its head spun around and it was an owl. . . . The car behind me . . . hit it. . . .
> I came back around and it was unconscious but still breathing. And so I had my hazards on and was blockin' the road and standin' out there wavin' cars away and called for the sheriff's office to come. . . . I will always step up because I know what the right thing to do is. . . . I would like to continue to work in my chosen field.

Sustaining did not mean Marsha was entirely free from distress. Her financial situation, to which she attributed 75 percent of her distress, left her feeling insecure and anxious. Despite actively looking for work, she was denied many jobs (including cashier and traffic guard) and had found no paid work in almost six months. She had made her three months of severance pay last five months, and was now paying bills and her mortgage with the help of friends and family. She was also preparing to withdraw all the money in her retirement account ($5,000) so she could pay her mortgage; the early withdrawal penalty would leave her with only about $3,000 to do so.

Marsha had tried to hold it together financially and emotionally, but she fought back tears as she told me that her teenage daughter, Tenille, had paid some of the household bills: "Tenille has been working part-time . . . and has been payin' for our gas, payin' our phone bill when it needs it, payin' all the things that I just don't have money for. . . . It's been very disheartening. I hate . . . for her first job, for her money, to be being spent on upholding our household, but she's been great and . . . it's takin' a big huge . . . fall for me." Sustaining could reduce identity-related distress, but not financial distress.

Finally, despite being a mother, Marsha did not shift to that identity, as Charlotte had done. Although as a woman, Marsha would have been likely to receive confirming feedback for that identity, she personally defined the meaning of mother (in part) as being a financial provider: "I think being a good woman is being strong and taking care of what you need to take care of . . . but I don't have the resources to do for my children what I would like to do. . . . I hate to see my kids do without. . . . I'm not really pleased with myself."

In essence, when she lost her job, she experienced both a time mismatch and a status mismatch (similar to many of the men in this study) because of her own definition of a "good woman." Because of what being a woman meant to her, she could not easily shift to a parent identity at the expense of the breadwinner or worker identities. So in order to feel like she was still the same person and in order to feel like a good woman, she likely had to sustain her occupational identity. Although doing so might not fully make her feel like a good woman (she still was not earning money), it did relieve the distress from her time mismatch. Overall, sustaining was the most available and effective coping strategy for Marsha.

I'm Still a Man

Besides threats to a general "worker" identity or a specific occupational identity, losing a job often threatened the male identity (as discussed at length in chapter 5). When men defined their masculinity in terms of work, sustaining a worker identity could also help sustain the male identity.

For example, as discussed in chapter 5, even when Saul, the former senior banker, took an exterminator job (which had much less prestige than his previous jobs), he once again felt like a man and a breadwinner, and went from a near-suicidal state to feeling positive: "I wanted to at least provide an honest living for the family. . . . I always said whatever I had to do to make it happen, I'll do whatever I can. As long as it's ethical and legal, I'll make it happen. . . . I look at it as a positive. . . . So I said boy, man, this [exterminator job] is turning out to be a golden opportunity. I'm looking at the bright side of things."

However, Saul was conflicted about being an exterminator because it created an education-based status mismatch. As noted in chapter 5, Saul hoped that his exterminator job at PestFree was temporary. As he used the exterminator job to sustain his male identity, he simultaneously used a "future self" (Markus and Nurius 1986) as a manager or entrepreneur to help him sustain his white-collar worker identity: "I'll get my hands wet on the technician end so at least I understand the application part of it, but I see management in the future. . . . In the back of my mind . . . I'm thinkin', boy, it would be nice . . . to have a PestFree in Africa or maybe expand in Jamaica. . . . Yes, I'm there as a technician, but [in] my mind, I'm a business, I'm an entrepreneur."

Recall that Paul had also sustained his male identity by reframing his online sales hobby as a business through which he became a provider, similar to unemployed men whose independent, self-reliant entrepreneurship reinstated their masculinity (Lane 2011, 45). Paul also told me that buying collectibles had once led to conflict with his wife, but that now (although he admitted she was still quite skeptical) she might start to see him as manly for doing so: "From my wife's point of view [the online site was] where I'm not the provider . . . something that took away a husband's time . . . a fantasy . . . and I don't think that was acceptable to her. . . . [Now] I think she may be understanding that, 'Wow, this guy is providing. . . . Maybe [online marketing site] is a good thing.'"

Like Charlotte and Lorna in chapter 6, Paul sustained his worker identity in a way that transformed a former "bad" identity (foolhardy collector) into something good (provider). In the process, he sustained his male identity.

Ken, the former CEO, also described how sustaining his worker identity helped him feel more like a man. Even though Ken's foray back into paid employment only consisted of one small contract job, it helped him claim that he was "back": he was a worker once again. Although he still expected himself to be a breadwinner and knew society expected the same, he was able to "worry less" about it; a small amount of work and accompanying positive feedback had helped him reestablish the male identity he had begun to lose a few months ago: "I think the societal expectation [of men] hasn't changed. I think . . . my expectation of myself . . . hasn't changed . . . [but] I think there's a direct relationship between . . . this consulting stuff and letting some of that go. . . . I called my wife after the [presentation] and I said, 'I'm baaaack!' . . . It was very reaffirming. . . . I worry less about [society's expectations of men] when I see some things happening."

Ken did not dismiss society's expectations of men, but he could put aside some of his fear about not being a "real man" because he was engaging in enough work-like activity to sustain his worker identity. Ultimately, Ken's story was one of success; he found work as a CEO after eight-and-a-half months of vigorous job seeking.[4] It is possible that sustaining his worker and male identities helped him to persevere and do what he needed to do to convince others that he was the right person for the job.

Is It Just a Delusion?

A modest amount of self-deception can benefit mental health (Robinson et al. 2009; Taylor and Brown 1988). But is it possible that sustainers had gone beyond that, lost touch with reality, and slipped into delusion?

Paul's demeanor and disposition were conspicuously different now than they had been three-and-a-half months earlier. I was intrigued by this striking change, so I asked him if I could come to his basement warehouse to observe his successful business in action and to help package and ship sold items. At this, Paul stood up, backed away from me, and put his palms toward me (as if to push me away), then said: "Only Jesus if he came and walked on this earth should be able to see my room. . . . That's where I live and it's incredibly disorganized, incredibly messy. It's a disaster area. . . . It's an area that should be just for living—television, relaxing, reading, bed—is really my shipping area. . . . I may be packing something on my bed. . . . Honestly, it's an archeological dig."

Paul was aware that his "successful small business" was not all he said it was. He had qualified his earlier claim about entrepreneurship with the statement that he was "not necessarily spinning," indicating that he knew others might not see his online activity as a legitimate business and that, to some degree, he was fooling himself. He then told me he was worried that if I visited his basement warehouse I would see him as "just some guy with a bunch of stuff in his basement. . . . What I'm sharing with you a lot has to do with perspectives and possibilities. . . . But it's the combination of me not being self-deceptive . . . and looking at myself as an entrepreneur."

Paul was saying that although he knew this was really a hobby, he was also intentionally thinking of that hobby as a business (and himself as an entrepreneur) to help him cope with his stress.

Even though Paul was not out of touch with reality, he may have had some other psychological issues. He hinted that he was a hoarder and compulsive shopper, and that he suffered from chronic low self-esteem: "Maybe some of the baggage I've had in the past is a compulsion to collect or buy, thinking I'm . . . adding value to myself by something that I perceived as possessing that is valuable." However, it is unlikely that Paul was seriously mentally ill or truly delusional.

He had seen a counselor during the past few months and he told me he had never been diagnosed with any kind of mental illness. He seemed aware of the real advantages and disadvantages of his online activities. He was also aware of the limited amount of income he brought in from these activities and spoke about the reality of his unemployment.

Similarly, Ruth was also aware that she was not really employed. She made it clear that she was trying to "trick herself" into feeling like she was still a worker by "working" at her job search in the library. Despite her awareness, sustaining still reduced her distress. Although she made her first trip to the library because she thought the environment would be conducive to job searching:

RUTH: Once I got there, it was like, oh, this feels like work. . . . [So now] I'm trying to trick my mind by going to the library and pretending like it's work every day. . . . But I understand that I don't have a job. . . . I'm not really fooling myself here.

ME: So when you realized that you were tricking yourself, did that not work as well or did it continue to work?

RUTH: It continued to work.

Although it may be tempting to chalk up sustainers' experiences to delusion, the evidence shows otherwise. People may have sustained their worker identities by "spinning" or "tricking themselves," but they were fully aware that they were doing so, and the mental health benefits they got from sustaining were real.

Summary

Having consistency in your identity is important to mental health. Some areas of identity consistency that help support positive well-being are: a sameness of self across time (Burke 1996; Swann 1983); consistency between who we are and who we wish or expect ourselves to be (Higgins 1987; Large and Marcussen 2000; Marcussen 2006); and consistency between who we believe ourselves to be and how others treat us (Burke 1991, 1996).

In the United States, people see "chemistry" between their jobs and identities (Sharone 2013a, 2013b), so sustaining worker identities should help support the self-consistency and feedback needed for well-being. All the unemployed people in this study who sustained their identities felt less distressed by doing so. This may help explain the tendency for some unemployed people to identify as entrepreneurs (Lane 2011) and attend certain types of job seekers' groups (Garrett-Peters 2009; Lane 2011; Sharone 2013a).

Many of our identities are based in institutional roles, such as manager within a company or father within a family (Stryker 1980). Although some people were able to sustain their identities without an institution that offered them a work-related role, institutional roles (when available) made it easier for people to understand and be sure of their identities, especially when other people in the institution gave them confirming feedback for performing those roles. For example, Paul's networking groups provided a structured setting through which he could perform leadership roles and get feedback that he was a "marketing man."

Social institutions were also vital to Marsha's and Ken's prospects for sustaining their identities. Educational institutions where Marsha took EMT, paramedic driver, and other public safety–related courses provided her with roles in which she could perform tasks similar to those she had done in her old job. Ken's office in his former workplace provided a position that allowed him to sustain his worker identity while he was unemployed.

Status was also important to the sustaining process. Being a man (in the way that Paul and many men of his generation defined it) would have made it hard for Paul or Ken to shift emphasis to a father identity. Furthermore, the fact that their children were adults would make that even harder to do. Being men also made it important for them to continue to be providers in order to avoid a status mismatch.

Like Paul and Marsha, Ruth did not have any obvious alternate roles into which she could shift her identity. Ruth was married, but had no children, so the status-congruent mother role that had worked so well for Charlotte was unavailable to Ruth, and she did not mention any hobby or leisure groups that could have provided a shifting option. Her involvement with FaithWorks! helped her stay positive, but it did not provide a new role into which she could shift, nor did it provide a work-like role that could help her sustain her worker identity (as it did for Paul). With limited institutional involvements, Ruth may have been less likely to shift and more likely to sustain in order to cope with the identity damage caused by the layoff. Ruth had not identified strongly with her specific job title ("information analyst"), but rather with the label "workaholic." So in order to sustain, Ruth only needed to find or create an environment roughly similar to the one in which she had previously worked.

Almost all sustainers had access to a social institution that provided a clear role that supported their efforts to sustain; Ruth was unique in her ability to sustain without one. Her story highlights the creative ways in which people perform identity work. She was able to construct the idea that she was still a worker by reframing a non-work setting (the public library) as a workplace, redefining her job search activity as work, and performing work-like behaviors (dressing for work, giving herself a timed lunch break, etc.).

There is likely a time limit on how long sustaining will work. For example, Ofer Sharone (2013a, 52) found that the emotional benefits gained from job seekers' networking groups only lasted about two to three months, although

Lane (2011) documented several people who had comfortably sustained the entrepreneur identity for up to five years. Structure played an important role there too, given that many of the men in Carrie Lane's (2011) study could do so because their wives' employment allowed them to remain financially comfortable. At some point, for most people, the financial realities of unemployment probably produce distress that overrides whatever emotional help sustaining can provide. Many people descend into depression after about six months of unemployment (Cassidy 2001; Sheeran and McCarthy 1990), possibly in part because their finances are becoming strained. But as a short-term strategy, sustaining (like shifting) may help alleviate some of the identity-related distress, including feedback, time, and status mismatches.

Sustaining may have other benefits as well. It could lead you to engage in activities that expose you to potential employers, keep your skills sharp (see, for instance, Garrett-Peters 2009 and Lane 2011), and provide you with new skills. All of these things may make it easier to land a new job. For example, volunteering at a fire and rescue organization could lead to a paid EMT position. Sustaining helps keep you "in the game" within your line of work. In contrast, if you do not continue to identify with your previous job, you may be less likely to look for paid work in the field in which you have the most experience, making it harder to find a job.

On the other hand, sustaining your identity as an employee may make you less likely to search for work. Many sustainers (like many shifters) abandoned their job searches. For example, as Paul sustained, he stopped searching for traditional work. Because he felt like he was employed (and even made some money from his online venture), he saw little need to look for work. However, the money he made—about $1,000 per month—was far less than he needed to pay his family's basic expenses. It was questionable whether Paul could ever make a solid living solely from his entrepreneurial online activities. And Paul's second potential business, YourMarketingMan, appears to have never gotten off the ground; even three-and-a-half years after the business cards were created, no such website existed. Sustaining is a complex phenomenon, and creates both advantages and disadvantages for unemployed people.

As you read in chapter 2, Pearlin's Stress Process Model (Pearlin 1999; Pearlin et al. 1981) highlights how social status affects exposure to stress, as well as our available coping options. In chapter 2, I also presented Peter J. Burke's (1991) Identity Control Theory, which proposes that day-to-day behaviors and feedback from others form and maintain our identities. The stories from participants in this study illustrate how status, feedback, and identities are interrelated in everyday life. In practice, the Stress Process Model and Identity Control Theory merge. Identity threats produce distress, and just as social support and material resources are used for coping, so are identities. Therefore, identity is important to consider when using the Stress Process Model.

All of the people in chapters 6 and 7 used identity to cope with distress. Their exact strategies depended on social statuses, the anticipated and actual feedback connected to statuses and roles, and the availability of social institutions. So what identity work options exist if you have lost your job but have few or no links to social institutions that could provide a status-congruent role? And what happens to your identity if you are not involved with institutions that could provide you with feedback that you are still the same person? This dilemma is the focus of chapter 8.

8

"Like You're Dead and Nobody Told You"

Identity Void

Chapters 3 through 5 focused on how job loss can threaten your identity and cause emotional pain. Chapters 6 and 7 showed how you can use shifting and sustaining as identity work to repair a damaged identity and improve your mental health. However, shifting and sustaining are not always viable strategies. Their availability depends on a combination of your statuses and the social institutions you are involved with. So what happens to your identity and mental health if you cannot shift or sustain?

This chapter illustrates the experience of identity void, a loss of all sense of self and profound confusion about who you are. When you have lost an important identity and cannot somehow sustain it or shift to another one, you are left with a disturbing hole in your identity. This kind of experience may be especially common for people who have involuntarily lost roles (see, for example, Duran-Aydintug 1995), such as those who have been laid off or fired. Furthermore, some research on the experience of identity confusion after losing a job (or after other transitions) supports the idea that social institutions and statuses may be critical to experiencing or preventing identity void (Baird 2010; Lane 2011; Riach and Loretto 2009).

This chapter revisits Charlie, whose attempts to shift and sustain were futile. I explain why these attempts were unsuccessful, and document the effects of his failed identity work. This chapter also introduces Janelle, who was caught in a distressing limbo between identifying with her former workplace and a new, unknown identity. Charlie and Janelle both suffered when they experienced identity void. I describe their experiences, and briefly compare and contrast them with the experiences of some of the people in previous chapters.

Returning to Charlie: "Shedding a Life"

Charlie's identity had been threatened by feedback, time, and status mismatches. He had been told he was not a good director, he felt like he was not the same person he had been for twenty-four years, and he felt less like a man. These things left him depressed and anxious.

But Charlie did not passively sit by, claiming there was nothing he could do about his threatened identities or his emotional pain. He tried to shift to other identities, such as father. He did not succeed. He also tried to sustain his employee identity by maintaining contact with his former workplaces and colleagues, sometimes in hostile, unproductive ways. He did not succeed here either. His identity remained threatened, and he fell ever more deeply into an upsetting identity void.

Identity void left him confused about who he was, as well as depressed and grief-stricken: "I'll be the first to say that I clearly was depressed. . . . I needed to disengage [from the job], but disengagement didn't feel good. I mean, that's not who I am. Disengage from the job and from that whole identity. That is almost like shedding a life, a skin. And so I had to—and I knew this intellectually—I had to mourn."

Charlie was in an "in-between" stage, neither here nor there in terms of his identity. This left him with an "in transition" identity. He was aware that if he was not the person he had been for twenty-four years, he needed to find out who he was: "I think I'm coming to a new identity. I guess the word I wanna use is I wanna be authentic. So what do I want that story to be?"

At first, several people in this study, including Charlie, engaged in what I call the "just me" phenomenon. For example, Charlie tried to simply detach who he was from work, claiming that he could be "just Charlie": "I just became Charlie Duncan . . . as opposed to . . . executive. . . . I tried to say I am not my job. . . . A good [Charlie whispers] guy, talented guy. . . . Don't need a job to be that guy."

Others echoed this idea. Cindy (the former travel executive featured in chapters 3 through 5) said: "Cindy is Cindy . . . and I can be myself, whatever that is. I'm not [Cindy sighs] defined by external-type things." Ideally, Cindy wanted to be "just Cindy," without anything else to define her. However, as shown in previous chapters, this left her confused about who she was, as indicated when she described her identity as "whatever that is."

Nancy, a forty-nine-year-old white former marketing director also struggled to define herself outside of other roles. She noted that since she had lost her job: "I feel like I'm more . . . Nancy . . . or more fully Nancy. . . . Work took up a good portion of, or defined a lot of Nancy. . . . I'm still figuring that out [who I am]. . . . I don't know quite yet, 'cause honestly I'm not sure what I want to do. . . . Sometimes I still don't know what I wanna be when I grow up." This identity confusion harmed her mental health. She said felt her worst when: "I feel confused about what I should, could, want to be doing."

Charlie, Cindy, and Nancy were unable to become "just me." This left them in an identity void. Many identities are strongly based on roles (Stryker 1980) and without them it can be hard to know who you are. Shifting to a new identity embedded in a social institution's role could have been a way out of this void. Unfortunately, Charlie was not sure which roles could fulfill his identity needs, and so he was in a transitional process of "discernment," a term he co-opted from his Catholic faith: "Discernment is a term that's used in the Catholic Church to determine whether or not you have a vocation. . . . That period of deciding whether or not you're gonna be able to commit to [the priest] lifestyle is called discernment. . . . I just look at this stage of my life as a discerning stage."

Charlie's discernment solidified into a more permanent identity void. Identity void is similar in some ways to the "vacuum identity" experienced by many people who leave roles voluntarily (Ebaugh 1988). Vacuum identities are temporary, and occur as people seek new roles, try them on for size, and experience anticipatory socialization to learn how to behave in the new roles (Merton 1957). Ultimately, all of this helps them decide to leave their current roles (Ebaugh 1988). But Charlie had been involuntarily pushed out of his role; he was no longer in it. The relative suddenness of his transition made it hard for him to take his time seeking and trying out alternative roles. Because he had largely lost his Smith Organization employee identity and had not moved into a new identity, he was left with identity void.

It is difficult to get others to validate an "in transition" identity (Baird 2010), so telling others that he was "in discernment" would probably not have been well received. This may be why he did not want to discuss his identity process with other people until he knew for sure who he would become: "When I sort of arrive at something, then I'm perfectly happy to announce it or talk about it or whatever. But until that time, I guess I'm not all that interested in talking about [the] process."

Trying to Shift: "Anybody Can Be a Father"

Charlie decided to work toward an identity attached to a role, and tried the strategy that Charlotte and Lorna found helpful—shifting. When I first interviewed him, he offered a laundry list of possible roles into which he could shift: "I started shifting away from the job to a different future. . . . I'm a good dad. I'm a good husband. I'm a good brother. I'm a good citizen. I'm a good financial guy . . . good businessman. I'm a good friend. I'm a good parishioner. . . . I started moving more of my sort of heart and interest into the family."

He initially tried to shift into the father identity. However, this left his mood, as he put it, "flat" because he was unable to fully identify this way:

I began to disengage . . . and to refocus toward . . . a different future. . . . Spend more time with family. Get more involved in, like, scouting and things to Little League . . . things that would help my daughter as well. . . . It was really a difficult transition. . . . I have to say that when I see my kids excel at something . . . there's no pleasure greater than that. But I can't say that day in and day out . . . that it sustains me. . . . The shift was very hard. . . . I had a really, really hard time transferring significance and importance to this because I always said to myself . . . anybody can be a father.

Although Helen Rose Fuchs Ebaugh (1988) found that existing relationships are important when seeking new roles, she gives little explicit attention to the social institutions and statuses that may be critical to the process. For example, Charlie's failed shift may have been because he believed fatherhood was not a sufficient identity, on its own, for a man. During his first interview with me, Charlie had said: "I think for men especially for [fatherhood] to be paramount in your life and to be pretty much your single identifier and to find that inner strength . . . and to strip out the ego [is hard]."

Although having a family made the father role available to Charlie, his status as a man made it tough for him to shift to it. In fact, when Charlie tried to describe his identity during my second interview with him, he began by emphasizing roles and social institutions and ended by getting choked up about the idea of himself in a domestic role, despite his wife's support for his situation: "Identity comes from, I think, a couple different sources. . . . Who you are in relation to other people—your family, your job, your community, your church, whatever your sort of micro worlds are. . . . Nine-to-fiving it and bringing home the bacon. Or I'm at home [Charlie chuckles, then laughs in a way that sounds like crying]. My wife seems to [Charlie laugh-cries again] accept me as a hausfrau."

In contrast to Charlie's difficulty shifting to a more domestic identity, Nancy's status as a woman may have helped her move past her identity void by easing the way for a shift into the mother identity. Although in her first interview Nancy had said she was "still figuring out who she was," three months later her identity void had disappeared. She described her mood as "very good," and she told me she was happiest when "everything around me—primarily with . . . my immediate family members—is coming along. You know, being a mom and a wife. . . . That confusion around who I am I guess doesn't exist [any more]."

For his part, Charlie tried to brainstorm other identities he could shift to. He added hobbyist to the mix in an attempt to find another identity. But just as with the father identity, he found he could not really latch on to it, nor could he simply pick activities "out of the blue" to identify with: "I own some property . . . a little tree farm. . . . [I could] get more involved in that, create some hobbies.

I do a lotta stuff but I don't really have a passion for it. I'm not a woodworker. I don't have to ski. . . . I couldn't say the day that I leave [my job] I will [Charlie laughs] buy a lathe and make hand-tooled staircases."

Although status and social institutions had supported several women's identity shifts to wife and mother, they made Charlie's attempted shifts problematic. None of the roles Charlie mentioned fulfilled his identity needs, perhaps because none of them addressed the breadwinner aspect of being a man. Additionally, many of the hobbies he mentioned were not embedded in social institutions, which would have made it more difficult for him to interact with others in a way that reinforced those identities.

Charlie did not know who he was. Six months after losing his job, he had sunk deeply into identity void. He mourned the death of his worker identity, and he had no new identity with which to fully replace it. He felt lost, depressed, and confused.

Who Am I Not?

Charlie's identity was unclear to him, but he was certain about who he did not want to become. He was not ready to call himself retired, and he did not want to be an unemployed person: "Getting too caught up in titles and all that kind of stuff, in this town it's pretty hard not to do that. . . . Whereas if I said, I'm retired, I'm not working, then would I be dismissed as 'He's not working. He's nobody'?"

He equated these identities with a "removal from the world" similar to identity void: "I'm not quite ready to say I'm retired. . . . I'll make that decision . . . when I've eliminated other possibilities. So I'm not ready to say that. Although I am [currently retired]. Because I looked it up in the dictionary and it said 'to remove oneself from the world.'"

Like Cindy, who said that low-level "retirement" jobs would not help her "feel valued again," Charlie believed that to be retired would leave him without an identity, valueless, and disconnected from the world. When older people in the study mentioned retirement, they usually did so in the context of not wanting it and not being ready for it, while admitting that "early retirement" could be a last resort if they could not find work again.

If retirement was an undesired identity for Charlie, an identity as an unemployed person was an anathema. Being unemployed is particularly harmful to men's mental health (Creed and Moore 2006; Thoits 1986), and Charlie feared being seen as worthless or a "slug" if people even found out he was unemployed. This left him unable to identify with it, for the risk to his self-esteem was too great.

The "unemployed" identity may have seemed especially distasteful when combined with his status as an "older person." Advancing age is typically viewed negatively in U.S. society (Gergen and Gergen 2000), and older people face stereotypes and age discrimination in the workplace (Palmore 1999). Members of stigmatized groups, such as older people and unemployed people, might easily internalize that stigma and belittle themselves. However, people have a need to see themselves positively, so some people use downward social comparisons—they compare themselves to others in a way that makes them seem "better"—to cope with the threatening situation of membership in a stigmatized group (Tajfel and Turner 1979, 1986).

Charlie had few options for successfully coping with identity threats, but he did what he could by distancing himself from the "older unemployed person" identity. He described the other older people at his job seekers' networking group as "unemployable" and "desperate," and psychologically separated himself from them: "I don't want to say I'm superior, but . . . I stayed in five-star hotels. . . . [The other older workers] haven't looked for a job in a long time. . . . They're not self-reflective. They don't have a resumé. . . . I probably would not hire them. . . . They're so totally clueless and so naïve. . . . They're desperate. . . . So I look at [them] and I go [Charlie whispers] 'Wow. [Charlie speaks in a normal volume] Good luck.'"

I attended the group many times and did not see any difference between them and Charlie in how they presented themselves, their experience, or their job qualifications. There likely was little, if any, difference. But Charlie knew that, as an older unemployed person, he could be judged harshly. By thinking about himself as "better" than them, he tried to push away the "unemployed" identity (especially as it related to his age) in order to maintain his self-esteem and some semblance of a positive identity.

When I visited Charlie's church, I realized that his fears of being judged for being unemployed may have been justified. Charlie did not tell most people that he had lost his job, but his wife had told a few people at their church. This agitated Charlie because he thought they might see him as "a slug." When I asked Charlie if I could spend a day with him, he invited me to attend Catholic services with his family.

On Sunday, I walked down the city sidewalk toward the well-manicured lawn of the Catholic church to which Charlie and his family belonged. As I entered the alcove, a priest in gold-trimmed white robes greeted me. Shortly thereafter, I met with Charlie, who introduced me to his wife, son, and daughter, all of whom were very friendly and exceptionally polite. Just before the service, Charlie's wife took a comb to their son's hair, ensuring that every strand was in place. About two hundred upper-middle-class attendees sat in the pews of the ornate, high-ceilinged chapel.

Charlie acted like the "good parishioner" he had claimed to be. As I sat in the wooden pew to his right, he prayed out loud, devotedly, and corrected his son when he fidgeted or lost track of his place in the hymnal. Charlie volunteered his family to help take up collections. All went smoothly during the service itself.

After the service, as Charlie and I waited in a long line for the reception which offered doughnuts and coffee, he introduced me to a fellow parishioner who had lost her job. After he told her what I was studying, she and I began to discuss unemployment. She was one of the few parishioners who knew of Charlie's plight. But when she turned to Charlie and asked him if her unemployment experience was similar to his, he did not respond and instead turned his entire body away so his back faced us. She repeated the question, to no avail.

After getting our refreshments, Charlie and I sat at a round table with about six of his acquaintances. As we made small talk, a polished-looking middle-aged Asian woman dressed in a business suit walked from table to table trying to sell ties to the church patrons. She was met with harsh reactions. Two women just to Charlie's right angrily told her to leave the church as she protested, "But I'm unemployed! I have to make money somehow!" After she left, the two angered women began an animated discussion about the plentiful availability of work and the laziness of people who were unemployed. Charlie remained silent. When I later asked him if they knew about his job loss, he said he had told no one at the table.

Charlie could not take on the identity of an unemployed person, even though he was, in fact, unemployed. It was much too risky to identify this way, given the potentially harsh judgment of his peers and his own negative evaluation of unemployed people. Charlie could not be "just Charlie." He could not successfully shift, nor could he identify with unemployment or retirement. So Charlie tried to find a way to sustain an identity connected to his former workplace.

Trying to Sustain: Websites, Lunches, and Lawsuits

In chapter 7, Paul, Marsha, and others found ways to sustain identities as workers even though they were unemployed. This form of identity work seemed especially helpful to people who could not shift to other identities because the roles available to them did not match expectations for their statuses. But in order for sustaining to be a viable identity work option, people usually needed social institutions that would validate their "worker" identity claims with reinforcing feedback and a structure within which to perform work-like tasks.

Charlie could not use his job seekers' group to sustain a worker or leader identity that paralleled his old job because he strongly distanced himself from other group members, as well as from the category "unemployed." His former employer, the Smith Organization, had been part of Charlie's identity for a very long time, and after he lost his job he tried to remain connected to it in several ways.

Charlie realized that it was extremely difficult to purposely shed his Smith Organization identity. During his first interview with me, Charlie had mentioned that, regarding identity, "There's sort of a hangover from your work life." Although he may not have been completely conscious of the link between his attempts to connect with his former workplace and efforts to sustain his worker identity, he did recognize this connection to some degree: "[It] doesn't mean that you're not still sort of living in the afterglow of that [work-related identity] as you make your adjustments and all that kinda stuff. . . . There's unresolved kinds of things, 'cause I'm still proceeding with legal action on a defamation case."

This "hangover identity" (Ebaugh 1988, 149) experience—having part of your old identity linger—is common for people who voluntarily leave a role, and it may even be sought out by people who, like Charlie, involuntarily lose roles (Duran-Aydintug 1995). Charlie had mixed feelings about continuing to identify with the Smith Organization. He wanted to move on, but it was hard to leave the old role completely behind. Perhaps this is why Charlie continued to try to connect with his old job in several ways, even though these ways were ultimately unproductive or counterproductive.

Charlie repeatedly visited the Smith Organization's website, and even looked for the vacancy announcement that offered his old job to new applicants. Even after six months of unemployment, Charlie continued to visit the site: "Once in a while I'll think to myself, 'Gee, I'm really curious what they're doing with the [specialty name] department, 'cause supposedly they were gonna revamp it.' And there were a couple times I was looking for something else. . . . I was on the site, so I thought, 'Well, I'll just see if they've done anything with it.' . . . Every once in a while I'll think, 'Hey, you should see . . . what they're doing for the regional meetings.'"

Charlie also tried to arrange lunches with his former colleagues. After three months of unemployment, he described having lunch with another Smith Organization employee who lost her job as "kind of a support group, what next kinda group." But as time went on, lunching with former employees, as well as people who still worked there, became unpleasant because they only reminded him that he was no longer really a part of the organization and reinforced his identity void:

> There was a really nice woman [from work] and we were kind of friends. We went to lunch. . . . I've tried to kinda keep a network going . . . [Charlie inhales] 'cause I think it's good psychologically. . . . We were talking about family and a bunch of other stuff. And then she started talking about the Smith Organization, and she goes, "Do you mind if I talk about this?" and I said, "Sure." She goes, "Are you interested?" and I said, "Not really." But I said, "You can talk about it. . . . I certainly know all the players and I'm happy to listen." But I said . . . "I don't really . . . care all that much." I mean, if somebody said to me "Hey, I heard [Charlie chuckles/scoffs a little] s-somebody's getting fired or somebody left or they totally redid the [specialty name] department," I'd say "Oh, yeah? . . . How is that?" I'd be interested enough to follow through. . . . [But] that's dead

and gone. . . . When I think about it . . . it is kind of inert. It's just kind
of a black hole. . . . So I thought, "It's about time to have lunch with Linda
again." . . . And then I thought, "All she's gonna talk about is the Smith
Organization. I don't really give a sh—."

The lunches became less frequent, and after five months of unemployment, he stopped going to them. This contradictory "approach-and-avoid"
stance in which study participants sought out contact with former people,
websites, or other media connected with their old workplace and then quickly
tried to separate themselves from it, was common for people who experienced
identity void (see also Janelle in the next section of this chapter), especially
those who were ultimately unable to shift or sustain. Participants may not have
been consciously trying to sustain an employee identity. In fact, sometimes they
claimed they were trying to prove to themselves that they could reengage with
their former employer without emotional harm, and that they could then simply "walk away" from that contact. However, these kinds of interactions may
instead signify a conflicting state of identity in which former employees had
one foot in their previous "worker identity" camp and one foot in emptiness—
no other new identity to replace it. They attempted to link up with their workplace identity again. When that failed, they were left in identity void in which
their worker identities were "dead and gone" and they were in a "black hole."
They then tried to cut themselves off from those situations and interactions.

Just two weeks after Charlie lost his job and continuing through six months
of unemployment, he filed several lawsuits against his former employer. Charlie
felt he had been wronged, and was angry. Working toward justice briefly helped
him feel a little better because of the regained sense of control that is impera-
tive for mental health (Pearlin et al. 1981): "I had to do it for myself. I had to do
it for justice [Charlie laughs], the American way. I just couldn't roll over. And I
think maybe that's why my mood improved and I think because I was doing
something. I wasn't helpless." He said that filing a lawsuit would make it as if
he "didn't go away," thereby potentially sustaining his Smith Organization identity: "We were going to continue the discussion. So I just wanted to make [them]
sweat, that I didn't go away easily."

Like the lunches and the website visits, this way of sustaining some form of
worker identity was ill fated. Although this was not necessarily a fully conscious
attempt to sustain some form of Smith Organization identity, Charlie may have
had a subconscious desire to stay connected to his old employer. But he went
about it by filing lawsuits, and this was ultimately detrimental to his identity
because the only feedback he got from these interactions was contentious and
mediated by lawyers. In short, sustaining in this way reminded him of his failed
work identity rather than providing him with experiences that made him feel
like a Smith Organization employee. The attempts to sustain his former work

identity did not work. He knew that although his old identity still lingered in his background, it really was in his past: "The past is the past. It is there. It's kinda like Chernobyl. You seal it in concrete and it's there. You look at the best of it and you just seal it off and you just move on."

Charlie could not sustain that past identity, and he could not replace it. Charlie's discernment process had been largely unsuccessful, which left him with a deepening identity void: "I get sort of flummoxed when [Charlie clears his throat] . . . I'm in kind of a professional situation and people say 'What do you do?' . . . I really [Charlie chuckles] have a long ways to go. . . . I guess I would have thought that [by his second interview with me] I might have a little clearer idea, or that something would have kind of dropped in. . . . But it's still very ambiguous. . . . Ambiguity is kind of unpleasant."

Charlie could not identify as "just Charlie" because that identity was not connected to a role in a social institution. And it was too emotionally risky for Charlie to identify as retired or unemployed. He tried to shift his identity to father, and considered identities as parishioner, hobbyist, friend, and brother. But his status as a man, along with some of these roles' lack of connections to social institutions, made those kinds of shifts unworkable. And although Charlie tried to sustain his Smith Organization identity through various attempts to stay connected to his old workplace, the methods he chose were unsustainable and sometimes antagonistic, and only resulted in feedback that confirmed he did not belong there. Charlie remained in identity void.

Janelle: "In Limbo"

Janelle, a vibrant thirty-nine-year-old African American woman, had loved her job. Since childhood, she had aspired to work for a specific television channel, SZTV. She had achieved her dream by working there as an online programming manager.

Janelle's job combined fast-paced multitasking with creativity and technical skills:

> My job was to do the online show pages—coming up with the content, making it interesting, making it interactive, and updating them. . . . [I did] the promotion of the page, working with the network, forecasting new shows. . . . Myself and my coworker . . . we would be the first people to get there [in the morning]. . . . We had 50 million emails. . . . We would go through the emails and then we would start updating the page. . . . There were occasions when you had to update from home. . . . And then they have a daily newsletter . . . and you have to get your text in like the day before or that morning at the latest. . . . There's a lotta phone meetings. . . . You might have a meeting at 10:00, another one at 1:00. . . . You're multitasking. . . . There's a lotta fires. This link is broke. You gotta

fix it right now. . . . You're constantly stopping what you're working on to put out a fire that is more urgent.

Her job was a major part of her identity: "I think when you like your job, you're associated with your job. . . . I grew up watching SZTV and I was like 'I'm gonna work there one day.' . . . I'm always like 'Miss SZTV.'"

During my first interview with Janelle, six months after she lost her job, we sat outside on a park bench on a cool spring evening. I was surprised by how young she looked. She was thirty-nine, but looked like she was in her early twenties. Her trendy outfit—a black scoop-neck shirt, billowing pants that became skin-tight below the knee, and a military-print jacket with matching sling-back sandals—furthered this impression. But her eyes looked puffy and tired, as if she had been crying. Nevertheless, she seemed energetic and ready to share the story of the day she lost her job.

She told me that one day, just after returning from vacation, she was called to the Human Resources office. At first, she had no idea that they were calling her to lay her off: "My first thought was 'Something must have happened when I went on vacation and they're gonna tell me about it. Maybe somebody got sexually harassed or somethin'.'"

But Janelle had been laid off once before in her past, and when another coworker half-jokingly mentioned layoffs, Janelle began to worry: "My coworker looked at me and she said, 'Is this how it happened the first time?' And that's when I realized . . . uh-oh. I think you're about to get canned. . . . And I'm still tryin' to think positive. . . . And [then] I see a folder with my name on it and I see the word 'termination.'"

Like several other people in the study, the first thing Janelle felt was shock: "It was like somebody kicked me in my stomach. . . . It's like Charlie Brown when they go 'Mwa mwa mwa mwa, mwa mwa mwa mwa.' And you don't hear. . . . And I remember sitting down and I remember saying [out loud to the HR staff] 'Yesterday was my birthday. But I just got back from vacation.' . . . I guess I was in shock."

As the reality of losing her job sunk in, Janelle began to experience identity mismatches. She had identified as "Miss SZTV" for a long time and others also used that as her nickname. About a month after she lost her job, Janelle ran into an acquaintance who called her "Miss SZTV," which reminded her that she was no longer that same person: "I ran into somebody and they're like 'Miss SZTV!' And I was like . . . 'I'm not there anymore.' So it is tough when you really like your job. . . . So it is kinda that . . . parta' your identity."

Part of what created this time mismatch for Janelle was losing her connection with her colleagues, who had been a big part of her social life. Their absence reminded her of her lost identity, and pushed her further toward identity void. Like others, Janelle spoke of identity void in terms of death and final separation, by saying it was "like a divorce" or "like somebody died": "You're like 'Oh man. What are you gonna be doin' next? What are you—?' . . . You kinda party together. You kinda hang out in the same areas. You kinda live in around the same spots and it's kinda cliquish. . . . So when you're not there anymore, you're really not part of the clique. . . . You're not parta' that group anymore. It's kinda like a divorce. Or, I hate to say it, but it's almost like somebody died."

In addition to the time mismatch Janelle experienced, losing her job also triggered status mismatches involving age. For example, when Janelle got into a car accident, the other driver asked for her business card so they could exchange information. But because Janelle did not have a job, she no longer had a business card. For her, this meant she was not the kind of person she "should" be at almost forty years old, and this made her feel embarrassed: "So it was like, [Janelle re-creates the crying voice she had at the accident] 'I don't have a business card.' . . . I was embarrassed. . . . All those feelings came back. . . . You're a temp. . . . You're forty years old. You don't have a business card. You're just like, whattya you been doin'? And the guy looked at me when I said, 'I don't have a business card.' . . . That's like tellin' somebody you're drivin' and you don't have insurance."

Janelle was not simply embarrassed because she had no job. Instead, not having a job triggered a status mismatch. For Janelle, to be almost forty meant you should be established and at a high level in your career. Being almost forty was about identity—who she was, who she believed she should be because of her age, and who she was not. For Janelle, nearing forty was "a milestone. Like I feel like you shouldn't be starting over. . . . You should already be firmly where you're supposed to be at. . . . Bein' established. And I feel like I'm not established."

Identity Mismatches, Looking for Work, and Trouble Finding a New Identity

Identity mismatches were also triggered when Janelle looked for a new job. Janelle was very actively looking for work, and usually applied to two or three jobs each day. She hoped to find work in her field that would utilize her bachelor's degree in communications. But by the time of my second interview with her, she had been unemployed for nine months and was becoming financially desperate. She had begun to receive food stamps and was worried that she would have to move back in with her parents. So Janelle had expanded her job search to a wide variety of jobs. This further threatened Janelle's identity by creating a status mismatch. She said applying for a part-time bank teller position was a "low point" for her because it did not match who she "should be" for her age: "I filled out a job—this is a low point—part-time bank teller. . . . I mean, a respectable job. But I just was feelin' a low point because when I see the people that are bank tellers, they're like really young. They're like . . . high school, in college . . . really young. So I was just like—[Janelle sighs a little]."

Janelle also applied for an advertised position as a "beauty and fashion advisor" to work at events. Janelle prided herself on being current with the latest fashions, and thought that even though this part-time position only paid about $11 per hour, it might be an opportunity for her to get back into a trendy field that involved communications, marketing, and events. But when she was interviewed, she quickly realized that the job was not what had been advertised:

> The interview was inside a [large box store]. . . . I was tryin' not to think about it. But I was like, really? Has it come to this? And the girl that comes out [and] interviews me, her name was Bess. And she was like twenty-one, very scraggly, clothes very just kinda thrown on and she's like the manager. . . . She calls me in the back . . . where all the machinery is—the produce, the sticker guns, the stocking equipment. It's dirty back there. . . . There's like really nowhere for me to interview at. . . . We sit down and she starts askin' me about how do I keep up with fashion trends. And I'm thinkin' to myself "Are you kidding me? You're asking me about fashion trends? . . . You're all wrinkled up . . . I drove in a car with no air conditioning and I still look better than you."

Despite the disappointing start to the interview, Janelle maintained her professionalism and gave her best effort to winning the job. When Bess asked her to demonstrate her selling ability, Janelle complied:

> She gives me a pack of paper clips . . . and says "Here. Pretend this is a product. Sell it." . . . I [thought] "Are you kidding me? For $10 an hour?" . . . [But] I just went with it. I took the paper clips. They were plastic and they were color coated. . . . and I spread 'em across her desk and I just started talkin'. I said, "Excuse me, ma'am? Have you tried our new paper clips? . . . Do you have any kids? They make great projects. You can color code your bills, pink for your clothing receipts, blue for your husband's dry cleaning," . . . She was sittin' there literally with her mouth open.

Then Janelle discovered the real nature of the job. Once Bess recovered from Janelle's marketing speech, she said:

> "I'm gonna tell them that you'll be a good candidate, but we don't have any more health and beauty positions. This one's for food." After alla that. I was like you gotta be kidding me. . . . She's like, "Can you make a hamburger? . . . Well, it would be like product demonstration, makin' hamburgers, handing out samples and coupons. . . . Sometimes it's dog food. Sometimes it's protein bars. . . ." So I smiled. Came back home. . . . By three o'clock the phone rang. They offered me a job. . . . I never called back.

Janelle decided not to take the job—not just because it was a less than desirable position, but because it threatened her age identity: "What if I see somebody from my old job at [the big box store job]? Am I gonna be like duckin' between the—Like 'Oh, my God. It's really bad. I saw Janelle like handin' out hamburger patties.' . . . It was horrible. And I was like maybe if I was twenty. Maybe if I was twenty-five. But I'm forty."

Janelle was also concerned about what it would mean for her as a college-educated African American woman to take such a low-level job. In this case, it was not just an education-based status mismatch she was worried about, but rather that taking the job would reinforce society's stereotypes about racial minorities, education, and low-wage work: "Bein' a minority . . . I'm very sensitive to that. And I don't wanna get stuck . . . in that box. . . . It's hard enough as it is. . . . It's not what I went to school for."

At first Janelle had tried to find a job that would help her maintain some kind of professional marketing or communications identity. As her bank account shrank, she looked for almost any job she could get, but those jobs were too threatening to her identities as a forty-year-old and a college-educated African American.

Experiencing Identity Void

After Janelle had been unemployed for nine months, I asked her what it meant to her to not have a job. She replied: "It's hard. . . . Sometimes I feel like I'm in the Twilight Zone. Like maybe I died and nobody told me."

Janelle felt like she did not exist, had no identity, and had lost her sense of self. Janelle's comments echoed the use of death and disconnection metaphors used by other people who experienced identity void. For example, Charlie had described his identity as "at sea" and like "shedding a life." Minnie (see chapter 3) had said she felt "like a ghost" when she attended staff meetings after learning that she would lose her job. And Cindy (see chapters 3 through 5) echoed disconnection and confusion when she said that wondering "Who am I?" was the hardest part of losing her job.

When Janelle lost her job, she also felt as though she lost who she was. She did not feel like the same person she used to be, and she did not know who she would become next. She had trouble fully letting go of her SZTV identity. She tried but, like other people forced out of their roles (Duran-Aydintug 1995), she was conflicted and held on to some items that reminded her of who she had been. Toward the end of my first interview with Janelle, she pulled her small black-and-silver tote bag onto her lap, opened it up, and pulled out several pieces of SZTV memorabilia. Enthusiasm, fondness, and anger mingled as she described the meaning of each piece, as well as SZTV-related items she had discarded in her attempts to get rid of her SZTV identity:

This is my five-year plaque. When I lost my job, I like cleaned up . . . It's over . . . It's like [a boyfriend] does that thing that you cannot forgive . . . I got rid of all my T-shirts . . . jackets, coats, put it in a bag, took it up to the little Goodwill . . . I guess it was a cleansing . . . [But] these are the things that I kept. [Janelle motions to the things in the tote bag and pulls out a booklet.] This was the twenty-year celebration . . . and I always kept this, my little ticket. It's like a yearbook, and that's me. [Janelle points to a small picture of herself.] . . . And let's see what else . . . [She pulls out a paperweight.] . . . It says "team spirit." I got the team spirit . . . I was proud of that award . . . [but] I shoulda took it and clubbed it up somebody's head.

Janelle had put on a brave face throughout the interview. But then she handed me a card her mother had given her. I read the handwritten note inside it out loud: "Dear Janelle, within the power of a dream is the power to make it come true. Follow your heart and your dreams won't be left behind. Congratulations on your job. May you find happiness and contentment. Love, Mom."

When I asked Janelle to tell me what that meant to her, she paused for a few moments, then began to quietly cry. She revealed that she had been trying hard not to show the sadness and conflicting feelings she had known she would feel during the interview: "I was like 'I'm not gonna cry.' [Janelle pauses for another few seconds] Hard work . . . [Janelle's voice wavers and is shaky] Movin' down here, takin' a chance . . . [Janelle sniffles] I think most people woulda said the heck with it. . . . But you know, I guess that's it . . . I'm done. No. I'm done. . . . It wasn't just a job."

Even though Janelle's identity was still connected to SZTV in many ways, she knew she needed to move on, and she tried to break her links with her old company: "I think I'm kinda mov[ing] away. I'm tryin' to distance myself. . . . I make myself watch SZTV for maybe five minutes and then I'll turn. Tryin' to think of other companies that I would wanna work at that would value my experience. . . . What else am I doing to distance? I don't get so involved in the [SZTV] gossip."

Janelle had tried to do identity work. She tried to "move away" from her SZTV identity by getting rid of some of her work-related items, but could not bring herself to part with all of them. She forced herself to watch SZTV and then forced herself to pull away from it. She tried to come up with ideas about working at other companies. But none of these things really worked.

No Shifting, No Sustaining

Janelle fell deeper into identity void as she was unable to fully distance herself from her SZTV identity, yet was also unable to shift to a new identity or sustain some form of her old work-related identity. Without successful identity work, Janelle did not know who she was, which disturbed her.

It was not possible for Janelle to successfully shift to the wife and mother identities as Charlotte and Lorna had done. Janelle was single and had no children. Furthermore, her parents and siblings did not live nearby, so she only very rarely had opportunities to even engage in the daughter or sister roles that a family would provide. And she could not shift to an identity based on a new lower-level job because of what those jobs would mean for her identities as a forty-year-old, a college graduate, and an African American woman.

Janelle also had little involvement in other social institutions, such as sports teams, volunteer organizations, or recreational groups that could have offered shifting opportunities. And although she attended two job seekers' groups, Janelle did not feel like a leader or marketing professional there. Instead, she felt shame at being one of the last remaining original members of the group after all the others had found work (or so she assumed). When removed from her former coworkers, her social connections were extremely limited. Janelle recognized that disconnection from social institutions and interactions with other people left her unsure whether she was "in the land of the livin'," and that this was problematic:

> It is like a *Twilight Zone* episode where like the ship crashed and all the astronauts, like nobody told them that like you guys are crashed or whatever. But it is bein' in limbo because you can't really make any plans. . . . I guess you're kinda like in your own little space. And then when I will go to the grocery store or somethin' like that . . . just bein' out in the mix . . . I'm like, oh, okay. I'm still in the land of the livin'. . . . I know I'm still here when I go out, which isn't that often . . . and that might not be good either, 'cause I'm like in my own little world. I'm single. I don't have any kids.

Minnie, the sixty-three-year-old former editor described in chapter 3 who lost her job after making three minor errors, experienced identity void similarly to Janelle. For both women, work had been the main social institution with which they were strongly involved. Minnie, like Janelle, was single and had no children. Without strong connections to other social institutions, it was hard to shift. Given that they also could not sustain their former work-related identities, they remained in identity void. Interestingly, Cindy, who also experienced identity void, was involved with several groups, including her religious community and a support group of women who were in the process of making transitions. But it may be that they did not offer roles that were fully socially acceptable, or the same types of "identity magnets," that motherhood provided for Charlotte and Lorna.

In contrast, Nancy, the forty-nine-year-old former marketing director described earlier in this chapter, had been in identity void when I interviewed her the first time, but had moved out of it by the second time I met with her.

She had shifted into wife and mother identities, and she recognized how much social institutions shaped her identity. When she discussed what her identities had been like before she lost her job, she pointed to social institutions: "I think work defined my time. . . . When I was at work I thought of work. . . . I was 'Nancy Work.' . . . And when I came home I was 'Nancy Mom,' 'Nancy Wife' . . . 'Non-Work Nancy.'" Now she was home, and the social institution where she spent most of her time, family, had anchored her more firmly to the "wife and mother" identities.

Shifting was typically the first form of identity work people attempted. If they were unsuccessful, they often then tried to sustain their work-related identities. But, as shown in chapter 7, to successfully sustain they usually needed a social institution that could support their identity in a structured way that provided them with "props," such as Ken's office, and validating feedback from others, such as people who called Paul "Marketing Man." Janelle, Minnie, and Cindy (the former travel executive featured in chapters 3 through 5) were not involved with any groups or organizations that provided these options, and therefore they could not sustain and succumbed to the distressing experience of identity void.

One route to sustaining that at first seemed plausible was Janelle's volunteer marketing and communications work that she did from home after nine months of unemployment. Each morning, she posted interesting news items for a marketing company's clients so she would have something recent to put on her resumé.

Having a connection to a potential new role can help people fully transition into that new role (Ebaugh 1988, 147–148). But Janelle needed more than a new role; she needed a new identity or a sustained identity as a marketer. Chapter 7 showed that new roles that are similar to people's previous workplace roles can help people sustain their former employee identities. But Janelle's volunteer role was disconnected from the aspects of a social institution, such as coworkers and interactions, which could have supported her marketer identity. So although volunteering improved her mood a little because it helped her stay busy, it did not address her identity, and so it did not alleviate her identity void: "I can feel like, okay, if I don't do anything else today. . . . I still have to do that volunteer job. So I do feel like it is makin' me get up and do something. . . . The cons are I'm by myself. . . . I miss the interaction. I miss getting up and going out and getting dressed. . . . When I'm home I might not even take a shower. Or if I do, I'll take a shower and put on clean pajamas."

Janelle's experience with volunteer work shows just how critical structured social institutions and feedback are for successful sustaining.

Most of Janelle's social life had revolved around her work associates. When she lost her job, her contact with them gradually grew less frequent, and she lost many of the interactions that could have potentially helped her sustain her worker identity. But even those friendships might not have been enough. For example, Minnie had friends outside of work who cheered her up, but she remained in identity void because there was not enough of a structured role within her friendship circle for "friend" to become a sufficient major identity. Friendships simply might not have done enough to sustain their worker identities, and may have even made it harder to move to a new identity.

When she first lost her job, Janelle continued to see her former colleagues socially from time to time. In a way, this contact sustained her SZTV identity, but only by reminding her of what she had lost. These forced reminders made it hard for her to fully distance herself from her SZTV identity: "When I see the [SZTV] commercials or the events or when coworkers email me . . . it's kinda like if it was a divorce, his side of the family that's still tryin' to be nice. . . . You can't really make a clean break."

Forced reminders also occurred when friends and acquaintances described her to other people as "having been with SZTV": "So this one lady wanted me to meet with a friend that she knows that's in marketing. And I could hear her on the phone, makin' the pitch. And she's like 'Oh Janelle, she's got a lotta great ideas. She used to work at SZTV.' [Janelle sighs] I was like, all right. Here we go again."

These forced reminders continued when Janelle went to the unemployment office, applied for food stamps, and even when she got interviews:

Volunteer job interview last Thursday. The very first question she asked me—and she only asked two questions—"Are you still at SZTV?" . . . Like somebody kicked me in my stomach. . . . To some people . . . that's all they wanna talk about. . . . It's been almost a year and people are still asking me about this. . . . I was like, I'm never gonna get away from it. . . . It's like, oh man, [Janelle claps her hands] . . . with my hardest attempts, I still can't even distance myself. . . . I feel like I'm "Miss [Janelle laughs] Ex-SZTV." . . . I don't know what's goin' on. I'm not involved in the activities. But I'm still associated with it. . . . I understand why divorced women go back and change, go back to their married names.

But perhaps the worst forced reminder of Janelle's SZTV identity was an unfortunately worded postcard that arrived in the mail seven months after she lost her job. The postcard had such an impact on her that she saved it for two months so she could show it to me: "I got a postcard from [parent company of SZTV] . . . sayin' that I left something behind. . . . It's a advertisement for 401k rollover."

The slightly oversized, brightly colored postcard was addressed to "recipient." The card was intended to remind her that she had not yet rolled over her retirement funds into a new account now that she was no longer with SZTV. She handed the card to me and I read it out loud: "You left something behind at [parent company]: Your money."

Janelle was angry at what the card implied, and that it reminded her of the SZTV identity she was trying so hard to cast off:

> First of all, I didn't leave. You guys kicked me out. . . . This is like it's my fault [Janelle quietly claps her hands], like I left it behind. . . . "Loosey-goosey airhead, you left your money behind." . . . I mean, it's just like "Come get it. Roll it over. Take charge of your life." Like, you guys screwed up my life. . . . This pisses me off. . . . I don't wanna get any more mail from you guys. I'm done. And just when you're tryin' to turn over your life and envision yourself workin' somewhere else, you get this in the mail. . . . I wish I had [more SZTV memorabilia] to throw away when I got this.

Janelle could not shift to a new identity, nor could she sustain her SZTV identity in a positive way. She had no social institutions to support a shift. Her volunteer job was not structured enough to help her sustain, and the paid jobs she applied for as she became financially desperate would have threatened her identity because of the ways they related to her age, education level, and race. Yet she was continually confronted with forced reminders that she had once been an SZTV employee, and this made it hard to fully exit that identity. Identity void was painful at worst and, at best, it left her in between identities, unable to move on and fully claim a new identity: "The best way to describe it is like bein' in limbo. . . . I guess my mood is in limbo too."

Putting It Together

Threatened identities can create distressing feedback, time, and status mismatches. But people do not just sit back and passively accept their situations; in some circumstances people successfully perform identity work, such as shifting or sustaining. Doing so helps them manage their identities and feel happier and more comfortable. However, people's statuses and their access to social institutions influence their likelihood of success in identity work efforts, and without identity work, people may get stuck in identity void.

Helen Rose Ebaugh's (1988) landmark work on identity transitions focused on roles that people purposely left. Before leaving those roles, people searched for new roles into which they could invest their identities. She identified four stages in this process: (1) first doubts; (2) seeking alternatives; (3) turning point; and (4) establishing the ex role, and recommended expanding this line of research to involuntary role loss. The people in my study show that the process is indeed somewhat different for people who lose roles involuntarily.

When people have no choice about losing a role, they typically do not have first doubts (Drahota and Eitzen 1998; Duran-Aydintug 1995). Although a few people in my study (Charlie and Cindy, for example) had some doubts about remaining in their jobs, they typically did not really want to leave them, and only began to doubt their roles once identity-threatening events occurred, such as Charlie's not being promoted to vice president. Also, many people in my study did not know they would lose their jobs, so they had no time for first doubts. Role loss and identity threats were thrust upon them suddenly, without much time to engage in the anticipatory socialization (Merton 1957) that could have helped them make a smoother, more gradual, and more successful identity transition. They had to react relatively quickly and use the tools they had at hand, including social institutions and statuses.

The "seeking alternatives" stage is also different for people who lose roles involuntarily compared to those who choose to leave their roles. Instead of seeking out new roles, people who do not want to lose their roles try to hold on to them (Drahota and Eitzen 1998; Duran-Aydintug 1995). However, I found that people who lost their jobs involuntarily also sought alternative new roles. This is what Charlie was trying to do during his "discernment." Structural factors influenced whether they found and adopted one of these roles as an identity. If people were involved in a social structure that offered a role they believed "matched" their statuses, they shifted. For example, Nancy's family provided her with wife and mother roles that were socially acceptable for a woman. Essentially, these roles that were available and that "fit" a status acted as identity magnets. In contrast, even though Charlie highly valued fatherhood, he could not shift his identity to "father," possibly because of male breadwinner expectations. Family thus provided him with a role, but it would have created a status mismatch involving his manhood. When Nancy shifted, her identity void disappeared and her distress decreased. Charlie could not shift and his distressing identity void intensified.

People who had limited involvement in social institutions when they lost their jobs had trouble shifting, but they also had trouble sustaining. For example, even though Janelle and Minnie (see chapter 3) had friends, these friends were not part of a more established group with identifiable, structured roles. Janelle and Minnie were both single and had very limited involvement in groups or organizations outside of work, such as a sports team or a volunteer organization. Furthermore, even when Janelle did volunteer work, she performed it at home, alone, without the support of a "setting," "props," or feedback from others that could have helped her sustain her marketing/communications identity (Burke 1991; Goffman 1959). In contrast, Ken (the former CEO described in chapter 5) had access to an office and gained identity-affirming feedback from a very brief stint as a consultant during his unemployment. This feedback may be especially important to sustaining identities based on roles that are lost involuntarily (Hockey 2005; Stier 2007).

Most of the people I spoke with were uncomfortable with the "in transition" identity that Baird (2010) documented. Rather, they believed they needed to go ahead and choose a "replacement" identity. Social institutions may have been what made this possible. Social institutions may be a more specific manifestation of what Ebaugh (1988, 147–148) refers to as a "bridge to a new role"—something that helps people decide to finally leave a role. But the people I interviewed had no choice about leaving; the role exit had already occurred. What had not yet occurred was the identity transition, and participants grasped at whatever social institutions they had to help them perform successful identity work. Social institutions provided a bridge to a new identity or helped them sustain identification with their old jobs. People connected with very few social institutions more often experienced identity void than those who had those valuable connections.

When people leave a role on purpose, part of the old role is often still part of who they are and part of how others treat them. In other words, as Ebaugh (1988) illustrated, they become "exes"—ex-nuns, ex-alcoholics, and so on—in addition to their new identities. For most of the shifters in my study, new identities became primary identities, even though most of them also still hoped to return to their former professions. Because of that hope, most of them did not consider themselves "exes." Sustainers also did not consider themselves "exes" because they were still able to feel like employees. However, some people who experienced identity void, such as Janelle and Charlie, did feel like "exes." For example, Janelle referred to herself as "Miss Ex-SZTV" and Charlie said he still had "sort of a hangover" from his work life, indicating that part of his past work identity lingered. Despite their attempts to shift away from past work-related identities and/or to sustain them, they got stuck in between past and future identities, with nothing but "ex" to claim, leaving them with an identity void.

Most of the people Ebaugh (1988) interviewed also experienced what she called a "vacuum identity"—a concept that is distinct from, but similar to, identity void. Vacuum identity was a "last glance backward" at the role people were preparing to leave (ibid., 143), and was often a necessary stage in being certain they were ready to leave their role. During vacuum identity, people felt lost, as if their identities were "suspended" (145). The vacuum identity often occurred during what Ebaugh called the "turning point," or the final decision (after much deliberation) to go ahead and exit a role. This temporary stage routinely occurred for most people who were making transitions as they moved toward the role they were considering. In contrast, identity void usually took more time to develop, seemed to last longer than the temporary stages documented by Ebaugh (1988), and usually happened after people tried unsuccessfully to perform identity work. Rather than being an expected, routine stage in moving from one role to another, identity void seemed more like a place people got stuck, without a clear idea of how to get out, when repeated identity work attempts had been unsuccessful (although some people, like Nancy, eventually moved out of identity void).

Not everyone's identities are threatened after losing a job. In fact, some people exhibit remarkably resilient identities in the face of job loss. Appendix B explores this, and examines alternative explanations for distress after losing a job, such as financial problems, family emergencies, and mental illness that existed before being laid off or fired.

Chapter 9 brings the book to a close by summarizing what these many people who selflessly shared their stories can teach us about the connections between job loss, identity, and mental health.

9

Conclusion

This final chapter of the book examines the stories you read earlier, in the context of three themes: historical context; cultural discourse and the meaning of work; and social institutions and status. The chapter also explores the overall importance of identity (especially identity mismatches) for mental health after losing a job, as well as the relative importance of subjective and objective factors in this process.

Historical Context and Job Loss

I undertook this research shortly after the official end of the Great Recession—the toughest economic period the United States has experienced since the Great Depression (Grusky et al. 2011a). Between World War II and the mid-1970s, jobs were generally secure. But since the 1970s, employment in the United States has become increasingly unstable and precarious as the burden of risk in jobs shifted from the employer to the employee. Decades ago layoffs were generally confined to the secondary labor market, which was composed of very low paid, sometimes temporary jobs that required little skill or training and that supported more stable, permanent jobs. But today technological advances and deregulated trade have enabled companies to lay off white-collar U.S. workers in the primary labor market and send those jobs around the globe, replace those workers with machinery or computers, or relegate those positions to temporary work. This means that even mid-level managerial jobs in the United States are now prone to elimination, leaving middle-class people to experience unprecedented financial instability (Kalleberg 2009).

The Great Recession further stressed this already volatile situation, and ultimately became the straw that broke the camel's (or the U.S. economy's) back. During the Great Recession, middle-class people suffered disproportionately (Wolff et al. 2011). For example, the managerial unemployment rate doubled between March 2008 and March 2010 (Hout, Levanon, and Cumberworth 2011, 72), and during the aftermath of the Great Recession (in March 2010) college-educated people were unemployed for an average of eight-and-a-half months—one week longer than the average unemployment duration for high school graduates during the same month (ibid., 74).

Prior to the Great Recession, banking deregulation had tightly intertwined the housing and mortgage industries with the overall economy. This led to a nationwide economic collapse once the housing bubble burst (Fligstein and Goldstein 2011, 23; Krugman 2012). At that point, companies and individuals who had borrowed heavily could no longer rely on high property values to serve as a buffer against their debt, and they dramatically reduced their spending in order to pay down that debt. The sudden sharp decrease in spending sent the American economy into a free fall, which was exacerbated as companies began to lay off employees (Krugman 2012, 126).

The significance of housing for the Great Recession is well represented in the kinds of people who participated in my study. Before they lost their jobs, several participants had worked in banks and mortgage companies—parts of the financial sector that took an especially strong economic hit (Hout et al. 2011, 78). Additionally, several people in my study could no longer afford to pay their mortgages, were foreclosed upon, lost their homes, or could not afford rent (and so had to live with relatives). This "double whammy" of unemployment and housing problems may have been extremely confusing and upsetting to well-educated people who had always had good jobs, thought they could rely on their high education levels for employment security, and believed they were taking the right steps to wealth management by investing in homes and borrowing against their home equity to make more purchases.

Because mid-level professional jobs typically require a four-year college degree (or even a graduate or professional degree), these former employees may have seen themselves as immune to job loss because of their credentials and because of where they lived. My study was centered geographically in and around one of the most highly educated and wealthiest urban areas in the country. Additionally, the era in which my participants grew up may have affected their ideas about the likelihood of losing a job. Many of my participants were old enough to recall the era of lifetime employment, as they may have watched a parent spend an entire career with one loyal employer. For all these reasons, they were probably unprepared for the economic and psychological shock that awaited them, even though they may have been aware that jobs today are unstable.

With the advent of the Great Recession, highly educated workers experienced heightened unemployment (Grusky et al. 2011a, 12–13). As mid-level white-collar jobs in the United States have begun to disappear, most new positions are either in the low-wage service sector (for example, food service worker) or are well-paid positions requiring extremely high education levels and specialization (for example, neuropsychologist) (Hout et al. 2011). Neither of these options fit well with former mid-level workers' skills and expectations.

Today's unprecedented economic and historical context may cause people who are in the middle to later stages of their careers to encounter problems they never thought they would have to deal with. Although they may not expect to lose their jobs, they may be aware that they cannot simply get another job quickly, and may thereby resort to short-term individualistic identity work strategies that help them get by until they find work.

There are many parallels between the experiences of the middle-class people in this book and those of working-class unemployed people who bore the brunt of earlier workplace transformations. Prior to the 1980s, General Motors (GM) autoworkers in Linden, New Jersey (Milkman 1997), Chrysler autoworkers in Kenosha, Wisconsin (Dudley 1997 [1994]), and steel mill employees in southeastern Chicago (Walley 2013, 7) had obtained high-paying factory positions prior to the 1980s without a college degree during a postwar era of economic prosperity. During that time there were good jobs available for people who had little formal education, as long as they were ready to work hard. The widespread availability of jobs like these left them with no reason to expect that these jobs would vanish or someday pay low wages.

These workers had done what they thought they were supposed to do—work hard to make a good living—and they expected their prosperity to continue as long as they did so (Dudley 1997 [1994]; Milkman 1997). But by the 1980s, the idea that hard work was enough was no longer a reality. As technology made it possible to replace people with machines and outsource jobs to locations outside the United States, as unions weakened, and as demand shifted to smaller, more fuel-efficient car models, employees were offered buyouts (in other words, paid to leave) (Milkman 1997). Deindustrialization also led to more than 100,000 layoffs in the Chicago steel mills (Walley 2013). These former employees did not expect the shock of losing the job stability, prosperity (Milkman 1997; Walley 2013), and sense of community (Walley 2013, 157–158) they thought would continue forever.

Although only a few of the former GM workers actually became unemployed (most continued to work either at GM or at other companies in lower-level positions), their standard of living was drastically reduced. Many of the GM workers had not found a great deal of meaning in their work; instead, they were there because they made good money. But the company's reorganization left them with limited low-paying options that pushed them out of a middle-class lifestyle (Milkman 1997). Nevertheless, as demonstrated by some of the steelworkers and ex-Chrysler employees whose identities were at least partially based on their occupations, individual and community identities tied to these working-class jobs were threatened by deindustrialization (Dudley 1997 [1994]; Walley 2013, 157–158). Some people managed to continue to identify with their jobs (Walley 2013, 74). Others suffered emotionally, in part because they lost their work-related identities (Dudley 1997 [1994]; Walley 2013). In all cases, the specific historical era, geographical location, and cultural expectations influenced how they felt about losing their jobs and/or the middle-class lifestyles they had once been able to afford. That era offered few options for regaining what employees had valued in their work because most of them had little formal education. The shock of downward mobility was strong for former factory workers who could no longer count on what they had always assumed was part of the social contract—hard work for good pay (Dudley 1997 [1994]; Milkman 1997; Walley 2013).

GM autoworkers (as well as K'Meyer and Hart's [2009, 138] working-class participants) knew by the mid-1990s that "they cannot simply walk away from the credentialist standards that are applied to everyone in this society" (Dudley 1997 [1994], 181). But the power of those same educational standards today may be weaker than my study participants grew up believing. At one time, college degrees may have practically guaranteed employment, leading to a perceived "degree guarantee." But laws and regulations have continued to move in favor of employer flexibility (Kalleberg 2009), which has essentially made this guarantee null and void.

In the past, factory workers who thought hard work guaranteed job stability and good money were shocked when that ceased being the case. Similarly, the change in the degree guarantee leaves middle-class professionals stunned at how quickly they can lose a job and how long they can remain unemployed—issues they thought they would never have to deal with because they had degrees. Most of the people in my sample were very highly educated, but that did not prevent them from losing their jobs. Like many Americans, they probably saw their degrees as "badges of ability" (Dudley 1997 [1994], 181) that validated their worth. As time passed with no results to show from their job search efforts, they may have begun to realize that their degrees no longer guaranteed employment or secure work-based identities. Like the factory workers earlier in history, the people who spoke with me had done what they probably thought they were supposed to do, but did not receive the rewards they had likely been taught would be attached to their efforts. The social contract surrounding work had once again been redefined.

Cultural Discourse and the Meaning of Work

The way in which we think about work is couched in specific historical contexts (Walkerdine 2006). As today's white-collar jobs become increasingly obsolete in the United States, do middle-class workers adapt to this new structural situation by no longer expecting continuous, stable middle-class employment? This certainly did not happen for middle-class unemployed people during the 1980s, who saw unemployment as an individual, personal failing. Nor did it happen with former blue-collar Chrysler autoworkers. Although they experienced a change in their pay and the availability of the types of jobs they had always done, their values and expectations about work and its meaning remained the same (Dudley 1997 [1994], 176). It did not happen for laid-off air traffic controllers in the 1980s either. Rather, they transferred the blame to the government while taking on proud collective work-related identities and resisting others' control of them through labor strikes (Newman 1999 [1988]).

Carrie Lane's (2011) work on unemployed middle-class professionals contrasts with this; they certainly appeared to adapt their values and identities to an unstable job market by expecting to be "companies of one." And so did some of Tracy E. K'Meyer and Joy L. Hart's (2009) working-class participants at International Harvester and Johnson Controls. They believed the absence of job security in the 1980s and 1990s meant they had only themselves to rely upon. But similar to other authors' results (for example, Ezzy 2001; Newman 1999 [1988]; Sharone 2013a), the expectations and values of the middle-class people I spoke with stayed the same, despite their awareness of a changing economy. Even though most middle-class people recognize that the availability of mid-level white-collar jobs is decreasing, and know intellectually that they are vulnerable to outsourcing and layoffs, in their hearts they may still expect that educated middle-class people will be immune to unemployment (and certainly to long-term unemployment). In other words, simple awareness of a changing job market may not lead people to immediately abandon the values and expectations that had been cultivated throughout their lifetimes. In fact, during the time my mostly older Generation X and Baby Boomer participants were entering the workforce, educational credentials were touted as the mainstream value on which hiring, promotion, and a middle-class lifestyle would be determined (Dudley 1997 [1994], 177–178).

If today's cultural discourse still holds that our identities should be centered in work, the current historical circumstances may be pushing us to be more adaptable in our work-related identities. Perhaps, as Lane (2011) so skillfully shows, people may develop a more flexible sense of the "self as the company"—or a "company of one"—rather than basing their identities strongly on a role within a conventional company. It may also be that Millennials (Lancaster and Stillman 2010; Pahl 1995, 194) and the upcoming Generation Z will feel less of a need to base their identities as strongly in work because they highly value a work-life balance. However, most authors (for example, Ezzy 2001 and Sharone 2013a) show that, despite increasing economic and employment instability, work remains central to most people's identities. Perhaps this is because the identities that form earlier in life are the ones that become "sedimented" (Walkerdine 2006, 34–35). We tend to think of them as our "true" identities, making it harder to change in any way that challenges them (ibid., 37). This implies that it could be very hard to enter into a new occupational identity, and that the loss of a former work-related identity could leave people with poor mental health unless they find another similar job or find some way to psychologically sustain their former worker identity.

My study hints that as a society, we may be at a "halfway" transitional point—a point between two extremes: work being central to who we are and work becoming less relevant to who we are. Middle-aged people in this study still based a great deal of their identities on work, but in the short term their identities were relatively malleable. Work is important, but perhaps we have, out of necessity, developed the flexibility to move in and out of work-based identities, sometimes shifting, sometimes sustaining. However, our ability to do so depends on what is available to us historically, as well as through our statuses, access to social institutions, and feedback.

Although the participants in my study used creative, agentic approaches to quickly repair their identities and salvage their mental health, their strategies were individualistic, perhaps in part because middle-class unemployed people are especially likely to blame themselves and become confused about their identities (Newman 1999 [1988], 94). Therefore, although these strategies may work for a short time, I question their long-term success because they do not ultimately address the structural causes behind the problems. Although Lane's (2011) IT professionals reframed themselves as entrepreneurs in a "company of one," these largely individualistic strategies to manage identities (and, in Lane's [2011] case, finances and careers) may be destined to fail in the long run.

Social Institutions, Status, and Job Loss

As Douglas Ezzy (2001) emphasized, the way people interpret and talk about losing a job is important. However, as he also pointed out, this subjective side of things can only go so far in coping with identity threats and mental health problems in the face of unemployment. *Job Loss, Identity, and Mental Health* takes this proposition a step further by uncovering specific ways in which subjective ideas and choices are shaped by social structure and interaction. Not everyone can simply repair their identities through sheer will as (at first glance) seems to be the case with Lane's professionals. A combination of social status, access to institutions, and receipt of identity-affirming feedback—all of which occur in a specific historical context—are critical to how people try to repair their identities and to the course of their mental health after losing a job.

In contrast to the more collectively oriented workplace or industry-based identities of many factory workers (for example, the "union man") (Dudley 1997

[1994], 17, 20–26, 114; Walley 2013, 157–158), the middle-class people I spoke to typically framed their work-related identities in an individual fashion, not in relation to others in their companies or professions. Middle-class people often work autonomously and see their work as an expression of personal fulfillment rather than just a way to make money, as they are "trained to see identity as a matter of occupation" (Newman 1999 [1988], 93). This may lead to a more individualistic mind-set toward work identities. When a middle-class person loses a job and does not obtain a new one quickly, he may revert to seeing himself as a personal failure rather than one of a group of people who has been affected by a structural event (Sharone 2013a). This was borne out by my participants who rarely used the language of social structure when they spoke about losing their jobs (or obtaining new ones).

If you blame yourself for being unemployed, you also make it your responsibility to "pick yourself up by your bootstraps" and find work. In Lane's (2011) study, unemployed people internalized individualism and saw finding work as an individual matter, something to be dealt with by personally finding clients for themselves. Although they recognized the structural changes in the U.S. economy, they rarely suggested structural or policy solutions to unemployment. Similarly, in Marianne Cooper's (2014) study, unemployed people attempt to craft individual strategies to manage the impact of their job loss on their lives. However, their social class (a social status) influenced the strategies they used. My study builds on these important works by showing how people take individualistic strategies toward their identity work after losing their jobs, often without consciously realizing the strong role that statuses and social institutions play in shaping the specific strategies "chosen."

This book shows that people often try to respond actively and creatively to crises by using identity work, but that their likelihood of success is often enhanced or constrained by structural factors, namely, social institutions and the cultural meaning of various statuses. In other words, not all identity work is equally available to everyone. Figure 1 shows how the identity work process related to social institutions and statuses for the people who spoke with me.

When people's identities were threatened, they often tried first to shift to another identity, as scholars have theorized as a possibility (Gecas and Seff 1990; Schöb 2013; Sieber 1974). Status and access to social institutions were critical to these attempts, as Sheldon Stryker (1980) and Leonard Pearlin (1999) would likely have predicted. Shifting usually required involvement in a social institution (for example, family) that provided a role (such as mother) that they felt matched society's expectations for a specific status that they held (such as woman).

If people could not shift, they often gravitated toward sustaining their work-related identities. To succeed in doing so, they usually needed a social institution that provided a structured setting where they could interact with

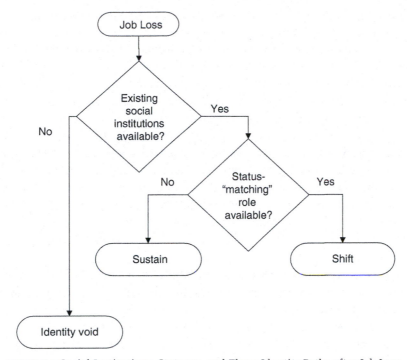

FIGURE 1 Social Institutions, Statuses, and Three Identity Paths after Job Loss.

others in a "workplace-like" way and receive identity-affirming feedback from those people. Lane's (2011) work implies that holding an identity attached to a company or workplace community may no longer be very important. However, her work also provides a good illustration of the continuing importance of occupational identity by describing how unemployed former high-tech workers helped bolster their professional identities via job seekers' networking groups. These groups were structured similarly to the business world and provided unemployed people with opportunities to continue to behave like professionals and leaders (Lane 2011, 90–91, 97–99). Ofer Sharone (2013a, 22–23, 27) shows a similar effect for unemployed people in job seekers' groups in the United States. Although analyzing these identity work processes was not the focus of their studies, it was central to my own work which builds on theirs by uncovering the conditions under which sustaining and shifting did or did not occur, as well as the emotional results of successful sustaining and shifting. My work also shows that if both shifting and sustaining failed, people often experienced a distressing identity void that seriously compromised their mental health.

Middle-class people are used to having a relatively large amount of control in the workplace. According to Gordon E. O'Brien, this sense of control carries over into unemployment, which helps middle-class people maintain positive mental health (O'Brien 1985). In theory, this should carry over into the way unemployed white-collar workers manage the identity aspects of losing a job. However, not all of my participants exhibited a strong sense of control in how they dealt with identity threats, perhaps because many aspects of personal control are based in locations in the social structure other than social class. For example, despite her high education level, Cindy felt like she had little control in sustaining her work-related identities because of her age. Her older age in a field that valued youth made it all but impossible to sustain her travel executive identity. The wide variety of social statuses that people hold, as well as their connection to identities, appears to have been downplayed in many of the theories that emphasize personal control as key to mental health after losing a job.

I propose that middle-class Baby Boomers and members of Generation X may still expect to avoid unemployment. Therefore, if they lose their jobs, their sense of control may decrease rather than staying strong and helping them cope with job loss, as O'Brien (1985) proposed. This means that aspects of social status, such as gender, race, or age, may come to the forefront when trying to manage identity-related distress after losing a job. For example, even though both Paul and Ruth were middle class and were involved in the same job networking group, Paul's status as a white male probably helped him be taken seriously as a leader and a "marketing man," whereas Ruth's statuses (African American woman) may have lessened the likelihood that others would react to her as a leader. This helped Paul sustain his employee identity (and strengthened his mental health), whereas Ruth did not have this avenue for sustaining. Fortunately, she found another way to do so—by reframing the library as a "workplace" and interacting with others there as if she was working.

My study also shows that these statuses do not necessarily play out in the expected ways (such as higher statuses automatically leading to more power, control, and options). For example, being male typically confers more power than being female, but it did not seem to help Charlie, who felt "impotent" without a job. Although finding new aspects of yourself (similar to "shifting" in this book) may help you cope with job loss (Walkerdine 2006, 36–37), some statuses make it easier or harder to do so, in certain social institutions. According to Charlie, being male made it impossible for him to shift to being a stay-at-home father, even though he had young children and his wife was working full-time. In contrast, Charlotte was able to shift to an emphasis on a full-time mother identity, despite having been the sole breadwinner for her family of four for years, and she believed others reacted positively to this because she was female. My study adds to the growing body of work on unemployment, status, and mental health by showing that the effects of statuses on coping and mental health are contextualized. It would be incorrect to simply assume that higher statuses always mean greater control over identity after job loss, and thus result in better mental health.

Furthermore, some middle-class people are not involved in social institutions that could boost their sense of control over their identities. But some are and, like the role of status in coping strategies, my study shows that this can play out in unexpected ways. For example, although Marsha did not have much money, she was fortunate to have access to organizations such as an EMT class that helped her sustain her worker identity and boost her mental health. In contrast, even though Charlie was in a very strong financial position, he could not sustain his worker identity because he had no links to organizations that gave him a role similar to his old position, and he could not maintain productive ties to former coworkers or his old organization. His mental health suffered as he fell into identity void.

The experiences of the people in this book show that the meaning of work to identity is not unidimensional, nor is it based only in the job itself. The job ties to many other aspects of identity, including our social statuses, others' feedback, and how we see ourselves across time. Although these topics have been touched upon in many studies of unemployment (for example, Cooper's [2014] focus on social status), their ties to identities have not been systematically explored by past research. *Job Loss, Identity, and Mental Health* is an attempt to take a step in that direction.

Finally, various theorists (for example, Jahoda 1981, 1982; Warr 1987) have proposed that work is central to how we define our identities and maintain good mental health. However, as Ezzy (2001) argues, these more psychological accounts of the relationship between work, identity, and mental health often neglect the historical context in which workplace relationships and employment options are embedded, as well as the subjective and active nature of how we think about and negotiate who we are in relation to work.

Although Marie Jahoda (1981, 1982) and Peter Warr (1987) initially suggested that the institutional engagement required for mental health occurs almost exclusively through the workplace, my work calls this into question (as Jahoda herself began to do in 1984 and 1986). Some of the people who told me their stories did not need an actual workplace in order to sustain their employee identities. Furthermore, it was not just the objective existence of an institution (workplace or other) that helped people sustain or shift, but rather their subjective interpretations of their roles in these institutions as they related to their social statuses (for example, Charlie's inability to shift into a father role in his family because of his definitions of "man" and "father"). This challenges the conventional approach to the meaning of work (and some theories of identity that emphasize institutional roles, such as Stryker 1980) in which inhabiting an organizational role within a workplace is a prerequisite for feeling like a worker. The subjective ways people thought about their worker identities were more creative than perhaps previously conceived, given that they did not necessarily need an actual, physical workplace or official position in order to sustain their worker identities.

This does not, however, mean that social institutions and social interactions were irrelevant to identity construction. Most of the people in my study did require some structural support (such as Ruth's use of the public library as a "workplace") and/or feedback (such as Paul being told he was a "marketing man") in order to sustain their worker identities. Without these supportive institutions and interactions, those same valiant efforts to hold on to treasured identities usually failed. Although the workplace is certainly one possible place to affirm your worker identity, other institutions and identity-affirming feedback may provide options for flexibly sustaining that identity after losing your job. The accounts in this book show that even though shifting and sustaining relied heavily on subjective interpretations, the ability to do so was ultimately structural in nature.

Identity as an Important Factor in Unemployment Research

Perhaps the single most compelling finding of this study is that identity was often critical to people's emotional experiences when they lost jobs. When they were told they were not the person they thought they were (feedback mismatches), when they felt like they were not the person they used to be (time mismatches), and when they felt like who they were did not match expectations for their gender, age, or other statuses (status mismatches), their identities were threatened and they felt depressed, anxious, and angry. These experiences were largely initiated by structural factors, such as the Great Recession and global competition, which led to layoffs and left people's identities in flux.

Job Loss, Identity, and Mental Health suggests that identity, and specifically identity mismatches, may be more important to the stress process and mental health than is typically recognized. It helps address calls for research that links identity change to mental health (Thoits 1999) and to role loss or gain (Burke and Stets 2009), especially when the loss is involuntary (Cantwell and Martiny 2010). It unearths explanations for distress that might go unnoticed in existing models of stress and coping that do not address identity, such as the Stress Process Model (Pearlin et al. 1981). This book also emphasizes the importance of combining David A. Snow and Leon Anderson's (1987) concept of identity work with theories involving identity mismatches or discrepancies (for example, Higgins 1987; Marcussen 2006), and with Identity Theory's (Burke 1991) focus on feedback and distress.

This book also points out that cultural meanings and subjective perceptions are important for how we experience distress, and for the behaviors we "choose." As the Stress Process Model (Pearlin et al. 1981) proposes, objective status, such as social class location, influences the coping options available to us when we lose jobs (Cooper 2014). But as Cooper skillfully illustrates, objective and subjective aspects of status are interrelated, and should be co-examined. *Job Loss, Identity, and Mental Health* presents several ways that social institutions and statuses connect to subjective identity processes, including those involving interactions, feedback, and perceived meaning. The Stress Process Model (Pearlin 1999) emphasizes the objective aspects of status. Stryker (1980) highlights objective structure as well by focusing on the importance of social institutions and the number of connections we have within them. But Peter J. Burke's (1991) Identity Theory, as well as Identity Discrepancy Theory (Higgins 1987; Marcussen 2006), highlights subjective experiences involving feedback, social institutions, and other aspects of structure and interaction. This book illustrates that making more explicit connections between identity theories and the Stress Process Model could enhance our understanding of distress that occurs after losing a job or other roles. In reality, both subjective and objective factors are important to identity and to mental health after losing a job. To ignore either one leaves our insight into distress, as well as our abilities to solve mental health problems at the societal and individual levels, incomplete.

Identity is not just a theoretical concept separate from real-life consequences. It can have real and powerful effects on mental health. The Stress Process Model (Pearlin et al. 1981) highlights material resources and social support as important avenues for coping. The people in this book show that identity work may offer yet another avenue for coping with stress. We want to feel good about ourselves (Rosenberg 1986 [1979]; Tajfel 1981) and we want to feel like we are generally the same people over time (Burke 1991; Rosenberg 1986 [1979]; Swann 1983). Identity work may help us achieve these things, if only temporarily.

After losing a job, we may head to a familiar well-worn path, starting with parts of ourselves that we believe are solid. Can we start with a status (such as female) and increase our identification with a role that "matches" it (such as mother), gaining approval from others and positive feedback for what women are "supposed" to do? If so, we may shift, and feel better about ourselves by increasing our self-esteem (Rosenberg 1986 [1979]; Tajfel 1981) and getting identity-affirming feedback that reduces distress (Burke 1991). After losing a job, can we manage to still feel like the same person we were before? Can we find ways to still subjectively see ourselves as employees? If so, we may successfully sustain our work-related identities, maintain identity consistency, and reduce distress (Burke 1991; Rosenberg 1986 [1979]; Swann 1983). Although it is unclear how long the mental health benefits of shifting and sustaining last, it appears that in the short term they may help people temporarily cope with extremely stressful role losses, and can therefore improve mental health.

This book supports classic theories of the relationship between self and society, and like Lane's (2011) and Sharone's (2013a, 2013b) work, shows how structure and social institutions influence our behaviors and self-concept after losing a job. It also shows that identity and mental health are processes, not static conditions. Future research would benefit from conceiving of these concepts as dynamic. Identity is a fluid performance; during it, we create and confirm who we are by interacting with others (Goffman 1959). When people's routines are disrupted, they try to rebuild their shattered sense of reality (and identities) by grounding them in social institutions (Berger and Luckmann 1966), and by interacting with others in the ways that are expected for their roles and statuses.

Job Loss, Identity, and Mental Health also supports the idea that people may use agency to creatively respond to identity challenges by taking on specific roles (Mead 1934). As they do so, they think about the generalized other (ibid.). For example, Janelle and Amber preemptively worried about society's suspicion of college-educated food service employees. People also think about how specific others might view their unemployment, as when Ken worried that if his neighbors knew he was unemployed, they might wonder what he did wrong. Like some of the people Ezzy (2001) studied, the people in this book used past and possible future selves to motivate themselves and reduce their distress. They also sometimes relied on their past role socialization to help them with their identity work. For example, Marcus already volunteered as a coach and so he knew how to perform that role. This helped him more easily shift to emphasize his coach identity more strongly after he lost his job. Finally, when people were aware of and agreed with others' negative judgment of a specific role (Rosenberg 1986 [1979]), such as the "unemployed" role, they avoided it as an identity because it would likely harm their self-esteem (ibid.). They made efforts to limit that harm by shifting their emphasis to other identities or subjectively sustaining their work-related identities and, at least in the short term, this helped them cope with the emotional pain of their job loss.

Losing a job can be devastating. It can ruin you financially, strain your relationships, harm your physical and mental health, and threaten your identity. In a culture that equates self-worth with what we are paid to do, unemployment can lead people to feel like pariahs. In an increasingly competitive global economy, during a time when job security is extremely hard to come by, and in an era in which risk is increasingly being shifted from the employer to the employee (Kalleberg 2009), the number of people who will experience the many hardships brought on by losing a job will likely only increase. It may be you who faces it next. It may be me. As I complete this book, the university that I joined just two years ago is undergoing historically large budget cuts, and some of our state system's other campuses have begun to lay off faculty. It is up to all of us to push for the large-scale social changes that will help to ensure job security and a good standard of living for everyone.

APPENDIX A: METHODOLOGY

In chapter 1, I provided a broad description of my methodology. This appendix gives additional detail on the methods I used to collect and analyze the data on which this book is based. Between the summers of 2010 and 2011, I conducted forty-eight semi-structured in-depth interviews at two points in time (about three months apart) with unemployed people who were once in middle-class professions. I interviewed twenty-five people for the first wave of the study, and twenty-three of those same people for the second wave (92 percent retention rate). I supplemented these interviews by observing groups and specific participants. I obtained Institutional Review Board approval prior to beginning the study, and obtained informed consent before conducting each interview and each observation that involved a specific participant.

As noted in chapter 1, I recruited participants at job seekers' networking groups and a local unemployment office, as well as through personal contacts, snowball sampling, and referrals from personnel recruiters. I entered all participants into a drawing for $25 Target gift certificates. I randomly selected one winner from the first round of interviews, one from the second round, and one from the observations of specific participants.

I screened prospective participants to ensure that they: (1) were currently unemployed or underemployed; (2) had lost their jobs within the past six months (median duration of unemployment at first interview = three months); (3) had formerly worked in white-collar professions that typically require a college degree; (4) had been regularly employed for at least thirty-five hours per week before losing their jobs; (5) were age thirty or older; (6) were not considering retirement at the time I screened them; and (7) had rated their past job as important to their identities, either at the time of screening or in the past.

My sample contained women and men, as well as African American and white participants, between the ages of thirty and sixty-three (median age = 52). All participants had at least some college education, and all but three participants had a bachelor's degree or higher. Most participants' pretax household incomes were higher than $100,000 before losing their jobs. Participants' family structures and the circumstances of losing their jobs (for example, being fired versus being laid off) varied, but all participants said they lost their jobs involuntarily. Sample details are documented in tables A1 and A2.

The questions I asked participants in the first interview centered on several themes: their typical daily experiences in their last job; the process that led to job loss; what job loss was like for them; the hardest part of job loss; what their gender, age, and education meant to them; job search activity; and emotions, distress, and distress relief.

To the greatest extent possible, I allowed themes involving identity to spontaneously emerge, and I usually waited up to one hour before asking identity-specific questions. When identity was important to the participants, they usually brought it up on their own within thirty minutes into the interview. When inquiring about identity, I asked whether they felt like the same person they were before they lost their jobs, whether they felt like they were the person they should be and wanted to be, what it felt like to be a man/woman, forty-year-old, etc., without a job, and how other people had treated them since they lost their jobs. I also asked specifically about their social support, financial situation, whether any other major events had occurred recently in their lives, and whether they had ever been diagnosed with mental health problems.

At the second interview, I reminded participants of the date of their last interview and asked them to update me on what had happened in their lives since then. I focused on questions that reflected the most important emergent themes for each specific participant, as indicated by my analysis of the first set of interviews. I explored any new themes that participants said were important, as well as thematic connections between interviews. In the second interview, I often asked many of the same questions I had asked at the first interview in order to determine if objective or subjective changes had taken place over time. I focused primarily on changes versus consistency in: distress; identities; coping; involvement in social institutions, roles, and activities; and the job search. At the second interview, I also presented each participant with verbatim quotes from the first interview that related to themes I had identified from the first batch of interviews, or had seemed particularly emotionally powerful for the participant at the first interview, and I asked participants to tell me where each of them now stood on that quote. This allowed me to evaluate changes over time in participants' perceptions. A full interview guide is available upon request.

During my observations at two job seekers' networking groups, as well as at the state unemployment office, I paid special attention to: interactions among participants; participants' self-presentation; the general organizational "mood"; participants' and leaders' topics of concern and attitudes toward unemployment, job seeking, and coping with job loss; connections between

Summary Statistics for Sample

	Percentage
Gender	
Female	60
Male	40
Race	
White	64
African American	36
Age (median = 52)	
30–44	24
45–54	32
55–63	44
Marital status	
Married	48
Divorced	32
Single	16
Separated	4
Has children	
Yes	64
No	36
Highest level of education	
Professional degree (PhD, JD, etc.)	8
Master's degree	24
Bachelor's degree	56
Some college (but no degree)	12
Household income before job loss (pre-tax)	
$100,000+	56
$50,001–99,999	36
$50,000 or less	8
Household's sole breadwinner	
Yes	52
No	48
Unemployment duration at first interview (median = 3 months)	
2 weeks to 1 month	16
>1 month to 3 months	44
>3 months to <6 months	12
6+ months	28
Has experienced job loss before	
Yes	76
No	24
Method of job loss	
Laid off	64
Fired for cause	28
Resigned because anticipated being fired	8
Received advance notice of job loss	
Yes	36
No	56
Other (N/A—resigned)	8
Working for pay by time of second interview	
Yes	28
No	64
Unknown (no second interview available)	8
Underemployed at time of second interview (of the 7 working)	
Yes—underemployed	43
No—working at level appropriate to education	57

TABLE A2
Description of Participant Characteristics

Pseudonym	Gender	Race	Age (time 1)	Former occupation/field	Unemployment duration in months (time 1)	Method of job loss
Marsha	Female	White	41	Middle manager/public safety	1	Fired
Paul	Male	White	56	General manager/publishing	3	Laid off
Uma	Female	White	62	Systems engineer/government defense contractor	11	Laid off
Ken	Male	White	57	CEO/nonprofit organization	1 ½	Fired
Theo	Male	White	60	Senior programmer and software engineer/small private tech company	2 ½	Fired
Minnie	Female	White	63	Staff editor/publishing	2	Fired
Marcus	Male	African American	47	Operations director/environmental technology industry	7	Laid off
Charlotte	Female	White	41	CFO/nonprofit organization	4 ½	Resigned—anticipated getting fired
Amber	Female	White	30	Staff editor and reporter/local newspaper	2 weeks	Fired
Saul	Male	African American	48	Senior mortgage banker/housing lender	6	Laid off
Corey	Female	African American	46	Director of affirmative action programs/education	2 ½	Resigned—anticipated getting fired

Name	Gender	Race	Age	Position		Status
Charlie	Male	White	62	Director of training/nonprofit organization	3	Laid off
Foluke	Female	African American (from Liberia)	52	Contracts administrator/pharmaceutical industry	6 ½	Laid off
Connie	Female	African American	56	Director of human resources/government contractor	3	Fired
Cindy	Female	White	62	Account executive/travel industry	2 ½	Resigned—anticipated getting fired
Norman	Male	White	51	Senior financial manager/trade association	4 ½	Laid off
Skip	Male	White	53	Vice president/banking	3	Laid off
Janelle	Female	African American	39	Online programming manager/TV station	6	Laid off
Margie	Female	White	57	Director of corporate business communications/mortgage lender	2	Laid off
Louie	Male	White	60	Area manager/small engineering company	1	Laid off
Ruth	Female	African American	43	Information analyst/government contractor	6	Laid off
Stanley	Male	African American	34	IT specialist/government contractor	1	Laid off
Nancy	Female	White	49	Marketing director/mortgage lender	3	Laid off
Kaci	Female	White	57	Health insurance manager/health insurance company	5 ½	Laid off
Lorna	Female	African American	51	Production supervisor/broadcast music and entertainment	6	Laid off

identities and work or unemployment; and positive or negative highly charged "flash point" topics or moments, including disagreements. I also conducted two observations with specific participants in environments they had suggested.

I made audio recordings of each interview, and I wrote and recorded field notes subsequent to each observation. Right after each interview, I also audio-taped my initial impressions of participants, themes from the study, and how both related to other interviews. I then transcribed all interviews verbatim, and summarized my field notes. I examined my transcripts and field notes to find recurring themes/patterns.

I approached this analysis with "anticipatory data reduction" in mind, and took a deductive, theory-based approach (Miles and Huberman 1994, 430). This is an ideal methodology when the goal is to examine many similar cases and when concepts of interest (such as identity work and discrepancies) are already well delineated (Miles and Huberman 1994). My analysis was case-focused and generalized. In other words, I examined topics within the context of partici-pants' lives and located general themes across cases that led to potential gen-eral truths (Weiss 1994). This was an ideal way to approach my analysis because it leads to typological description of categories (ibid.), such as shifting versus sustaining as types of identity work.

I wrote analytic memos to summarize ideas about each interview immedi-ately after the interview was completed (Miles and Huberman 1994), and took an iterative approach to data analysis, examining transcripts line-by-line mul-tiple times. In my first round of analysis, I began by coding for the themes I had identified from the literature. I also performed open coding to identify addi-tional themes (Esterberg 2002; Lofland et al. 2006), followed by focused coding to connect all the themes I had identified (Esterberg 2002; Lofland et al. 2006), and to ensure that I had accounted for both confirming and disconfirming evidence. I used ATLAS.ti 6 to assist with coding.

I used cross-case analytic procedures—primarily data matrices (Lofland et al. 2006; Miles and Huberman 1994)—in my analysis. I focused on finding simi-larities and variation between cases (Lofland et al. 2006; Miles and Huberman 1994). I used data matrices to cross-classify the key themes (such as identity mismatches, social statuses, involvement in social institutions, and distress level) by placing these themes in rows and columns, along with corresponding examples and quotes (Lofland et al. 2006). This helped me determine how the themes fit together, whether the "shape" of each case was similar to or different from others (Miles and Huberman 1994), and to create ideas about how the process unfolded—from unemployment to identity work to distress. In order to ensure validity, I continued to actively search for disconfirming evidence (Creswell and Clark 2007) using the methods noted above.

APPENDIX B: ADDITIONAL
CONSIDERATIONS

Although there are many facets to unemployment, I made conscious choices to emphasize the aspects discussed in previous chapters in order to maintain focus and keep within the scope of my research questions. Unfortunately, this leaves other intriguing ideas and experiences related to unemployment less fully explored, but they are worthy of research in their own right. This appendix is meant to answer some of the questions you may have had while reading the book, as well as to serve as a starting point for discussing important issues that were related to the book's topic but were outside the scope of my focus. I hope this section invites further conversations about these and other issues on the topics of job loss, identity, and mental health.

The experiences shared by the people in this book show how important identity is to mental health and the stress process. It affects the kinds of stresses we experience, as well as how we cope with those stresses. People may be very resilient in the face of adversity. They may actively use identity to repair the damage done by job loss and by doing so may improve their mental health.

Most people who spoke with me experienced identity threats, including feedback, time, and status mismatches. Of those who experienced these threats, almost half described them as the hardest part of unemployment. When their identities were threatened, they felt depressed, anxious, angry, and confused, and experienced low self-esteem. But many of them used identity work—shifting or sustaining—to cope with these threats and regain a sense of self. Statuses and access to social institutions influenced the success of their efforts to shift or sustain. When identity work failed, people often fell into identity void.

Large-scale structural forces in society affect our individual well-being. For example, a macro-level recession affects meso-level workplaces, resulting in layoffs that harm individuals. But not all people will experience these events similarly, nor will they all react to them in the same way. Some of the people I spoke with had highly resilient identities after losing their jobs; others did not. Furthermore, structural changes that lead to losing a job can trigger troubles not directly related to identity, such as major financial problems, that can also harm mental health. There may be other things going on in people's lives (unrelated to losing a job or to identity) that cause emotional pain, such as a death in the family or mental health problems that existed before job loss. This appendix explores these situations.

When Identities Were Not Threatened: "Just a Person without a Job—That's All"

Even though I had screened participants to make sure that their work was important to their identities (or had been before they lost their jobs), some people did not feel that losing their jobs had harmed their identities. For example, Theo, a divorced sixty-year-old white former computer software engineer who had been fired almost three months before I interviewed him, told me his identity was strong, and that losing his job had not changed who he was:

> I have a pretty strong, pretty solid core of my identity and I know who I am. I'm glad I am who I am. . . . I still have all these ideas. . . . I still have my computer system at home, my laptop, my desktop. I've got lots of good software tools, lots of good books. There's nothing other than time to prevent me from going right home and working on a client-server program. . . . I think of myself primarily as a learner, and next as a visionary . . . and those roles haven't changed at all. . . . I have so many other interests and projects on the fire, good ideas in my notebook [Theo sniffs], being out of work is just a blip.

Theo's mood during both interviews was positive, upbeat, and almost jolly. It was not that he was unconcerned about being unemployed, and it was not that he never felt upset by things, but losing his job simply did not affect his identity. His lifelong tendency to be, as he put it, a "nonconformist" and "a former hippie" may have strengthened his ability to shrug off how society might view a man without a job.

Uma, a married sixty-two-year-old white former systems engineer for a government contractor, also separated her identity and self-worth from her job. Uma was the sole participant who had been unemployed for longer than six months when I first interviewed her. Due to a miscommunication before the interview, I thought she had fit the six-month time frame, but she had actually been laid off eleven months before I interviewed her. Previous research (Sheeran and McCarthy 1990) implies that she should be highly distressed by being out of work for this length of time. But Uma was resilient and relatively positive. This may be because Uma was an exception to Americans' tendency to blame themselves when they are out of work (Sharone (2013a, 2013b). Rather, she was more like the laid-off blue-collar employees who blamed the government for their plight (K'Meyer and Hart 2009): "I see it as a failure of the federal government. . . . They didn't protect the jobs that we had in this country. They let them go away and they didn't care. . . . I feel betrayed by the politicians. I did my part. They didn't do their part. . . . I am the same person. . . . I like who I am. . . . I'm just a person without a job. That's all."

Although Uma told me she had felt anxious about whether she would get another job and that she sometimes felt down, these emotions were not about identity. They were more about money and the experiences of age discrimination while searching for work. Her principal emotion was anger at the government for the policies that had left her, a woman with two master's degrees and high-level technical expertise, in this position.

Connie, a fifty-six-year-old single African American woman, also had a highly resilient identity. She told me that losing her former job as a human resources director three months ago did not affect who she was or her self-worth. She attributed her attitude partially to the way her parents had raised her, and partially to a "bad fit" between herself and her former employer:

CONNIE: I was not gonna allow that experience to define me. . . . I was in the wrong environment and the wrong company. . . . I don't think that that two-year stint speaks to who I am and what I can do. I know that I bring a lotta value to the table, to any company, and I will not allow [the job loss experience] to be . . . me. I'm just not gonna allow it to be me. It's not who I am.

ME: Where do you think you get such a strong sense of feeling good about who you are?

CONNIE: My parents. . . . They've always said that you can do whatever you wanna do and that nothing should stop you. You stop yourself. . . . I think that's where I get it from. . . . It's like, Connie, you're gonna get through this. This too shall pass.

Race, Resilience, and Job-Seeking Experiences

African American women, like Connie, seemed to have particularly resilient identities. They typically attributed this to being brought up to believe in themselves and to realize that unjust things could happen to them simply because of their race. This awareness of potential discrimination may have ultimately strengthened their identities by helping them develop a strong self-esteem that could prevent emotional devastation from the negative things they could encounter.

For example, Corey, a forty-six-year-old divorced African American woman who had formerly been a director of affirmative action programs, struggled with threats to her identity, but rarely succumbed to any serious emotional distress because of them. She was aware of racial discrimination and described the "black tax" her parents had told her about when she was young: "[My parents] said, 'You have to study hard. You have to do the right thing. . . . Remember, the rules don't apply to you. You're always gonna get that extra tax.' We call it the black tax. . . . The rules don't apply to you. You cannot do the same thing as your counterparts do and get away with it. If you do that, it will become a felony. If they do it, it's a misdemeanor or a looking the other way. That's just the way it is."

African American women knew that race could affect their job searches. Corey described her race as being at "the forefront" of her job seeking experiences: "I always think that they're gonna think that automatically I screwed up because I am black. . . . [Race is at the] forefront for me. . . . I've literally in my lifetime had people say [at the in-person interview] 'I didn't know you were a black woman.' . . . I will have to explain [being unemployed] even more so because I am a woman of color."

She believed she had to present herself as better than her white counterparts when looking for work because of racial discrimination:

COREY: And so you have that in the back of your head. . . . They're gonna blame this on [race. They'll say] "Of course she's gonna give you substandard stuff because she's black."

ME: Do you internalize that as well, or no?

COREY: No. You get used to it, but, but that's why we work extra hard. . . . We always have to be 150 percent better in order to get to the same spot because people always come to the conclusion that we don't have what we need to before we get there. . . . [Corey uses a snobby, critical voice] "Where did you go to law school?" That's the question you get. Not [Corey uses a friendly and inquisitive voice] "Oh, where'd you get your degree?" [Instead I get] [Corey uses critical voice] "Where did you go? . . . How did you get in there?" . . . Sometimes people'll say stupid things like that. You'd be surprised.

Being African American could present challenges, but African American women often transformed adversity into strength. Even Janelle, who suffered the pain of identity void, thought about race in a way that helped her cope with the stress of unemployment. After my second interview with her was over and the tape recorder was off, she told me she wanted to show me something in her kitchen. As we entered, she showed me her collection of Aunt Jemima memorabilia—plaques, figurines, magnets, potholders, and poster ads—that she had been collecting since age sixteen. She told me that when she had hard days at SZTV, and now while she was unemployed, the women these images represented served as inspirations and sources of strength. She said that she knew they had had it much harder than she did, and if they could get by, then she also could get through anything.

When Distress Is Not about Identity

Many things other than identity can harm people's mental health. Because of this, when I asked people what it was like to be without work, I initially avoided bringing up identity to prevent bias, by seeing if people would bring it up themselves. Most people who brought up distress involving identity did so spontaneously, without my asking about it, within the first thirty minutes of the interview. Because the focus of my study was identity, if they did not bring it up after about one hour into the interview, I would ask them directly if losing their jobs had affected their identity. Usually, if they had not brought it up, they would say no and they would describe a little bit of detail about why it did not relate to identity. I would then move on to other topics that they had said were more relevant to them.

To ensure that I captured a variety of issues that could affect mental health (and not just identity), I asked people explicitly about their financial situations as well as whether they had recently experienced other negative or difficult events in their life. Some had undergone major financial problems or other personal crises such as deaths in the family, and these occurrences—not identity—caused their distress. Others were relatively financially stable or even well off, and/or had not had personal crises in their lives other than losing their jobs.

Although the topic of this book is how identity relates to job loss and mental health, it is critical to not lose sight of the material problems that job loss creates, and the extreme stress associated with financial difficulties. (For more thorough explorations of financial problems during unemployment, see Cooper 2014; K'Meyer and Hart 2009; and Newman 1999 [1988], among others.) For example, Stanley, a married thirty-four-year-old African American man who had worked in information technology but had been laid off one month before I interviewed him, said he felt like the same person he had always been, but that he felt his worst when "going through bills." He said the hardest part of unemployment was "just looking at my bank balance and just seein' it shrink and shrink and shrink and shrink and shrink. . . . It just takes the enjoyment outta life. . . . I'm not as happy as before, but I feel like basically the same person."

Foluke, a fifty-two-year-old African immigrant and divorced mother of three adult children, had been a contracts administrator before she was laid off. After being unemployed for ten months, she had to cancel our original date for a follow-up interview because her electricity had been turned off when she could not pay the bill. She had borrowed against her retirement account, and was trying to make sure her rent was always paid. She was living in fear of what could happen if she was unable to do so, and she turned to prayer to help her cope with this:

> I just been trying to pay my rent. . . . Remember when I told you
> about my electricity had been turned off? That was one of the telling

times. . . . I was saving it for rent. And if I had started taking monies out to pay this, pay that bill then I would have really been in serious trouble. . . . I'm really scared of that kind of situation. . . . I prayed about it. . . . I said, "Jehovah, if I take the money out—" I said, "But we can't be without lights. 'Cause we can't cook. We have to eat. . . ." So I realized I had to pay it.

Other people I spoke to who were depressed or anxious were more affected by personal crises happening in their lives—many of which had nothing to do with losing a job—than by identity threats. For example, the second time I interviewed Connie, her identity was still strong. But she arrived with dark circles under her puffy eyes, and began to cry right away when we sat down together at the library. The first thing she told me was "My father died," and she described the terminal cancer that had claimed him, and how this affected her mental state:

> As my father was dying those were some bad days. . . . I knew my father wasn't gonna live. . . . My father also was a "wonderful recipient" of Agent Orange 'cause he was in Vietnam. I wanted my father to be at peace. And I always questioned why he would have to be in so much pain, 'cause I thought that was wrong. . . . Right after the funeral that Saturday night, I remember sitting on the back deck and my mother was like, "What are you doing?" And I looked at her and I said, "Drinking. What else could I do?" . . . I had a bottle of this wine. . . . I put it in a paper bag. . . . I intentionally was sitting on the back deck and drinking out of the bottle in a paper bag. And I told mother, I said, "Daddy'd appreciate this one." And she kinda chuckled. She said, "Yeah. He would."

Some people had major financial and personal crises simultaneously. Kaci, a divorced (and now engaged) fifty-seven-year-old white woman who had been a health insurance manager before losing her job, had lived a troubled life and had overcome many obstacles, including a controlling ex-husband and a cancer diagnosis. During my first interview with Kaci five-and-a-half months after she lost her job, her fiancé had moved to a larger city several hours away for a job, and she had to sell her home because she needed that money to live on: "I have to sell my house which just upsets me tremendously 'cause I love where I live. . . . [My fiancé] got an apartment [in another city]. It's very expensive. So you add the expense of the apartment and our house. Unemployment . . . it's not enough to cover all the health insurance stuff. If it wasn't for him carrying the expenses— which it's killin' us now."

By the second time I interviewed Kaci, she had a large credit card bill and she and her fiancé had split up, leaving her to prepare her old house for its new residents:

Ended a relationship with [my fiancé]. Prep the house. . . . Can't find a job. . . . [Kaci sighs] Had like one or two weeks to find an apartment to move into . . . place to store the stuff. . . . Abandonment, in a sense of this should have been a collaborative effort because [my fiancé and I] own the house together. So that made me angry that I couldn't do anything about it. . . . No support. . . . I was up at 1:30 in the morning and staying up late. . . . And then I had hurt my back so I just tried to push through it all. . . . Very, very stressful.

Like Kaci, Connie was also very stressed about money. She spoke quietly in a scared voice that periodically cracked as she told me that the hardest part of being without a job was the possibility of losing her house:

CONNIE: My savings I think . . . next month, it's gone . . . and I'm scared . . . I'm gonna lose my [Connie's voice breaks and she moans the next word while crying] home.

ME: What's the scariest part right now?

CONNIE: [in a thin, frightened voice] Losin' my house. And where would I go? What would I do? . . . July's it. I'll make my mortgage payment for July, and then that's it.

For some people, personal or financial problems, not identity, were their biggest concerns. Still other people I spoke to had financial problems and/or personal crises, but identity threats added yet another source of distress. For example, both Marsha (see chapters 4 and 7) and Amber (see chapters 5 and 6) had financial problems that threatened their living situations. Marsha was even potentially facing home foreclosure while trying to support her two children as a single parent, but she still experienced a time mismatch. Clearly, identity threats can occur even when people are under serious and immediate financial stress.

Some people who were undergoing personal crises not directly related to losing their jobs also experienced identity threats. For example, Marcus (see chapter 6) had had several deaths in his family, Cindy's (see chapters 3 through 5) husband had recently been diagnosed with a serious health problem, and Paul (see chapter 7) was dealing with marital problems and a permanently disabled adult child. Yet all still also experienced the extra stress of threatened identities.

Ultimately, the existence or absence of financial hardship or personal crises did not relate to whether people experienced identity mismatches. It is possible that some experiences of severe financial or personal stresses, such as Foluke's electricity being turned off or Kaci's having to quickly sell a house and move out of it, take precedence over and mask identity threats. However, I have no evidence for this, and so I have chosen to take these participants' words at face value—that they did not experience identity threats.

Preexisting Mental Health Problems

In contrast to the idea that unemployment causes mental health problems, the rehabilitation approach (Tiffany, Cowan, and Tiffany 1970) proposes that mental health problems cause people to perform poorly at work and lose their jobs. In other words, the high rate of mental health problems among unemployed people is not caused by unemployment itself, but merely reflects the likelihood that people with mental health issues struggle to hold jobs.

For this reason, it was important to find out whether people in my study had struggled with mental health problems in their pasts. Sometimes, without my asking, people mentioned that they had once battled depression or other extreme moods, said they had sought counseling in the past, or even told me they had been clinically diagnosed with a mental illness. If they did not, at the end of the interview I asked if they had ever been diagnosed with a mental health problem. If they answered yes, I asked for details including the diagnosis, when it was made, how long they had experienced the problem, and information about treatment of the problem. Most people seemed very forthcoming about their experiences with mental health issues, when they had had them.

I tried to separate mental health issues that had existed before job loss from emotional pain brought on by identity threats after losing a job. A little more than one-quarter of the people I spoke with said they had been diagnosed with mental health problems in the past, including borderline personality disorder, bipolar disorder, depression, and anxiety. Most of them no longer suffered from those problems, or were managing them with therapy or medication. Most importantly, distress that came from identity threats was about equally likely for people who had a history of mental health diagnoses versus people who did not (71 percent versus 67 percent, respectively).

Furthermore, the people I spoke with were usually very clear in attributing specific emotions or types of distress to specific things, including feedback, time, or status mismatches. This made it easier to separate distress that came from preexisting mental health problems, recent personal crises, and/or financial problems from distress involving identity.

People who have mental health issues are not immune to the effects of role loss. Because mental illness is stigmatized, it may be tempting to think that people who have received mental health diagnoses experience the world very differently from those who have not. But people who struggle with depression, anxiety, and other problems still hold role identities, still experience interactions with other people, and still receive the same cultural messages about things like jobs and gender and age. It would be wrong to simply assume that the social psychological factors and processes that are important for most people suddenly do not apply to people who have been diagnosed with a mental illness or emotional problem. The data used to write *Job Loss, Identity, and Mental*

Health cannot answer whether poor mental health leads to job loss. However, the data do support the idea that prior mental health history does not necessarily determine whether someone will experience identity threats after losing a job. Furthermore, the data support the idea that processes involving feedback, consistency of identities over time, meanings of statuses and roles, and the stress process generally still apply to people with a history of mental health problems.

NOTES

CHAPTER 2   WHY IDENTITY?

1. Charlie, Cindy, and Marsha are not all included in every chapter because not every participant experienced all three types of identity threat.

CHAPTER 3   "THAT'S NOT THE WAY WE DO IT AT GENTAY": FEEDBACK MISMATCHES

1. Typically, in layoffs, many people lose their jobs at once. Layoffs are done to increase company profits by cutting labor costs (Kalleberg 2009), not because the laid-off employees performed poorly.

2. A severance package consists of money and/or benefits (such as health insurance or life insurance) that a company may offer to someone they are laying off. This is usually proposed by the employer, written up in a contract, and is often non-negotiable.

3. You may find yourself condemning Charlie's behavior or even disliking Charlie. Certainly there is much to dislike about some of his attitudes and actions. But Charlie, like most people, had both good and bad characteristics. Charlie loved his wife and children deeply, worked hard to be a good Christian, and strived to behave morally. Overall, he genuinely meant well. Real people are complex beings, and even when they behave poorly or make bad decisions, they suffer just like anyone else. Charlie is one of these real people, with real failings and real suffering.

4. Despite Charlie's own disillusionment about his work, he still expected people to treat him as the employee he still (technically) was.

5. Charlie told me his boss referred to his termination as a layoff, but there is strong evidence to suggest that he was really fired "for cause," or because of his behavior.

6. A merger is the joining of two or more companies. Mergers are often accompanied by layoffs.

7. Because Cindy no longer felt like she was the person she used to be (travel industry executive) this also reflects a time mismatch (see chapter 4). Although they are conceptually distinct, the three types of mismatches often overlapped or co-occurred.

8. Cindy was reluctant to share details about her severance package.

CHAPTER 5   "ME CAVEMAN . . . I CLUB DEER": STATUS MISMATCHES

1. A small amount of recent scholarship challenges the strength of the connection between breadwinning and men's identities (Demantas and Myers 2015; Lane 2009, 2011).

2. Interestingly, Theo instead relied on other traditional views of manhood, stating that manhood meant "defending your woman," "exploring and getting out in the world," and "seeing how things work."

3. It is possible that subtle, indirect messages may have reinforced the idea that manhood was tied to employment. For example, Charlie mentioned that he had heard Janette tell their children that Charlie was "working at home." This may have implied that a man who is simply at home, not working for pay, is defective.

4. Alternately, some middle-class people are relatively comfortable with moving into lower-level jobs (Lane 2009, 2011).

CHAPTER 7   "IT WAS LIKE I WAS STILL WORKING": SUSTAINING

1. Unfortunately, Paul also had a new expense: a $300 per month payment toward COBRA healthcare coverage. COBRA refers to the Consolidated Omnibus Budget Reconciliation Act, which allows people who have lost their jobs to keep their employer-provided health insurance for up to eighteen months by paying the same monthly cost (often hundreds of dollars) that their employer would have paid for the insurance (U.S. Department of Labor 2012).

2. A site called "YourMarketingMan" does exist, but this is not Paul's actual domain name.

3. Marsha also told me that her children were with their father for those three days, and that being alone may have contributed to her depression.

4. The difference between Paul's abandoned job search and Ken's and Marsha's vigorous searches is hard to explain. Financial hardship alone does not explain the difference: Ken was affluent, Paul was middle-class (but starting to struggle financially), and Marsha was barely able to pay her mortgage. Given that unemployed men in Lane's (2011, 40) study tried to avoid risking low corporate job security by becoming entrepreneurs, it is possible Paul also avoided searching in order to avoid risk. Paul blamed himself for losing his job, so it may have seemed too risky to be potentially rejected by another employer. Conversely, in Ken's and Marsha's situations, discrimination contributed to losing their jobs. They knew this was unjust, and so may never have questioned their qualifications. If they also thought that the bigotry they had encountered was atypical, seeking a job probably did not seem risky, and so they simply continued to search vigorously.

REFERENCES

Alexander, Mary Jane, and E. Tory Higgins. 1993. "Emotional Trade-Offs of Becoming a Parent: How Social Roles Influence Self-Discrepancy Effects." *Journal of Personality and Social Psychology* 65: 1259–1269.

Amundson, Norman A. 1994. "Negotiating Identity during Unemployment." *Journal of Employment Counseling* 31: 98–104.

Baird, Jim. 2010. "Identity Work for 'Boomer' Professionals: Career Transition in the Restructured Economy." PhD diss., College of Arts and Sciences, Georgia State University.

Bambra, Clare. 2011. *Work, Worklessness, and the Political Economy of Health.* New York: Oxford University Press.

Barbulescu, Roxana, and Herminia Ibarra. 2009. "Identity as Narrative: Overcoming Identity Gaps during Work Role Transitions." *Academy of Management Review Journal* 35 (1): 135–154.

Bennett, Kate Mary. 2010. "'You Can't Spend Years with Someone and Just Cast Them Aside': Augmented Identity in Older British Widows." *Journal of Women & Aging* 22: 204–217.

Berger, Ellie D. 2009. "Managing Age Discrimination: An Examination of the Techniques Used When Seeking Employment." *Gerontologist* 49 (3): 317–332.

Berger, Peter L., and Thomas Luckmann. 1966. *The Social Construction of Reality.* New York: Anchor Books.

Blau, Zena Smith. 1973. *Old Age in a Changing Society.* New York: New Viewpoints.

Blumer, Herbert. 1962. "Society as Symbolic Interaction." In *Human Behavior and Social Processes*, edited by A. M. Rose, 179–192. Boston: Houghton Mifflin.

———. 1969. *Symbolic Interactionism.* Englewood Cliffs, NJ: Prentice-Hall.

Burke, Peter J. 1991. "Identity Processes and Social Stress." *American Sociological Review* 56: 836–849.

———. 1996. "Social Identities and Psychosocial Stress." In *Psychosocial Stress: Perspectives on Structure, Theory, Life-Course, and Methods*, edited by Howard B. Kaplan, 141–174. San Diego: Academic Press.

Burke, Peter J., and Michael M. Harrod. 2005. "Too Much of a Good Thing?" *Social Psychology Quarterly* 68: 359–374.

Burke, Peter J., and Jan E. Stets. 2009. *Identity Theory.* New York: Oxford University Press.

Cantwell, Allison M., and Sarah E. Martiny. 2010. "Bridging Identities Through Identity Change." *Social Psychology Quarterly* 73: 320–321.

Cassidy, Tony. 2001. "Self-Categorization, Coping, and Psychological Health among Unemployed Mid-Career Executives." *Counselling Psychology Quarterly* 14: 303–315.

Cast, Alicia D. 2003. "Power and the Ability to Define the Situation." *Social Psychology Quarterly* 66: 185–201.

Cast, Alicia D., Jan E. Stets, and Peter J. Burke. 1999. "Does the Self Conform to the Views of Others?" *Social Psychology Quarterly* 62: 68–82.

Castel, Philippe, Brigitte Minondo-Kaghad, and Marie-Françoise Lacassagne. 2013. "Socio-Psychological Counseling: How to Manage Identities?" *Psychology* 4 (3): 356–362.

Clark, Tom, and Anthony Heath. 2014. *Hard Times: The Divisive Toll of the Economic Slump.* New Haven, CT: Yale University Press.

Cooper, Marianne. 2014. *Cut Adrift: Families in Insecure Times.* Berkeley: University of California Press.

Cottle, Thomas J. 2001. *Hardest Times: The Trauma of Long-Term Unemployment.* Westport, CT: Praeger.

Creed, Peter A., and Dee A. Bartrum. 2008. "Personal Control as a Mediator and Moderator between Life Strains and Psychological Well-Being in the Unemployed." *Journal of Applied Social Psychology* 38: 460–481.

Creed, Peter A., and Kelli Moore. 2006. "Social Support, Social Undermining, and Coping in Underemployed and Unemployed Persons." *Journal of Applied Social Psychology* 36: 321–339.

Creswell, John W., and Vicki L. Plano Clark. 2007. *Designing and Conducting Mixed Methods Research.* Thousand Oaks, CA: Sage.

Cruikshank, Margaret. 2013. *Learning to Be Old: Generation, Culture, and Aging.* 3rd ed. Lanham, MD: Rowman & Littlefield.

Demantas, Ilana, and Kristen Myers. 2015. "'Step Up and Be a Man in a Different Manner': Unemployed Men Reframing Masculinity." *Sociological Quarterly* 56: 640–664.

DeNavas-Walt, Carmen, Bernadette D. Proctor, and Jessica C. Smith. 2012. "Income, Poverty, and Health Insurance Coverage in the United States: 2011." Current Population Reports, September. Retrieved February 26, 2015 (http://www.census.gov/prod/2012pubs/p60–243.pdf).

Dooley, David. 2003. "Unemployment, Underemployment, and Mental Health: Conceptualizing Employment Status as a Continuum." *American Journal of Community Psychology* 32: 9–20.

Drahota, Jo Anne Tremaine, and D. Stanley Eitzen. 1998. "The Role Exit of Professional Athletes." *Sociology of Sport Journal* 15: 263–278.

Dudley, Kathryn Marie. 1997 [1994]. *The End of the Line: Lost Jobs, New Lives in Postindustrial America.* Chicago: University of Chicago Press.

Duran-Aydintug, Candan. 1995. "Former Spouses Exiting Role Identities." Journal of Divorce & Remarriage 24: 23–40.

Ebaugh, Helen Rose Fuchs. 1988. *Becoming an Ex: The Process of Role Exit.* Chicago: University of Chicago Press.

Eisenberg, P., and P. Lazarsfeld. 1938. "The Psychological Effects of Unemployment." *Psychological Bulletin* 35: 358–390.

Esterberg, Kristin G. 2002. *Qualitative Methods in Social Research.* Boston: McGraw-Hill.

Ezzy, Douglas. 1993. "Unemployment and Mental Health: A Critical Review." *Social Science and Medicine* 37: 41–52.

———. 2001. *Narrating Unemployment.* Burlington, VT: Ashgate.

Feldman, Daniel C. 1996. "The Nature, Antecedents, and Consequences of Underemployment." *Journal of Management* 22: 385–407.

Feldman, Daniel C., Carrie R. Leana, and Mark C. Bolino. 2002. "Underemployment and Relative Deprivation among Re-Employed Executives." *Journal of Occupational and Organizational Psychology* 75: 453–471.

Feldman, Daniel C., and William H. Turnley. 1995. "Underemployment among Recent Business College Graduates." *Journal of Organizational Behavior* 16: 691–706.

Fishman, Charles. 2012. "The Insourcing Boom." *The Atlantic*, December, 44–52.

Fligstein, Neil, and Adam Goldstein. 2011. "The Roots of the Great Recession." In *The Great Recession*, edited by David B. Grusky, Bruce Western, and Christopher Wimer, 21–55. New York: Russell Sage Foundation.

Folkman, Susan, and Richard S. Lazarus. 1985. "If It Changes It Must Be a Process: Study of Emotion and Coping during Three Stages of a College Examination." *Journal of Personality and Social Psychology* 48: 150–170.

Fraccaroli, Franco, Alexis Le Blanc, and Violette Hajjar. 1994. "Social Self-Description and Affective Well-Being in Young Unemployed People: A Comparative Study." *European Work and Organizational Psychologist* 4: 81–100.

Fraher, Amy L., and Yiannis Gabriel. 2014. "Dreaming of Flying When Grounded: Occupational Identity and Occupational Fantasies of Furloughed Airline Pilots." *Journal of Management Studies* 51 (6): 926–951.

Gabriel, Yiannis, David E. Gray, and Harshita Goregaokar. 2013. "Job Loss and Its Aftermath among Managers and Professionals: Wounded, Fragmented, and Flexible." *Work, Employment, and Society* 27 (1): 56–72.

Garrett-Peters, Raymond. 2009. "'If I Don't Have to Work Anymore, Who Am I?': Job Loss and Collaborative Self-Concept Repair." *Journal of Contemporary Ethnography* 38: 547–583.

Gecas, Viktor, and Monica A. Seff. 1990. "Social Class and Self-Esteem: Psychological Centrality, Compensation, and the Relative Effects of Work and Home." *Social Psychology Quarterly* 53: 165–173.

Gergen, K. J., and M. M. Gergen. 2000. "The New Aging: Self Construction and Social Values." In *The Evolution of the Aging Self: The Societal Impact on the Aging Process*, edited by K. W. Schaie and J. Hendricks, 281–306. New York: Springer.

Goffman, Erving. 1959. *The Presentation of Self in Everyday Life*. New York: Doubleday.

Grusky, David B., Bruce Western, and Christopher Wimer. 2011a. "The Consequences of the Great Recession." In *The Great Recession*, edited by David B. Grusky, Bruce Western, and Christopher Wimer, 3–20. New York: Russell Sage Foundation.

———. 2011b. *The Great Recession*. New York: Russell Sage Foundation.

Hanisch, K. 1999. "Job Loss and Unemployment Research from 1994 to 1998: A Review and Recommendations for Research and Intervention." *Journal of Vocational Behavior* 55: 188–220.

Higgins, E. T. 1987. "Self-Discrepancy: A Theory Relating Self and Affect." *Psychological Review* 94: 319–340.

Hockey, John. 2005. "Injured Distance Runners: A Case of Identity Work as Self-Help." *Sociology of Sport Journal* 21: 38–58.

Hout, Michael, Asaf Levanon, and Erin Cumberworth. 2011. "Job Loss and Unemployment." In *The Great Recession*, edited by David B. Grusky, Bruce Western, and Christopher Wimer, 59–126. New York: Russell Sage Foundation.

Ibarra, Herminia, and Roxana Barbulescu. 2010. "Identity as Narrative: Prevalence, Effectiveness, and Consequences of Narrative Identity Work in Macro Work Role Transitions." *Academy of Management Review* 35 (1): 135–154.

Iceland, John. 2013. *Poverty in America: A Handbook*. 3rd ed. Berkeley: University of California Press.

Iyer, Aarti, Jolanda Jetten, Dimitrios Tsivrikos, Tom Postmes, and S. Alexander Haslam. 2009. "The More (and the More Compatible) the Merrier: Multiple Group Memberships and

Identity Compatibility as Predictors of Adjustment after Life Transitions." *British Journal of Social Psychology* 48: 707–733.

Jahoda, Marie. 1981. "Work, Employment, and Unemployment: Values, Theories, and Approaches in Social Research." *American Psychologist* 36: 184–191.

———. 1982. *Employment and Unemployment*. Cambridge: Cambridge University Press.

———. 1984. "Social Institutions and Human Needs: A Comment on Fryer and Payne." *Leisure Studies* 3 (3): 297–299.

———. 1986. "In Defence of a Non-Reductionist Social Psychology." *Social Behaviour* 1 (1): 25–29.

Kalleberg, Arne L. 2000. "Nonstandard Employment Relations: Part-time, Temporary, and Contract Work." *Annual Review of Sociology* 26: 341–365.

———. 2008. "The State of Work (and Workers) in America." *Work and Occupations* 35: 243–261.

———. 2009. "Precarious Work, Insecure Workers: Employment Relations in Transition." *American Sociological Review* 74: 1–22.

Kanter, Rosabeth Moss. 1977. *Men and Women of the Corporation*. New York: Basic Books.

Kelvin, Peter, and Joanna E. Jarrett. 1985. *Unemployment: Its Social Psychological Effects*. Cambridge: Cambridge University Press.

Khanna, Nikki, and Cathryn Johnson. 2010. "Passing as Black: Racial Identity Work among Biracial Americans." *Social Psychology Quarterly* 73: 380–397.

K'Meyer, Tracy E., and Joy L. Hart. 2009. *I Saw It Coming: Worker Narratives of Plant Closings and Job Loss*. New York: Palgrave Macmillan.

Krekula, Clary. 2009. "Age Coding: On Age-Based Practices of Distinction." *International Journal of Ageing and Later Life* 4 (2): 7–31.

Krugman, Paul. 2012. *End This Depression Now!* New York: W. W. Norton.

Lancaster, Lynne C., and David Stillman. 2010. *The M-Factor: How the Millennial Generation Is Rocking the Workplace*. New York: HarperCollins.

Lane, Carrie M. 2009. "Man Enough to Let My Wife Support Me: How Changing Models of Career and Gender Are Reshaping the Experience of Unemployment." *American Ethnologist* 36 (4): 681–692.

———. 2011. *A Company of One: Insecurity, Independence, and the New World of White-Collar Unemployment*. Ithaca, NY: Cornell University Press.

LaPointe, Kirsi. 2013. "Heroic Career Changers? Gendered Identity Work in Career Transitions." *Gender, Work & Organization* 20 (2): 133–146.

Large, Michael D., and Kristen Marcussen. 2000. "Extending Identity Theory to Predict Differential Forms and Degrees of Psychological Distress." *Social Psychology Quarterly* 63: 49–59.

Lee, James Daniel. 1998. "Which Kids Can 'Become' Scientists?: Effects of Gender, Self-Concepts, and Perceptions of Scientists." *Social Psychology Quarterly* 61: 199–219.

Lofland, John, David A. Snow, Leon Anderson, and Lyn H. Lofland. 2006. *Analyzing Social Settings: A Guide to Qualitative Observation and Analysis*. 4th ed. Belmont, CA: Wadsworth/Thomson Learning.

MacKinnon, Neil J., and David R. Heise. 2010. *Self, Identity, and Social Institutions*. New York: Palgrave Macmillan.

Maharidge, Dale. 2013. *Someplace Like America: Tales from the New Great Depression*. Berkeley: University of California Press.

Manzi, Claudia, Vivian L. Vignoles, and Camillo Regalia. 2010. "Accommodating a New Identity: Possible Selves, Identity Change, and Well-Being across Two Life-Transitions." *European Journal of Social Psychology* 40: 970–984.

Marcussen, Kristin. 2006. "Identities, Self-Esteem, and Psychological Distress: An Application of Identity-Discrepancy Theory." *Sociological Focus* 40: 392–412.

Marcussen, Kristin, and Michael D. Large. 2003. "Using Identity Discrepancy Theory to Predict Psychological Distress." In *Advances in Identity Theory and Research*, edited by Peter J. Burke, Timothy J. Owens, Richard T. Serpe, and Peggy A. Thoits, 151–164. New York: Kluwer Academic/Plenum.

Markus, Hazel, and Paula Nurius. 1986. "Possible Selves." *American Psychologist* 41: 954–969.

McDaniel, Susan A. 2003. "Hidden in the Household: Now It's Men in Mid-Life." *Ageing International* 28: 326–344.

McFadyen, Ruth G. 1995. "Coping with Threatened Identities: Unemployed People's Self-Categorizations." *Current Psychology* 14: 233–256.

Mead, George Herbert. 1934. *Mind, Self, and Society from the Standpoint of a Social Behaviorist.* Chicago: University of Chicago Press.

Mendenhall, Ruby, Ariel Kalil, Laurel J. Spindle, and Cassandra M. D. Hart. 2008. "Job Loss at Mid-life: Managers and Executives Face the 'New Risk Economy.'" *Social Forces* 87: 185–209.

Merton, Robert K. 1957. *Social Theory and Social Structure.* Rev. ed. New York: Free Press.

Michniewicz, Kenneth S., Joseph A. Vandello, and Jennifer K. Bosson. 2014. "Men's (Mis) Perceptions of the Gender Threatening Consequences of Unemployment." *Sex Roles* 70 (3–4): 88–97.

Miles, Matthew B., and A. Michael Huberman. 1994. *Qualitative Data Analysis: An Expanded Sourcebook.* 2nd ed. Thousand Oaks, CA: Sage Publications.

Milkman, Ruth. 1997. *Farewell to the Factory: Auto Workers in the Late Twentieth Century.* Berkeley: University of California Press.

Mills, C. Wright. 2000 [1959]. *The Sociological Imagination.* New York: Oxford University Press.

Moore, Valerie Ann. 2001. "'Doing' Racialized and Gendered Age to Organize Peer Relations: Observing Kids in Summer Camp." *Gender & Society* 15 (6): 835–858.

Newman, Katherine S. 1999 [1988]. *Falling from Grace: The Experience of Downward Mobility in the American Middle Class.* New York: Free Press.

Nixon, Darren. 2006. "I Just Like Working with My Hands: Employment Aspirations and the Meaning of Work for Low-Skilled Unemployed Men in Britain's Service Economy." *Journal of Education and Work* 19: 201–217.

Norris, Dawn R. 2011. "Interactions That Trigger Self-Labeling: The Case of Older Undergraduates." *Symbolic Interaction* 34: 173–197.

O'Brien, Gordon E. 1985. "Distortion in Unemployment Research: The Early Studies of Bakke and Their Implications for Current Research on Employment and Unemployment." *Human Relations* 38 (9): 877–894.

O'Brien, Laurie T., and Mary Lee Hummert. 2006. "Memory Performance of Late Middle-Aged Adults: Contrasting Self-Stereotyping and Stereotypes Threat Accounts of Assimilation to Age Stereotypes." *Social Cognition* 24 (3): 338–358.

Pahl, R. 1995. *After Success: Fin-de-Siècle Anxiety and Identity.* Cambridge: Polity Press.

Palmore, Erdman Ballagh. 1999. *Ageism: Negative and Positive.* New York: Springer.

Pearlin, Leonard I. 1989. "The Sociological Study of Stress." *Journal of Health and Social Behavior* 30: 241–256.

———. 1999. "The Stress Process Revisited." In *Handbook of the Sociology of Mental Health*, edited by Carol S. Aneshensel and Jo C. Phelan, 395–415. New York: Kluwer Academic/Plenum.

Pearlin, Leonard I., Morton A. Lieberman, Elizabeth G. Menaghan, and Joseph T. Mullan. 1981. "The Stress Process." *Journal of Health and Social Behavior* 22: 337–356.

Pearlin, Leonard I., Kim B. Nguyen, Scott Schieman, and Melissa A. Milkie. 2007. "The Life-Course Origins of Mastery among Older People." *Journal of Health and Social Behavior* 48: 164–179.

Pearlin, Leonard I., and Carmi Schooler. 1978. "The Structure of Coping." *Journal of Health and Social Behavior* 19: 2–21.

Pritchard, Katrina, and Gillian Symon. 2011. "Identity on the Line: Constructing Professional Identity in a HR Call Centre." *Work, Employment, and Society* 25: 434–450.

Probst, Tahira M. 2000. "Wedded to the Job: Moderating Effects of Job Involvement on the Consequences of Job Insecurity." *Journal of Occupational Health Psychology* 5: 63–73.

Riach, Kathleen, and Wendy Loretto. 2009. "Identity Work and the 'Unemployed' Worker: Age, Disability and the Lived Experience of the Older Unemployed." *Work, Employment, and Society* 23: 102–119.

Robinson, Michael D., Sara K. Moeller, and Paul W. Goetz. 2009. "Are Self-Deceivers Enhancing Positive Affect or Denying Negative Affect? Toward an Understanding of Implicit Affective Processes." *Cognition and Emotion* 23 (1): 152–180.

Rosenberg, Morris. 1986 [1979]. *Conceiving the Self.* Malabar, FL: Krieger.

Ryan, Ellen Bouchard. 1992. "Beliefs about Memory Changes across the Adult Life Span." *Journal of Gerontology* 47 (1): 41–46.

Schieman, Scott, Tetyana Pudrovska, Leonard I. Pearlin, and Christopher G. Ellison. 2006. "The Sense of Divine Control and Psychological Distress: Variations across Race and Socioeconomic Status." *Journal for the Scientific Study of Religion* 45 (4): 529–549.

Schöb, Ronnie. 2013. "Unemployment and Identity." *CESifo Economic Studies* 59 (1): 149–180.

Sharone, Ofer. 2013a. *Flawed System/Flawed Self: Job Searching and Unemployment Experiences.* Chicago: University of Chicago Press.

———. 2013b. "Why Do Unemployed Americans Blame Themselves While Israelis Blame the System?" *Social Forces* 91 (4): 1429–1450.

Sheeran, Paschal, and Charles Abraham. 1994. "Unemployment and Self-Conception: A Symbolic Interactionist Analysis." *Journal of Community & Applied Social Psychology* 4: 115–129.

Sheeran, Paschal, and Eunice McCarthy. 1990. "The Impact of Unemployment upon Self-Conception: Evaluation, Affection, Consistency, and Involvement Dimensions." *Social Behavior* 5: 351–359.

———. 1992. "Social Structure, Self-Conception, and Well-Being: An Examination of Four Models with Unemployed People." *Journal of Applied Social Psychology* 22: 117–133.

Sieber, Sam D. 1974. "Toward a Theory of Role Accumulation." *American Sociological Review* 39: 567–578.

Simon, Robin W. 1997. "The Meanings Individuals Attach to Role Identities and Their Implications for Mental Health." *Journal of Health and Social Behavior* 38: 256–274.

Snow, David A., and Leon Anderson. 1987. "Identity Work among the Homeless: The Verbal Construction and Avowal of Personal Identities." *American Journal of Sociology* 92: 1336–1371.

Sorenson, Aage B. 2000. "Toward a Sounder Basis for Class Analysis." *American Journal of Sociology* 105: 1523–1558.

Stets, Jan E., and Peter J. Burke. 2005. "Identity Verification, Control, and Aggression in Marriage." *Social Psychology Quarterly* 68: 160–178.

———. 2014. "Emotions and Identity Nonverification." *Social Psychology Quarterly* 77 (4): 387–410.

Stets, Jan E., and Michael M. Harrod. 2004. "Verification across Multiple Identities: The Role of Status." *Social Psychology Quarterly* 67: 155–171.

Stier, Jonas. 2007. "Game, Name and Fame—Afterwards, Will I Still Be the Same?: A Social Psychological Study of Career, Role Exit, and Identity." *International Review for the Sociology of Sport* 42: 99–111.

Stryker, Sheldon. 1980. *Symbolic Interactionism: A Social Structural Version*. Caldwell, NJ: Blackburn Press.

Stryker, Sheldon, and Peter J. Burke. 2000. "The Past, Present, and Future of an Identity Theory." *Social Psychology Quarterly* 63: 284–297.

Sullivan, Teresa A. 2004. "Work-Related Social Problems." In *Handbook of Social Problems: A Comparative International Perspective*, edited by George Ritzer, 193–208. Thousand Oaks, CA: Sage.

Sum, Andrew, and Ishwar Kahtiwada. 2010. "The Nation's Underemployed in the 'Great Recession' of 2007–2009." *Monthly Labor Review*, November. Retrieved February 25, 2015 (http://www.bls.gov/opub/mlr/2010/11/art1full.pdf).

Swann, W. B., Jr. 1983. "Self-Verification: Bring Social Reality into Harmony with the Self." In *Social Psychological Perspectives on the Self*, Vol. 2, edited by J. M. Suls and A. G. Greenwald, 33–66. Hillsdale, NJ: Lawrence Erlbaum.

Tajfel, Henri. 1981. *Human Groups and Social Categories: Studies in Social Psychology*. Cambridge: Cambridge University Press.

Tajfel, Henri, and J. C. Turner. 1979. "An Integrative Theory of Intergroup Conflict." In *The Social Psychology of Intergroup Relations*, edited by W. G. Austin and S. Worchel. Monterey, CA: Brooks/Cole.

———. 1986. "The Social Identity Theory of Intergroup Behavior." In *Psychology of Intergroup Relations*, 2nd ed., edited by S. Worchel and W. G. Austin, 7–24. Chicago: Nelson-Hall.

Tausig, Mark. 1999. "Work and Mental Health." In *Handbook of the Sociology of Mental Health*, edited by Carol S. Aneshensel and Jo C. Phelan, 255–274. New York: Kluwer Academic/ Plenum.

Taylor, Shelley E., and Jonathon D. Brown. 1988. "Illusion and Well-Being: A Social Psychological Perspective on Mental Health." *Psychological Bulletin* 103 (2): 193–210.

Thoits, Peggy A. 1983. "Multiple Identities and Psychological Well-Being." *American Sociological Review* 48: 174–187.

———. 1985. "Self-Labeling Processes in Mental Illness: The Role of Emotional Deviance." *American Journal of Sociology* 91: 221–249.

———. 1986. "Multiple Identities: Examining Gender and Marital Status Differences in Distress." *American Sociological Review* 51: 259–272.

———. 1991. "On Merging Identity Theory and Stress Research." *Social Psychology Quarterly* 54: 101–112.

———. 1995. "Identity-Relevant Events and Psychological Symptoms: A Cautionary Tale." *Journal of Health and Social Behavior* 36: 72–83.

———. 1999. "Self, Identity, Stress, and Mental Health." In *Handbook of the Sociology of Mental Health*, edited by Carol S. Aneshensel and Jo C. Phelan, 345–368. New York: Kluwer Academic/Plenum.

Thompson, Jeffery A., and J. Stuart Bunderson. 2001. "Work-Nonwork Conflict and the Phenomenology of Time." *Work & Occupations* 28: 17–39.

Tiffany, D., J. Cowan, and P. Tiffany. 1970. *The Unemployed, A Social Psychological Portrait*. Englewood Cliffs, NJ: Prentice-Hall.

Tosti-Kharas, Jennifer. 2012. "Continued Organizational Identification Following Involuntary Job Loss." *Journal of Managerial Psychology* 27 (8): 829–847.

Townsend, Nicholas. 2002. *The Package Deal*. Philadelphia: Temple University Press.

U.S. Department of Labor. Employee Benefits Security Administration. 2012. "An Employee's Guide to Health Benefits under COBRA: The Consolidated Omnibus Budget Reconciliation Act of 1985." Retrieved February 25, 2015 (http://www.dol.gov/ebsa/pdf/cobraemployee.pdf).

U.S. Department of Labor. U.S. Bureau of Labor Statistics. 2008. "Involuntary Part-Time Work on the Rise." *Issues in Labor Statistics*, December. Retrieved March 9, 2012 (http://www.bls.gov/opub/ils/pdf/opbils71.pdf).

———. 2014a. "Long-Term Unemployed." Retrieved February 25, 2015 (http://www.bls.gov/bls/cps_fact_sheets/ltu_mock.htm).

———. 2014b. "The Rise in Women's Share of Nonfarm Employment during the 2007–2009 Recession: A Historical Perspective." *Monthly Labor Review*, April. Retrieved February 25, 2015 (http://www.bls.gov/opub/mlr/2014/article/pdf/the-rise-in-women-share-of-nonfarm-employment.pdf).

———. 2015a. "Labor Force Statistics from the Current Population Survey." Series ID: LNS14000000. Series Title: (Seas) Unemployment Rate, 1948–2015. Series Report 20150225194253. Retrieved February 25, 2015 (http://data.bls.gov/timeseries/LNS14000000).

———. 2015b. "The Employment Situation—January 2015." Retrieved February 25, 2015 (http://www.bls.gov/news.release/empsit.nro.htm).

———. 2015c. "Labor Force Statistics from the Current Population Survey." Series ID: LNU05026645. Series Title: (Unadj) Not in Labor Force, Searched for Work and Available, Discouraged Reasons for Not Currently Looking, 2005–2015. Retrieved February 26, 2015 (http://data.bls.gov/timeseries/LNU05026645).

Vaccaro, Christian A., Douglas P. Schrock, and Janice M. McCabe. 2011. "Managing Emotional Manhood: Fighting and Fostering Fear in Mixed Martial Arts." *Social Psychology Quarterly* 74: 414–437.

Wahl, Ingrid, Maria Pollai, and Erich Kirchler. 2013. "Status, Identification and In-Group Favouritism of the Unemployed Compared to Other Social Categories." *Journal of Socio-Economics* 43: 37–43.

Walkerdine, Valerie. 2006. "Workers in the New Economy: Transformation as Border Crossing." *Ethos* 34 (1): 10–41.

Walley, Christine J. 2013. *Exit Zero: Family and Class in Postindustrial Chicago*. Chicago: University of Chicago Press.

Warr, Peter. 1987. *Work, Unemployment, and Mental Health*. Oxford: Clarendon Press.

———. 2005. "Work, Well-Being, and Mental Health." In *Handbook of Work Stress*, edited by Julian Barling, E. Kevin Kelloway, and Michael R. Frone, 547–573. Thousand Oaks, CA: Sage.

Weiss, David, and Frieder R. Lang. 2012. "'They' Are Old but 'I' Feel Younger: Age-Group Dissociation as a Self-Protective Strategy in Old Age." *Psychology and Aging* 27 (1): 153–163.

Weiss, Robert S. 1994. *Learning from Strangers: The Art and Method of Qualitative Interview Studies*. New York: Free Press.

Westerhof, Gerben J., and Anne E. Barrett. 2005. "Age Identity and Subjective Well-Being: A Comparison of the United States and Germany." *Journals of Gerontology Series B: Psychological Sciences and Social Sciences* 60 (3): 129–136.

Williams, Robin. 1965. *American Society: A Sociological Interpretation*. New York: Alfred A. Knopf.

Willott, Sara, and Christine Griffin. 2004. "Redundant Men: Constraints on Identity Change." *Journal of Community & Applied Social Psychology* 14: 53–69.

Wolff, Edward N., Lindsay A. Owens, and Esra Burak. 2011. "How Much Wealth Was Destroyed in the Great Recession?" In *The Great Recession*, edited by David B. Grusky, Bruce Western, and Christopher Wimer, 127–158. New York: Russell Sage Foundation.

Woo, Jong-Min, and Teodor T. Postolache. 2009. "Mood Disorders and Suicide." In *Health and Happiness from Meaningful Work*, edited by Soren Ventegodt and Joav Merrick, 161–182. New York: Nova Science.

Wrench, Alison, and Robyne Garrett. 2012. "Identity Work: Stories Told in Learning to Teach Physical Education." *Sport, Education, and Society* 17: 1–19.

Yang, Sungeun. 2002. "Chaemyoun-Saving (Face-Saving) Due to Korean Job Loss: Listening to Men's Voices." *Journal of Comparative Family Studies* 33: 73–95.

INDEX

Page numbers in *italics* represent figures.

abuse, 40
age: age-related issues, 37; identity,
132–133, 138, 147, 150; social
expectations, 100, 152; social status,
9, 61, 101–102; stigmatized group,
124–125, 131. *See also* status mismatch
age discrimination, 72–73
agitation, 19
air traffic controller, 146
alcohol abuse, 5
Alzheimer's disease, 37, 69
Amber (newspaper reporter), 68, 71, 73, 75,
76, 92–94, 97, 98, 154
Anderson, Leon, 152
anger, 5, 14, 29, 37, 45, 71, 76, 82, 83, 128–129
anxiety: connection to unemployment, 5;
feedback mismatch, 36, 37, 38, 43, 45;
identity mismatch, 19; shifting, 78, 80;
status mismatch, 71, 76; sustaining, 102,
110, 111, 113; time mismatch, 57, 58
aspiration discrepancy, 18–19

Baby Boomers, 26, 44, 146, 150
Baird, Jim, 139
Bambra, Clare, 5; *Work, Worklessness, and the
Political Economy of Health*, 5
banking industry, 3, 5
bankruptcy, 53
Barbulescu, Roxana, 21
Barkley, Charles, 95
Bess (Janelle's interviewer), 132
bigotry, 172n4
breadwinner role, 33, 113, 150. *See also* men
Burke, Peter J., 19, 118, 153
buyout, 144

Castel, Philippe, 50
Charlie (training director), 1; feedback
mismatch, 25–32, 39, 41, 44–45, 61; identity
void, 120, 121–129, 139, 140; shifting, 124,
151; status mismatch, 62, 63, 64–65, 66,
67, 76, 77, 150, 151, 172n3; time mismatch,
46–52, 58–61
Charlotte (nonprofit CFO): feedback
mismatch, 39–40, 41, 42–43, 44–45;
identity void, 135; shifting, 79–87,
88, 90–91, 97, 99, 100, 113, 122, 150;

sustaining, 114, 117; time mismatch, 49, 51,
56, 59, 80
Cheryl (Charlie's boss), 25, 28, 29, 30,
31, 41
Chicago, Illinois, 144
China, 4
Chrysler autoworkers, 144, 146
Chuck (Marsha's subordinate), 54
church (as social institution), 17
Cindy (account executive): feedback
mismatch, 32–39, 44–45, 61; identity void,
121–122, 124, 133, 135, 136; status mismatch,
62, 68–73, 76, 150; time mismatch, 46, 49,
50, 56–57, 59, 171n7
Clark, Tom, 5; *Hard Times: The Divisive Toll of
the Economic Slump* (with Heath), 5
coach as role, 51
COBRA healthcare coverage, 172n1
college degree, 8–9, 10, 44, 68, 73–74, 133,
143–144, 145, 154
community organization (as social
institution), 17
consistent identity. *See* identity:
time-consistent
contract activities, 60, 106–107, 114
Cooper, Marianne, 148, 153
coping strategies, 9, 15–16, 50, 78–79, 111, 118,
150, 152, 153
Cottle, Thomas J., 7; *Hardest Times: The
Trauma of Long-Term Unemployment*, 7
culture: conception of leader, 110; discourse,
job loss in, 12, 67, 145–147, 148, 152–153;
meaning of manhood, 67

Daily Banner, 94
death metaphors, 48, 124, 130–131, 133
debt, paying off, 3, 143
dementia, 68–69
depression: connection to unemployment,
5; feedback mismatch, 36–37, 38, 41, 43;
identity mismatch, 19; identity void, 121;
mismatches, 7; shifting, 78, 84, 92, 94;
status mismatch, 64, 71, 73, 76; stress and
mental health processes, 14; sustaining,
106, 112, 118, 172n3; time mismatch, 50, 52,
57, 58, 60
deregulation, 3, 142

discernment process, 122, 139
"discouraged workers," 2
distress: identity-related, 20, 21–22, 110, 150,
    152, 153–154, 165; identity void, 139, 141;
    shifting, 79–84, 90; status mismatch, 61,
    62, 64, 76; sustaining, 99, 107, 111, 112–113,
    116, 118; time mismatch, 9, 46, 60–61
dramaturgy, concept of, 17

Ebaugh, Helen Rose Fuchs, 123, 138, 140
economic collapse, 3
economic deregulation, 2–3
economic recovery, 4
education, 26, 61, 74–75, 92, 93, 117, 133, 138,
    145, 150. See also college degree; status
    mismatch
"educational identity," 7, 135
elevator speech, 109
entrepreneurship, 60, 105, 106, 116, 118, 147,
    172n4
evaluative messages, 37
exes, described, 140
Ezzy, Douglas, 6, 7, 147, 151, 154; Narrating
    Unemployment, 7

faith. See religion
FaithWorks!, 103–104, 109–110, 117
family: identity void, 123, 139, 141;
    relationships, 23; shifting, 79, 88, 148;
    social institution, 8, 9, 12, 17; sustaining,
    100
father identity, 116–117, 123, 129, 139, 150, 151.
    See also manhood, meaning of; men
feedback, 19–20, 49–50, 147, 149, 153; identify
    void, 121, 126; importance of, 22; shifting,
    87–90, 99; sustaining, 100, 106, 109–110,
    116
feedback mismatch, 11, 23, 25–61, 77, 152;
    common themes, 39; identity void, 138;
    loss of job-related tasks, 41–42; monitoring
    self, 42–44; shifting, 80, 96, 97; status
    mismatch, 67, 69; sustaining, 101; while
    still working, 39–41
financial difficulties, 23, 26, 142, 151; identity
    void, 131, 141; shifting, 84, 85–86, 87,
    89–90, 94; stress and mental health as
    processes, 14; status mismatch, 63, 71,
    72, 73, 76; sustaining, 102, 111, 112–113, 118,
    172n4; time mismatch, 53, 55, 57, 58
fired from job, 55, 82–83, 111, 120
food stamps. See public assistance
foreclosure, housing, 4, 72, 143
Fraher, Amy L., 60
freelancing, 60
friendship, 6, 14, 65, 70, 86, 92, 107, 108, 113,
    127, 137, 138
frustration, 57
"functional model," 6

Gabriel, Yiannis, 60
Garn-St. Germain Act, 3
gender (social status), 9, 15, 61, 150, 152;
    shifting, 79, 87–89, 90–91, 92, 100;

sustaining, 101; traditional views, 66, 150.
    See also status mismatch
General Motors (GM), 144–145
Generation X, 44, 146, 150
Generation Z, 146
Gentay Travel, 32, 34–36, 38–39, 44
geographical location, 145
ghost metaphors, 41, 43, 48
Glass-Steagall Act, 3
global competition, 32, 152
GoDaddy.com, 104
Goffman, Erving, 17, 89, 99
Gramm-Leach-Bliley Act, 3
Great Depression, 2, 142
Great Recession, 2–5, 8, 10, 14, 44, 76,
    142–143, 152
Grusky, David B., 5; The Great Recession
    (Grusky, Western, Wimer), 5

hangover identity. See identity
Hank (Marsha's ex-husband), 52
harassment, 54
Hart, Joy L., 6, 146; I Saw It Coming
    (with K'Meyer), 6
Haylee (Minnie's boss), 40, 43
health insurance, 26, 171n2
Heath, Anthony, 5; Hard Times: The Divisive
    Toll of the Economic Slump (with Clark), 5
high-tech worker, 149. See also information
    technology (IT) professional
historical context, job loss in, 12, 142–145, 151
hobbies, 106, 115, 123–124, 129
home equity loan, 3
homeless identity, 109
housing: bubble, 3, 143; foreclosure, 4, 72,
    143; industry, 3, 143; values, 3, 5

Ibarra, Herminia, 21
identity: abandoning, 62; challenge,
    47; commercial, 109; defined, 16–18;
    described, 13–14; disengaging, 27–28, 47,
    59, 121, 123, 134; feedback, 19–20, 99, 147;
    hangover, 87, 127, 140; loss, 18, 37, 48–49,
    52, 78, 120; magnet, 78, 88, 92–97, 135;
    mental health relationship, 18; messages,
    37; mismatch, 7, 11, 16, 18–19, 22, 109, 130,
    131–133, 152 (see also feedback mismatch;
    status mismatch; time mismatch); models,
    6 (see also specific models); stress
    and mental health processes, 14–16,
    44; threat, 1, 8, 18, 79, 125, 139, 150, 154;
    time-consistent, 20–21, 22, 46, 50, 56,
    57, 60–61, 87, 93, 99, 109, 111, 116, 153;
    transition, 4, 138, 139; uncertainty, 79–84;
    unemployment research and, 152–154;
    vacuum, 122, 140. See also identity work
Identity Control Theory, 69, 77, 118
Identity Discrepancy Theory, 20, 153
Identity Theory, 19, 22, 35, 39, 47, 97, 152, 153
identity void, 12, 120–122, 133–134; identity
    mismatch, 131–133; in limbo, 129–131;

sense of self, 124–126; shifting, 122–124, 134–138; sustaining, 126–129, 134–138
identity work, 77, 148, 149, *149*; coping with identity-related distress, 21–22, 152, 153; shifting, 78, 84, 87, 89–90, 97, 99, 126; sustaining, 104
individualism, 13, 148
information technology (IT) professional, 147
insecurity, 37, 113
insurance companies, failing of, 3
International Harvester, 146
investment companies, failing of, 3
Israeli job search strategy, 7

Jahoda, Marie, 6, 87, 151
Janelle (broadcast programming manager), 120, 129–138, 139, 140, 154, 172n3
Janette (Charlie's wife), 64–65, 125
JCC (broadcast entertainment company), 81
Jenay (Marsha's first boss), 54
"jobless recoveries," 2
job loss. *See* unemployment
job outsourcing. *See* outsourcing
job search: American strategy, 7–8; constrained, 62; identity void, 125, 131–133; Israeli strategy, 7; shifting and, 86, 91; strategies, 7–8, 76; sustaining and, 102–103, 107, 109, 116, 117, 118
job security, 146, 154
job seekers' network (as social institution), 149, 150; identity void, 125–127, 135; importance of, 8; race and resilience, 163–164; research study, 10; social institution, 12; structural factor, 9; sustaining, 103–104, 107, 109, 116, 117–118
Johnson Controls, 146
Johnson County Weekly, 93

Ken (chief executive officer): status mismatch, 63, 65, 66, 154, 172n4; sustaining, 106–107, 111, 114–115, 117, 136, 139
Kenosha, Wisconsin, 144
K'Meyer, Tracy E., 6, 146; *I Saw It Coming* (with Hart), 6
"knowledge work," 10
Korean white-collar men, 19–20
Krekula, Clary, 70
Krugman, Paul, 5; *End This Depression Now!*, 5

Lacassagne, Marie-Françoise, 50
Lane, Carrie M., 8, 66, 105, 118, 146, 147, 148, 149, 154, 172n4; *A Company of One*, 8
layoffs, 25, 44, 72, 75, 100, 101, 120, 130, 142, 146, 171n1
life insurance, 171n2
life transitions, 5
Linden, New Jersey, 144
Lisa (Cindy's boss), 34, 35–36, 38
Lorna (broadcasting industry supervisor), 1; identity void, 135; shifting, 79–87, 89, 91, 97, 122; sustaining, 114; time mismatch, 48, 49, 51, 59, 83–84

manhood, meaning of, 7–8, 16; identity void, 129; shifting, 79, 88, 95, 96; social status, 150; status mismatch, 62–68, 76, 77, 151, 172n3; sustaining, 100–102, 105, 110, 113–115, 117; time mismatch, 51–52. *See also* men
Maharidge, Dale, 6; *Someplace Like America*, 6
Marcus (operations director), 51, 94–97, 154
Marsha (public safety manager): shifting, 113; status mismatch, 113, 151, 172nn3, 4; sustaining, 111–113, 117, 126; time mismatch, 52–61, 113
mastery, 15, 18
material resources, 14, 89, 119, 153
memory problems, 37–38, 68
men: as homemakers, 20; identity relationship, 18; impact of unemployment, 1; job loss relationship, 18; male breadwinner role, 12, 16, 20, 62–68, 79, 101–102, 105, 114, 124, 139; in relationships, 88; unemployment and mental health, 124. *See also* manhood, meaning of
mental health, 5, 14–16, 57, 62–68, 75, 77, 124, 168–169. *See* anger; anxiety; depression; distress; frustration
mentorship, 72, 95
merger, 32, 34, 44, 69, 101, 171n6
messages, 37
Millennials, 146
Minnie (periodical editor), 40, 41, 43, 44–45, 133, 135, 136, 137, 139
Minondo-Kaghad, Brigitte, 50
mismatch. *See* feedback mismatch; identity mismatch; status mismatch; time mismatch
mobility, downward, 76, 145
mood changes, 46, 81, 96, 105, 115–116, 122, 123, 128
mortgage: behind on paying, 85, 143; government's role, 5; industry, 3, 143; underwater, 3
mother identity, 51, 79–87, 99, 113, 117, 123, 124, 135–136, 139, 150

Nancy (marketing director), 121–122, 123, 135–136, 139, 140
Newman, Katherine, 6; *Falling from Grace*, 6
Nixon, Darren, 75

obligation discrepancy, 19
O'Brien, Gordon E., 150
outsourcing, 4, 13, 144, 146

Patenko Institute, 79
Paul (publishing company manager), 100–106, 107, 109, 110–111, 117, 118, 126, 136, 150, 172n4
Pearlin, Leonard I., 77, 97, 111, 118, 148
performance criteria, 35
personal resources, 14–15
PestFree, 75, 114

poverty, 52
promotion, 26
props, 17, 89, 99, 136, 139
public assistance, 58, 131, 137

race (social status), 15, 61, 110, 133, 138, 150, 163–164
religion, 122, 125–126, 129, 135
research study: described, 9–12; interviews, 11; methodology, 155–160; participants, 10–11, 24, 146; screening procedures, 10
resignation: forced, 54, 111, 152; voluntary, 41, 43, 55, 56, 78, 87, 122, 127
resilience, 163–164
retirement, 4; early, 124; funds, 5, 32, 71, 85; jobs, 124; redefined as "retired," 51, 129
Rod (Charlotte's former boss), 39, 79
role, 12, 16, 23, 26, 153–154; buffer, 78; defined, 17; identity based on, 51, 122, 138; importance of, 42; interdependent, 17–18; loss, 139; model, 95; shifting, 79–87, 99, 100, 148; status mismatch, 66, 69; sustaining, 116–117; time mismatch, 58–61; unemployment, 154. See also specific role
romantic narrative, 97, 109
Ruth (information analyst), 110–111, 112, 116, 117, 150

Samantha (Marsha's boss), 54–55, 56
Sandra (Lorna's boss), 82–83
Saul (senior banker): 63–64, 66, 68, 74–75, 113–114
school (social institution), 17. See also college degree; education
self: future, 21, 27, 28, 46, 154; getting back to self, 111–113, 116; identity void, 124–126; "just," 51, 121, 126, 129, 162–163; loss of (see identity: loss); past, 50, 154
self-blame, 36
self-deception, 115–116
Self-Discrepancy Theory, 18–19, 20, 22
self-doubt, 36
self-esteem: feedback mismatch, 27, 37; identity mismatch, 18, 21; identity void, 124; shifting, 78, 81, 92, 98, 153; status mismatch, 73; Stress Process Model, 15; sustaining, 101, 110, 115; time mismatch, 56; and unemployment, 5, 154
self-image, 16
self-worth, 63, 78
severance package, 26, 32, 38, 54, 84, 89, 104, 112, 113, 171n2
Shannon (Charlotte's boss), 39, 41, 42, 43, 44, 56, 80
Sharone, Ofer, 7–8, 67, 76, 104, 117, 154; Flawed System/Flawed Self: Job Searching and Unemployment Experiences, 7
shifting strategy, 9, 12, 78–79, 110, 149, 154; identity magnet shifts, 92–97; identity uncertainty and distress, 79–84, 148, 150, 153; identity void, 122–124, 134–138; making the shift, 84–87; repairing identities, 90–91; social institutions, status, feedback, 87–90, 97; wife and mother, 79–87, 99

"sign vehicle," 89. See also props
Skip (bank vice president), 62, 68, 71–73
Smith Organization, 26–32, 47, 59, 122, 126–129
Snow, David A., 152
social contract, 8, 145
social institution, 8, 9, 12, 22, 24; connections to, 60; defined, 17–18; identity void, 124, 126, 129, 135, 138–140; shifting, 79, 87–90, 93, 95–97, 99; status and job loss, 147–154, 149; sustaining, 100–106, 109, 111, 112, 116–117. See also family; job seekers' network; workplace
social relationships. See friendship
social resources, 14–15, 153
social status: feedback, 20; identity threat, 24; identity void, 120, 124, 126, 136–137; mismatch, 12; research study, 9; shifting, 79, 87–90, 100; social institutions and job loss, 147–152, 149, 153; Stress Process Model, 15–16; sustaining, 110, 117, 118; time mismatch, 61. See also age; education; gender; race
social structure, 26–27
socialization, 154
socioeconomic class (social status), 15, 89
sports team (social institution), 9, 95
spousal support, 64–66, 67, 80, 114, 118
status mismatch, 11, 23, 152; age-based, 62, 68–73, 77, 100–101; education-based, 62, 73–76, 77; gender-based, 62–68, 77, 101; identity void, 131, 138, 139; race-based, 110; shifting and, 92, 95, 97; sustaining and, 101, 113
stay-at-home mom. See mother identity
steel mill employees, 144
Stephanie (Charlie's subordinate), 29–30
stereotypes, 15, 64, 68, 73, 125, 133
stigmatized groups, 21, 60, 108, 125
stress, 14–16, 22, 36, 44, 60–61, 62–63. See anger; anxiety; depression; distress; frustration
Stress Process Model, 14–16, 22, 45, 76, 97, 118–119, 152–153
stress theory, 7
structural factors, 4, 9, 13–14, 79, 139, 148
structural identity theories, 22
structure, loss of, 57
Stryker, Sheldon, 42, 47, 148
student financial aid, 112
suicide, 5, 64
support groups, 50
sustaining strategy, 148–149, 151, 153, 154; coping mechanism, 9; identity void, 126–129, 134–138, 140; identity work, 12, 78, 99–100; male identity, 113–115; performing occupation, 109–113; self-deception, 115–116; still a worker, 100–109; time mismatch, 58
SZTV (television channel), 129, 133–134, 137

technology and job outsourcing, 4, 13, 142, 144
Tenille (Marsha's daughter), 113

Theo (computer programmer), 65–66
Thoits, Peggy A., 20
time: chunking, 47; identity and, 20–21; identity void, 121; relationship to unemployment, 9, 10; shifting and, 83–84; sustaining and, 111. *See also* identity: time-consistent
time mismatch, 23, 46–61, 152, 171n7; feedback mismatch, 36; identity threat, 11–12; identity void, 130–131, 138; shifting, 80; status mismatch, 77; sustaining, 111, 113
Tosti-Kharas, Jennifer, 21
tuition assistance, 112

Uma (systems engineer), 72
underemployment, 2, 4
underwater mortgage, 3
unemployment: checks, 84, 94, 104; historical context, 12, 142–145; identity and unemployment research, 152–154; long-term, 2, 4, 145; and men's mental health, 124, 129; rates, 2, 4; role, 154; social institutions and job loss, 147–152, 149; sustaining strategy, 100–106
unions, 144, 147

vacuum identity. *See* identity
violence, 4
"vitamin model," 6
volunteer activities: identity void, 125, 136, 137, 138, 139; identity work, 154; shifting, 79, 95; status mismatch, 71; sustaining, 103–104, 109, 111–112, 118

Warr, Peter, 6, 87, 151
Western, Bruce, 5; *The Great Recession* (Grusky, Western, Wimer), 5
Wimer, Christopher, 5; *The Great Recession* (Grusky, Western, Wimer), 5
women: in relationships, 88; shifting, 79–87, 89, 90–91, 124
work: doing, 12, 107–109; meaning of, 145–147
workaholic, 107, 117
worker, behaving as, 100–109, 117
work–life balance, 72, 146
workplace (social institution), 8, 17, 23, 60, 100, 106–107, 117, 121, 136, 139, 152
World War II, 4, 142

ABOUT THE AUTHOR

DAWN R. NORRIS, PhD, is assistant professor of sociology at University of Wisconsin–La Crosse. She takes both quantitative and qualitative approaches to study the sociology of identity, aging and the life course, mental health, and work and occupations, and is especially interested in identity discrepancies. She has published in journals such as *Symbolic Interaction, Research on Aging,* and *Teaching Sociology.*